Mind Over Markets

Uncovering Truths, Overcoming Biases and How to Ensure a Comfortable Retirement

Mike LeGassick

TABLE OF CONTENTS

Dedication ix

Foreword x

Part 1

Mastering Your Inner Cavemen: Emotions and Investing........... 1

Chapter 1

Human Nature: The Caveman Investor................................. 2

Chapter 2

The Evolutionary Pull of Bad News: A Further Glimpse into Our Cave-Dwelling Past.. 12

Chapter 3

The Alarming Stats: Brits' Misunderstanding of Investments 16

Chapter 4

Forget the Jargon. Speak My Language: Plain English Financial Definitions.. 21

Part 2

Clarifying Investor Basics.. 31

Chapter 5

Discover the Stoic Path to Investing Wisdom: Ancient Philosophy for Modern Financial Decisions 32

Chapter 6

Why on Earth Would Anyone Do This?............................... 39

Chapter 7

Unveiling Common Misconceptions: How First-Time Investors View the Stock Market....................................... 49

Part 3

Cultivating the Right Investor Mindset 54

Chapter 8

Nobody Ever Went Broke Saving Money 55

Chapter 9

From Pain to Prosperity – The Investment Journey 64

Chapter 10

Balancing Act: The Moral Tightrope of Profiting from Corporate Success 71

Chapter 11

Behaving Yourself to Wealth 76

Part 4

Adopting an Effective Investing Strategy 83

Chapter 12

The Virtues of Simplicity and Low Costs 84

Chapter 13

The Investment World's Best Kept Secret 89

Chapter 14

The Zero-Sum Game: Unravelling the Dynamics of Winners and Losers in the Financial Markets 95

Chapter 15

Investment Mistakes That Will Hurt Your Wallet 109

Chapter 16

The Winning Formula: Low-Cost Funds and Global Giants 125

Chapter 17

Auto Lane Assist for Your Investments: The Power of Portfolio Rebalancing........ 129

Part 5

Understanding Investment Risks and Returns........ 133

Chapter 18

Inflation's Creeping Constrictor: A Subtle Stranglehold on Our Financial Dreams........ 134

Chapter 19

From Incremental to Explosive: Harnessing the Full Potential of Compounding and Exponential Growth........ 144

Chapter 20

But I Deserve More!........ 158

Chapter 21

Beyond the Hype: The Ineffectiveness of Following Media's Financial Pundits........ 165

Chapter 22

The Illusion of Expertise – Don't Believe the Hype........ 169

Chapter 23

The Danger of Sensationalist Financial Headlines: Putting Perspective into Context........ 180

Chapter 24

The Investor's Dilemma – DIY or Working with a Trusted Professional........ 186

Part 6

Recognising and Overcoming Investor Biases........ 196

Chapter 25

Navigating the Investor Mind: Unveiling the Biases that Shape Financial Decisions 197

Chapter 26

The Performance Illusion 203

Chapter 27

Demystifying Risk - Understanding its True Nature in Investing 207

Chapter 28

The Stock Market Paradox: Unveiling the Peculiar Aversion to Investing in Great Businesses 212

Part 7

Achieving Long-Term Investing Success 225

Chapter 29

Decoding the Risk Levels: Unravelling the True Risks of Everyday Asset Classes 226

Chapter 30

Volatility Composure 232

Chapter 31

Redefining Risk 237

Chapter 32

The Relentless Healing Power of the Stock Market 246

Chapter 33

Diversification, Asset Allocation and the Danger of Fixed Income 252

Chapter 34

Equities vs. Bonds: Unleashing the Power of Ownership ... 258

Chapter 35

No Surefire Returns: All Investments Carry Some Degree of Risk ... 267

Chapter 36

The Two Big Investor Mistakes – The Importance of Understanding Risk and Reward ... 272

Chapter 37

The Fear of Loss: A Dominant Force in Decision-Making . 282

Chapter 38

Beyond the Crystal Ball: Unveiling the Secrets of Long-Term Investment Success ... 286

Chapter 39

Investing Excellence: How the Best Rise Above ... 292

Chapter 40

Live Long and Prosper: Battling Emotions as an Investor .. 297

Part 8

Planning for Retirement ... 302

Chapter 41

You Can't Simply 'Save' for Retirement, You Must 'Invest' ... 303

Chapter 42

Unlocking Financial Freedom: Multiply Your Annual Expenses by 25 and Embrace the 4% Rule – A Rough Guide. ... 315

Chapter 43

The Misconception of Retirement: Continuity of Investment 328

Chapter 44

Dream Today, Achieve Tomorrow: Cashflow Modelling for Retirement 333

Chapter 45

Are You Prepared to Weather a Temporary 50% Market Decline? 344

Part 9

Avoiding Financial Scams and Mastering Investor Psychology 357

Chapter 46

Guarding Your Nest Egg: Navigating the Minefield of Financial Scams 358

Chapter 47

It's About Behaviour, Not Brains – Master Yourself, Not the Market 362

Index 369

Dedication

For my wife Mary's endless love and support.

Thank you for always being there.

And in memory of my wonderful parents.

A sincere thanks to all my clients for trusting me.

"Far more money has been lost by investors preparing for corrections, or trying to anticipate corrections, than has been lost in corrections themselves."

Peter Lynch

"While money can't buy happiness, it certainly lets you choose your own form of misery."

Groucho Marx

Foreword

Imagine navigating any market with clarity, bypassing the noise to focus on what genuinely matters. This book is your map, turning investing from a daunting maze into a journey of understanding and growth.

Welcome to the intriguing realm of investing—a place where financial freedom awaits those ready to pursue knowledge. This guide equips both newcomers and experienced investors with the tools needed to excel.

Our individual experiences can skew our views on investing. But remember, our personal interactions with the market are just a speck in its vast history. While these experiences heavily influence our perceptions, it's essential to see the bigger picture to avoid emotional missteps. True market wisdom comes from acknowledging our biases and seeing beyond them.

From ancient civilisations storing grain for future use to today's savers diversifying their portfolios, our inherent desire has always been to secure the future. This isn't just about chasing returns; it's a journey towards stability and a dream of a safe tomorrow.

The capacity to delay gratification, highlighted in Walter Mischel's "marshmallow test", where children were given the choice to eat one marshmallow immediately or wait and get two marshmallows later, is a cornerstone of sound investing. Sacrificing today's pleasures for tomorrow's comfort is less about chasing numbers and more about fulfilling our psychological need for future security.

For most, investing transcends the mere thrill of growing numbers. It's the peace stemming from knowing the future is secure. Amidst the jargon and intricacies of financial markets, the predominant concern is the fear of running out of money. Beyond the complexities, people merely seek assurance for their and their families' futures.

By understanding our motivations and sidestepping common pitfalls, we don't just aim for financial success but align our journey with our core desires.

This book dispels myths clouding investment truths and introduces core concepts like simplicity, diversification, cost efficiency, and risk management. You'll learn about human behaviour's impact on financial choices and how to align actions with long-term goals.

While foundational principles are discussed, remember that investing is personal. It requires adapting strategies to individual risk appetites and goals. Investing is also a lifelong learning process. Armed with the strategies and insights from this book, you'll stay grounded amidst the media's chaos, focusing on the long haul.

Throughout, I share insights from my investment journey and client interactions. But while this guide provides a broad overview, it isn't a universal solution. Your financial path is unique. Always consult professionals for advice tailored to your objectives.

Join me on this quest to master our instincts, transforming them into our greatest assets in investing. Embrace clarity and confidence. Dive in!

Mike LeGassick Behavioural Investment Coach and Lifestyle Financial Planner

Part 1

Mastering Your Inner Cavemen: Emotions and Investing

Chapter 1

Human Nature: The Caveman Investor

"The biggest investing errors come not from factors that are informational or analytical, but from those that are psychological."

Howard Marks

Thousands of years ago, when our ancestors lived in caves, survival often depended on swift reactions. The difference between securing food and becoming food could hinge on mere moments. Our brains have evolved to prioritise immediate response to threats. Before we can even rationalise a situation, our brain's emotional and habitual centres are already on alert. The tiny gap between instinctual reaction and rational thought may only be a few milliseconds, but for our ancient forebears, those crucial moments could mean the difference between life and death.

Humans have evolved with both emotional and logical (rational) systems. The emotional system, often referred to as the limbic system, is more ancient and can react more quickly than our logical system, the neocortex. This fast emotional response was crucial in situations of immediate danger, like when early humans encountered predators. So, from an evolutionary perspective, emotions had a significant role in survival.

However, when it comes to investing, human nature often works against us. Our natural instincts frequently lead us astray, making it difficult to make rational financial decisions. When our investing goes awry, it's easy to blame ourselves, but in reality, our natural cognitive biases are to blame. We should not judge ourselves harshly - even experienced investors fall prey to instincts that lead to poor financial decisions. Our brains are simply not wired to intuitively grasp the best practices of investing. But the fault lies not in ourselves, but in our human nature. The key is to approach investing with that reality in mind.

Evolution has equipped us effectively for life in the wilderness, but how do we navigate the myriad stimuli in our contemporary world? Imagine watching the evening news, and the first image you see is a trader on the stock exchange floor, a tear tracing its path down his cheek. This visual tugs at your emotions instantly.

A similar emotional jolt occurs when a friend shares an alarming article, or when you check your pension value amidst this year's market volatility. The innate fight-or-flight response might urge you to exit the market or make significant changes. This issue extends beyond just investment—it influences financial, business, and personal decisions alike. We perceive a threat, and our instinct is to respond.

When starved of context or information, our feelings become the compass. Confronted with unsettling news, you reach out to your advisor. They reassure you, emphasising long-term goals. Yet, without a solid foundation in financial planning, their words might offer little solace.

By understanding our innate tendencies and consciously counteracting them through education, strategy, and discipline, we can override our faulty wiring. With self-compassion, patience, and good financial habits, we can triumph over our instinctive investing pitfalls. When we make poor financial choices, we should remember that it's not our fault - the fault lies in the limits of human nature. But we have the power to rise above our natural biases if we invest the effort.

Our financial missteps can be traced back to a time when our most pressing concerns were hunting mammoths and avoiding saber-toothed tigers. It's a puzzling thought, isn't it? How could our ancient instincts possibly influence our modern investing decisions?

The Value of Behavioural Advice

Just as we wouldn't leave all our doors and windows open hoping to get burgled to use our home insurance, behavioural advice from advisors plays a critical safety net role. Behavioural coaching can act as an insurance against our own instincts that might otherwise lead us to make poor investment choices. You wouldn't pay for insurance hoping for an incident to occur, would you? Similarly, you seek financial advice not hoping for a financial downfall, but to guard against one. And even if you never "need" the behavioural coaching and achieve your goals, it's likely you'd still be content, right? That's the essence of investing.

This understanding and prevention of behavioural mishaps tie back to our innate human nature. Let's explore this further.

Evolutionary Roots: Our brains evolved to help us survive in environments very different from modern financial markets. For early humans, quick, reactive decisions were often more beneficial than slow, analytical thinking.

Cognitive Load: Our brains have limited processing capacity. Making decisions about investments requires considering vast amounts of complex information. To manage this cognitive load, people often resort to mental shortcuts known as heuristics, even if they are not always logical or rational in the context.

Desire for Control: Humans have an inherent desire to feel in control of their surroundings and outcomes. The stock market, by its nature, is unpredictable. By making active decisions (even if they're not necessarily rational), people feel a sense of control over their investments.

Difficulty in Grasping Abstract Concepts: The idea of money and abstract financial instruments is, in the grand scheme of human history, relatively new. Concepts like compound interest, market fluctuations, financial risk, and volatility are not inherently intuitive. Many people struggle to fully grasp these concepts, leading to decisions that may seem irrational.

Temporal Discounting: Humans have a natural tendency to prioritise immediate rewards over future benefits. This psychological principle, known as temporal (or time) discounting, means that we might opt for a smaller payoff now over a larger payoff later. In the context of investing, it can lead to decisions that prioritise short-term gains over long-term growth.

Sense of Identity and Ego: People often tie their financial decisions to their self-worth and identity. Admitting to a bad investment decision or acknowledging a lack of understanding can be a blow to one's ego, leading them to double down on bad decisions or avoid seeking advice.

Cultural and Societal Factors: Cultural narratives and societal pressures can shape our understanding of success, wealth, and risk. In some cultures, or communities, for instance, not participating in a booming market might be seen as missing out or being overly cautious.

Misunderstanding of Randomness: Humans look for patterns; it's a fundamental way our brains make sense of the world. However, many events in the stock market are random or influenced by unpredictable factors. People may misinterpret these events as patterns or indicators, leading to irrational decisions.

Overwhelm and Information Overload: With the internet and 24/7 news cycles, investors are bombarded with information, opinions, and predictions. Sifting through this to determine what's relevant and accurate is challenging and can lead to decision fatigue or reliance on questionable sources. This can lead onto: Buyer's Paralysis.

"Buyer's paralysis" refers to the difficulty some investors have in pulling the trigger to make purchases due to analysis paralysis or fear of making the wrong decision. It stems from the endless amount of data and options in the financial markets, which can make choosing what to invest in and when paralysingly complex.

Some key traits of buyer's paralysis include:

- Endlessly researching and analysing investment options without ever buying them.
- Constantly looking for new information to make absolutely sure it's the right pick.
- Delaying decisions again and again out of fear of making a mistake.
- Finding reasons to doubt every potential investment, preventing any action.
- Letting great opportunities pass by while locked in indecision which leads to regret.

Endlessly analysing options, seeking absolute certainty, doubting choices, and repeatedly delaying decisions out of fear leads to buyer's paralysis - missing opportunities while stuck in perpetual indecision. The indecision of buyer's paralysis can result in missed chances and hasty, frustration-driven moves. It highlights the need for discipline, systematic decision-making, and the courage to act on rational choices despite lingering uncertainty. Having clear investing criteria and processes can help overcome the natural tendency toward buyer's paralysis in investing.

Consider these strategies to ensure your financial decisions are rooted in rationality rather than emotion:

Align Goals with Values: Reflect on what truly matters to you and tailor your financial goals accordingly. Goals misaligned with your values can result in behaviours that don't support them. While money is a valuable tool for enriching life, it shouldn't dictate its purpose. Establishing goals rooted in genuine values helps maintain focus, even when challenges arise.

Develop a Detailed Plan: Rather than a vague idea of what you desire, create a structured roadmap of your objectives. Assess the resources available and strategise their optimal use. Ask yourself: What specific steps will guide you towards achieving your goals? For financial assets, contemplate the "when" and "where." For instance, if you won't need funds for the next 10 years, consider enduring potential bear markets or investing further to capitalise on growth potential. Contemplating “where” can be a lengthy thought process, but it includes taking things like taxes and fees into consideration.

Regularly Review Your Plan: Periodically evaluate your plan. Is it still relevant after a year, two, or even ten? Determine what's effective and what needs refinement. Adherence to your plan is crucial, but so is adaptability. Modify goals if they no longer align with your values or desires and adjust strategies if they prove inefficient.

Stay Inquisitive: In today's digital age, information is abundant. But be cautious; sensationalism can often overshadow facts. Partner with a financial advisor who prioritises educating and guiding you. Never underestimate the power of asking questions.

Emotional Intelligence: The Underrated Asset in Successful Investing

In the world of investing, numbers, algorithms, and statistical models often dominate discussions. Yet, there exists an intangible asset that is often overlooked but plays an instrumental role in determining the success of investors: emotional intelligence (EI). Some of the most revered minds in both psychology and finance have delved into the profound impact of emotional intelligence on investment outcomes.

In the realm of investing, every decision carries both financial and emotional dimensions. A financial advisor's key role lies in balancing these aspects, providing expertise in analysing market trends and potential returns, while also addressing the investor's risk tolerance and emotional responses to market fluctuations. By guiding clients to align their investments with both their financial goals and personal values, advisors ensure that investment strategies are comprehensive, accounting for both the logical and emotional facets of financial decision-making.

By blending objective financial advice with empathetic understanding of a client's emotional needs, advisors create a holistic investment strategy that balances both the head and the heart. Let's explore how emotional intelligence shapes effective investment decisions:

1. The Role of Emotional Intelligence in Decision Making: Dr Daniel Goleman, who popularised the concept of emotional intelligence, has consistently emphasised its significance in decision-making. Investors, regardless of their analytical abilities, are not immune to biases and emotional triggers. Recognising one's own emotions and understanding their impact on decisions is paramount. For instance, an investor with high EI can recognise the signs of fear or greed, preventing rash decisions based on short-term market fluctuations.

2. Warren Buffett and the Temperament Factor: Warren Buffett, perhaps the most successful investor of all time, once said, "Success in investing doesn't correlate with IQ... what you need is the temperament to control the urges that get other people into trouble in investing." This temperament, largely rooted in emotional intelligence, allows investors to remain calm under pressure, to think long-term, and to avoid being swayed by market hysteria.

3. The Peril of Herd Mentality: Emotional intelligence equips investors with the self-awareness to avoid being sucked into the herd mentality, a phenomenon where individuals follow the majority in an emotional reaction, often leading to irrational market bubbles and crashes. Renowned economist Robert Shiller, in his works, highlighted how emotions play a role in economic decisions, including those in the stock market.

4. Navigating through Confirmation Bias: One of the pitfalls in investing is seeking information that only aligns with one's pre-existing beliefs, known as confirmation bias. A high EI investor recognises this tendency and actively seeks diverse opinions, ensuring that their investment strategy is well-rounded and not driven by ego. I cover the main behavioural biases that affect investors later in the book.

5. Maintaining Discipline and Patience: The cornerstone of successful investing lies in discipline and patience, two attributes closely tied to emotional intelligence. Dr John Gottman, known for his work on emotional intelligence and relationships, suggests that EI can be used to maintain calm and focus in the face of challenges. For investors, this translates to sticking with a sound investment strategy, even when the market seems to be moving in the opposite direction.

As investment tools and strategies continue to evolve with technological advances, the human element remains a constant. No matter how sophisticated our algorithms or models become, they cannot account for the emotional dynamics that play out in the markets daily. The ability to understand, manage, and harness these emotions through emotional intelligence is, and will continue to be, one of the most valuable assets an investor can possess.

By tapping into your emotional intelligence and incorporating it into your decision-making processes, you'll be better equipped to navigate emotional impulses. This empowers you to steer decisions towards rationality, ensuring they align with both your goals and values.

At their core, many of these factors are deeply rooted in our evolutionary history, cognitive limits, and the fundamental ways in which humans perceive and process information. Recognising these fundamental challenges is the first step in navigating them effectively. As if overcoming our instinctive caveman biases isn't enough, investors must also contend with the barrage of negative news flooding the media landscape.

Chapter 2

The Evolutionary Pull of Bad News: A Further Glimpse into Our Cave-Dwelling Past

"I am an old man and have known a great many troubles, but most of them never happened."

Mark Twain

In today's age of information overload, it's a common observation that bad news seems to dominate our media landscape. Headlines highlighting crises, conflicts, and challenges catch our eyes more often than those emphasising positivity and progress. It's not merely a media strategy to gain higher viewership; it taps into an evolutionary trait deeply rooted in our psyche.

Our ancestors, the early humans, lived in a world filled with potential threats: predatory animals, rival tribes, and natural disasters. Their very survival depended on being constantly aware of potential dangers around them. Evolution favoured those who could quickly detect threats, as they were more likely to survive and pass on their genes. Over countless generations, this trait was hardwired into our brains. When a caveman heard a rustling in the bushes, it was beneficial for him to assume it might be a lurking predator rather than merely the wind.

Those who were more alert and attentive to threats had a better chance of escaping and surviving. This constant state of vigilance, though essential in the past, has left an indelible mark on our modern minds. Fast forward to today, and while we no longer face the same daily life-or-death threats, our brains still operate with that age-old programming. Our evolved inclination is to focus on potential threats. Modern media taps into this by leading with bad news, which instinctively grabs our attention. This "negativity bias" is an evolutionary hangover from a time when paying attention to bad news was often a matter of life or death. However, while this evolutionary trait served us well in the past, it may not be entirely beneficial in our modern context.

Being constantly bombarded with negative news can lead to heightened stress, anxiety, and a distorted view of the world. It's essential to recognise this bias and seek a balance by also tuning into positive stories, developments, history, and achievements that highlight the progress and good in the world. Understanding our evolutionary roots can help us better navigate the modern information landscape, ensuring we stay informed without becoming overwhelmed. It's a reminder that while our cave-dwelling ancestors passed on their survival instincts to us, we have the power to adapt our focus and attention in the 21st century. Remember, while our evolutionary past might influence our decisions, understanding these influences gives us power over them. Knowledge is the first step to making informed, rational choices in the investment world and beyond.

The media's portrayal of events can often skew our perspective, leading us to believe that the world is more dangerous or negative than it really is. The technological advancements in communication have further amplified this effect. In mere seconds, news from thousands of miles away can be broadcast directly to our screens, making distant occurrences feel close to home. This constant flow of news means that while bad news might have once been a rare occurrence, it now seems omnipresent, saturating our perception.

Moreover, the rise of social media platforms means that we don't just passively receive news; we actively engage with it. We share, comment, and debate, and this constant engagement can amplify our emotional reactions. However, there's a silver lining. Just as quickly as a distressing event can spread, so can acts of kindness, innovation, and breakthroughs. These positive stories, unfortunately, often get overshadowed, but they're out there, playing a vital role in counterbalancing the grim narratives.

Furthermore, while it's essential to be informed, it's equally crucial to filter and critically analyse the information we consume. This is especially true in the financial world, where markets are driven not only by hard data but also by investor sentiment and perception. The herd mentality, another evolutionary trait, can cause drastic market fluctuations based merely on a piece of negative news. As investors, understanding the balance between fact and emotion, between historical data and present perception, can be the key to successful decision-making.

It's also worth noting that while we are predisposed to focus on threats, we're also capable of hope, optimism, and resilience. Throughout history, humans have faced adversities, and while the negativity bias kept us alert, our ability to hope and collaborate has propelled us forward. As consumers of media, we can choose to seek stories that reflect the full spectrum of the human experience: the challenges, yes, but also the solutions, innovations, and triumphs.

In summary, as we navigate the modern world with its relentless information flow, it's beneficial to be aware of our evolutionary biases, but also to remember our capacity for critical thinking, adaptation, and positive action. Whether it's in the realms of daily news or the intricacies of financial markets, a balanced perspective is not only healthy but essential for growth and progress.

Investing is not just about numbers and charts; it's also about understanding human behaviour and, by extension, your own behaviour. By recognising the evolutionary biases that might cloud our judgment, such as being overly reactive to negative financial news, we can make better, more rational investment decisions.

While our evolutionary hardwiring explains many investing pitfalls, ancient philosophies reveal timeless wisdom for overcoming them - the Stoics provide a rational framework for navigating the turbulent waters of the financial markets.

Chapter 3

The Alarming Stats: Brits' Misunderstanding of Investments

"If a man empties his purse into his head, no man can take it away from him. An investment in knowledge always pays the best interest."

Benjamin Franklin

There is widespread confusion and intimidation around investing. This is all because of a lack of education.

According to research conducted by Lloyds Bank in 2023, it was revealed that approximately 50% of the population in the UK feel intimidated by the concept of investing, while 38% of individuals find investment jargon confusing. The research revealed that the UK's most misunderstood investment term is 'asset class,' with 77% confused about its meaning. More than a quarter (29%) don't understand the term 'inflation', including 6% who have never heard of it.

Some 26% said it would be easier to learn an entirely new language or go on a first date (23%) than to start investing (21%), although more than half (51%) said that they would be open to learning the basics of investing if appropriate instruction and support was in place.

Nearly half of those without investments (48%) said they don't want to risk losing money, while 38% of Brits – rising to 44% of women – confessed that they are clueless about financial terms. Common investment terms that bewilder Brits include shares (31%), stocks (37%), portfolio (37%) and dividend (42%). Some of the other terms that Brits don't understand include gilts (70%), risk appetite (62%) and equities (59%).

Only one-in-five (21%) of those surveyed claimed to have high financial literacy regarding investing. In my personal opinion, I find it disheartening and a clear reflection of the inadequate financial education available when observing these statistics. Throughout the years, I have actively advocated for the inclusion of basic finance education in schools.

The pervasive misunderstanding and apprehension surrounding investments isn't merely a British issue; it's a global concern. Many individuals worldwide feel similarly daunted by financial jargon and the perceived complexities associated with investing. Such intimidation often leads to missed opportunities and hinders individuals from taking the initial steps towards building their wealth or securing their financial future.

The gap in financial education is a multifaceted issue. It stems not only from a lack of formal instruction in schools but also from societal norms that discourage open conversations about money. Many people grow up in households where discussions about finances are deemed taboo or too personal. This cultural mindset perpetuates the cycle of financial illiteracy and inhibits subsequent generations from seeking information or asking crucial questions.

Moreover, the rapidly evolving nature of the financial world and the emergence of new financial instruments, like cryptocurrencies and various online investment platforms, further widen the knowledge gap. While these innovations offer opportunities, they also present challenges in understanding and risk assessment for the uninitiated.

It's also pertinent to address the role of the media in shaping perceptions about investing. Sensationalist headlines about stock market crashes or investment scandals can overshadow the myriad success stories or the slow and steady growth that many investors experience. Such skewed representations further amplify fear and scepticism.

Empowerment through education is crucial. Seminars, workshops, and educational books are indispensable resources. However, we must also foster a society that encourages open dialogue about financial matters, removing the stigma attached to seeking help or admitting ignorance. Financial institutions, too, have a role to play in this, by adopting transparent practices and prioritising client education.

Lastly, the responsibility doesn't lie solely with educators or professionals. As consumers, we must adopt a proactive approach to our financial education. In the age of the internet, resources are plentiful; they're just waiting to be tapped into. By taking the reins of our financial education, we not only demystify the world of investments but also pave the way for informed and rational decision-making.

I have conducted seminars in colleges and universities where I have witnessed the alarming lack of fundamental financial knowledge among students, which is both distressing and concerning. However, I am not at all surprised by the widespread aversion to investing experienced by millions of people. This book aims to dispel the various myths and misconceptions surrounding investing. Nevertheless, the greatest challenge faced by professionals in this field is the excessive use of jargon.

The abundance of technical terminology only exacerbates the fear of the unknown that people naturally possess. It is understandable why millions of individuals approach investing with excessive caution and nervousness, as making an initial foray into the world of investments can be an intimidating experience.

In my opinion, some financial advisors use jargon in an attempt to impress clients, but it often ends up confusing them instead. They may also complicate matters unnecessarily to justify the fees they charge, making things seem more complex than they actually are. Investment language should be no different from everyday conversation, conducted in plain English. Hence, instead of deferring the explanation of terminologies until the end of this book, I have decided to break tradition and provide plain English explanations for many of the terms mentioned at the beginning.

Throughout the book, I have tried to avoid unnecessary jargon and explain any technical terms that may arise. However, to ensure clarity and alleviate anxiety, here are plain English definitions of the common terms you will encounter in this book. Once you grasp these concepts, you'll enhance your knowledge and gain confidence in your decision-making. This will help you avoid being among the unfortunate individuals mentioned in a Lloyds market research study.

Chapter 4

Forget the Jargon. Speak My Language: Plain English Financial Definitions

Stock Market:

The stock market is a place where people buy and sell parts of companies, called shares. It's like a big, global shop for owning bits of businesses.

Passive Investing:

Passive investing is a simple and cost-effective strategy where you buy and hold a mix of investments that follow the market's performance. You don't try to beat the market; instead, you aim to match its overall returns over time.

Index tracking Funds:

Index tracking funds, also known as index funds, take a passive investing approach. They replicate the performance of a specific stock market index, offering a low-cost and diversified investment option. They aim to match the market's returns over the long term without active stock picking.

Active Investing:

Active investing is a more hands-on approach to investing, where you aim to outperform the market by carefully choosing individual stocks, bonds, or other assets. The goal is to make strategic decisions based on research, market analysis, and the expertise of the fund manager or investor. Active investing involves more frequent buying and selling of investments to try and achieve better returns than the overall market. However, it often comes with higher costs and requires continuous monitoring and decision-making.

The S&P 500 Index:

The S&P 500 is a stock market index that tracks the performance of 500 large and important companies in the United States. It gives an overall picture of how these companies' stock prices are changing, which is used as a benchmark for the US stock market's performance and a broad indicator of how the global stock market is performing.

Bull Markets:

A bull market is when investment values are rising, and investors feel optimistic and confident about the future. It's a happy time in the stock market.

Bear Markets:

A bear market is the opposite of a bull market. It's a period when investment values are falling, and investors feel pessimistic and uncertain about the future. It's a challenging time in the stock market.

Asset Classes:

Asset classes refer to different types of investments that have similar characteristics. Common asset classes include stocks, bonds, property, and cash. Each asset class has its own potential risks and levels of expected investment return.

Investment Fund:

An investment fund is a way for many people to pool their money together and have it managed on their behalf. It's like a group savings account where the money is used to buy a large mix of different investments. Investment funds make it easier for individuals to access a diverse range of investments without having to manage them individually. Most people with personal pensions have their money invested this way.

Stocks, Shares and Equities:

Stocks, shares, and equities are essentially the same thing and represent ownership in a company. When you buy stocks or shares, you become a partial owner and have the potential to benefit from the company's success. The value of stocks can fluctuate based on various factors such as the company's performance, market conditions, and investor sentiment.

Investment Volatility:

The frequency and amount an investment's value fluctuates over time. Think of it as a roller coaster's ups and downs.

Market Capitalisation/Company size:

Market capitalisation (aka market cap) refers to the total value of a company's outstanding shares of stock. It's calculated by multiplying the current market price of one share by the total number of shares outstanding.

For example, if a company has 1 million shares trading at £50 per share, the market cap is £50 x 1 million = £50 million. So, in simple terms, market cap is used to indicate the size of a company. It represents the public consensus on the total market value of a company's stock.

The larger the market cap, the bigger the company by valuation. Market cap is commonly used to categorise companies as small-cap, mid-cap, or large-cap. It's a quick way to gauge a company's size.

Dividends:

Dividends are payments made by a company to its shareholders. When a company earns a profit, it can choose to distribute a portion of that profit to its shareholders as dividends. Dividends provide a way for investors to receive a share of the company's earnings. Most investors have these dividends reinvested back into their investment automatically to make it grow quicker.

Bonds:

Bonds are debt instruments issued by governments to support their spending and to meet obligations and corporations issue bonds to raise money for them to further invest in their business. When you buy a bond, you are essentially lending money to the issuer in exchange for periodic interest payments and the return of the principal amount at maturity. Bonds are generally considered less risky than stocks but offer lower potential returns.

Property:

Property refers to real estate assets, including land, buildings, and homes. It can be residential, commercial, or industrial in nature. Property ownership offers potential benefits such as rental income, property value appreciation, and tax advantages.

Cash or Money Fund:

Cash refers to money in the form of physical currency or funds held in bank accounts that are readily available for spending. It is the most liquid asset and can be used for immediate transactions or as a store of value. Cash provides flexibility and serves as a means of payment for goods and services.

GDP (Gross Domestic Product):

A country's economic report card. It shows the total value of goods and services a country produces in a year. A rising GDP means the economy is doing well, while a falling GDP indicates it might be struggling.

Inflation:

Inflation refers to the general increase in the cost of living over time, resulting in the decreased purchasing power of money. In simpler terms, it means that as time goes on, the same amount of money can buy fewer goods and services. Inflation is influenced by factors such as supply and demand, government policies, and economic conditions.

Real Rate of Return:

The real rate of return is the actual return on an investment after adjusting for inflation. It considers the impact of inflation on the purchasing power of your investment. For example, if your investment earns a 5% return, but inflation (the cost of living) is 3%, the real rate of return would be 2%.

Portfolio:

A portfolio refers to a collection of investments held by an individual. It typically includes a mix of the different asset classes mentioned above, such as stocks, bonds, and possibly other investments, with the goal of diversifying risk and achieving specific financial objectives.

Market Volatility:

Market volatility refers to the degree of price fluctuations in the financial markets. It indicates how much prices of assets, such as stocks or bonds, are changing within a given period. High market volatility implies larger price swings, while low volatility suggests more stable prices. Market volatility is largely influenced by factors outside of an investors control like economic events, market sentiment, and market conditions.

Compounding:

Compounding is the concept of earning returns on an initial investment and reinvesting those returns to generate even more returns over time. It's like putting your money to work and earning interest not only on your original investment but also on the accumulated returns. This process is similar to a snowball rolling down a hill, growing larger as it gathers more snow. In investing, compounding can lead to rapid and significant growth, allowing your wealth to build steadily and multiply over the long term.

Diversification:

Diversification involves spreading investments across different assets or asset classes to reduce risk. Some people may underestimate its importance or misunderstand how to achieve effective diversification. It’s the same as not putting all your eggs in one basket. Most investors choose to invest in funds that hold thousands of companies. This way, if some companies in the fund are not performing well, the others can help balance it out.

Risk Tolerance:

Risk tolerance is an individual's ability to endure volatility or potential losses in their investment portfolio. Many people misjudge their risk tolerance and may take on more risk than they can comfortably handle. Conversely, they might need more of their money invested to get the returns they seek.

Return on Investment (ROI):

ROI is a measure of the profitability of an investment, usually expressed as a percentage. Misunderstanding ROI can lead to unrealistic expectations or overlooking other factors like time horizon and risk. Imagine you decide to buy a bicycle for £200. After a year, you sell the bicycle for £250. To calculate the ROI, you subtract the initial cost (£200) from the final sale price (£250), which gives you a profit of £50. Now, you divide the profit (£50) by the initial cost (£200) and multiply by 100 to get the percentage. In this case, the ROI would be 25%.

Market Timing:

Market timing refers to the strategy of trying to predict the best times to buy or sell investments. It is often misunderstood as a reliable way to generate profits. It is virtually impossible to consistently time the market correctly without the aid of a crystal ball. If anyone could do this consistently, they would soon become extremely wealthy.

Investment Timeframes:

Short term investing is deemed to be between 1 and 5 years. Medium term investing is deemed to be between 5 and 10 years. Long term investing is deemed to be a minimum of 10 years.

Individual Savings Accounts (ISAs):

A Cash ISA is like a savings account where you can put your money and earn interest without having to pay any tax on the interest you earn. It's a safe and straightforward way to save money, but the interest rates may be lower compared to other types of investments.

An Investment ISA, on the other hand, is like a special account where you can invest your money in various ways, such as stocks, bonds, or funds. The money you make from these investments can grow over time, and you won't have to pay any tax on any profits you earn within the ISA.

In summary, a Cash ISA is for saving money without paying tax on the interest earned, while an Investment ISA allows you to invest your money and potentially earn higher returns without paying tax on the profits. Both can be useful for different financial goals and risk preferences.

Personal Pension:

A personal pension is a retirement savings plan that you set up to have money for when you retire. You regularly save and invest money, so it grows over time and provides you with income during retirement. One of the benefits is that you may get tax relief on the money you contribute, helping your savings grow even faster.

Annuity:

An annuity is like a financial contract or agreement that you make with an insurance company. You pay the insurance company a lump sum of money or regular payments over time. In return, the insurance company promises to give you a steady income for a specific period, which could be for the rest of your life or for a set number of years. It's like creating your own personal pension plan, where you get regular payments from the insurance company to support your retirement or other financial needs.

Flexible Access Drawdown:

Flexible access drawdown is a retirement option that allows you to access your pension savings while keeping the remaining funds invested. With this approach, you can withdraw money from your pension pot as and when needed, providing you with flexibility and control over your retirement income. It's an alternative to buying an annuity and offers the freedom to adapt your withdrawals based on your changing financial requirements throughout retirement.

Part 2

Clarifying Investor Basics

Chapter 5

Discover the Stoic Path to Investing Wisdom: Ancient Philosophy for Modern Financial Decisions

"The investor's chief problem — and even his worst enemy — is likely to be himself."

Benjamin Graham

In my journey as an advisor, I have always found solace and wisdom in the words of ancient philosophers. Their insight, formed under the lamp of introspection and experience, illuminates the path through the often-foggy landscape of investing. Among these philosophers, the Stoics have profoundly impacted my approach towards investing and life.

This book isn't intended to be a history lesson on the great philosophers of the past, although there are some historical references within. However, we can still gain useful insights from certain teachings of earlier thinkers when it comes to investing wisely. The timeless principles they set forth on human nature and rational decision-making remain quite relevant today.

Why the Stoics, you might ask? When related to investing, stoicism, at its core, emphasises rationality, control over one's responses, and acceptance of the unpredictable nature of the global economy and the markets—all crucial elements for a successful investor. I've found that applying these stoic principles to investing instils a sense of calm and clarity, allowing investors to make composed, well-informed decisions, even amidst the stormy fluctuations of the markets, and what happens to be going on in the world.

The teachings of Epictetus, Marcus Aurelius, Seneca, and other Stoic philosophers offer timeless wisdom that transcends the boundaries of time and context, landing squarely into the realm of modern investing. Their thoughtful quotes provide a compass which can help investors navigate the ever-changing currents of the market.

In my endeavour to share the profound connection between Stoic philosophy and investing principles, I aim to illuminate how the wisdom of these ancient philosophers can serve as guiding stars in your investment journey. By embracing these teachings, you can not only achieve financial success but also cultivate emotional resilience and develop a disciplined approach to investment, fostering a balanced and rewarding investor behaviour.

Incorporating the teachings of Stoicism into investing could lead to a strategic and composed approach, enhancing our decision-making abilities and creating a balance between risk and reward.

Epictetus's quote, "We cannot control the world around us; all we can control are our thoughts and reactions to it," is particularly relevant. In investing, we can't control market fluctuations, global events, or economic downturns. However, we can control our investment decisions, strategies, and how we react to these external events.

Marcus Aurelius' advice, “If you are distressed by anything external, the pain is not due to the thing itself, but to your estimate of it; and this you have the power to revoke at any moment.” If an external event, such as a market downturn or bad economic news, causes you distress, it's not the event itself that's causing the pain, but your perception of it. You have control over your reactions and your mindset. At any moment, you can change your perspective, re-evaluate the situation, and adjust your investment strategy accordingly. This can help you to manage your emotional responses to the volatility of the market, allowing you to make more rational and beneficial investment decisions.

Seneca's wisdom, "We suffer more often in imagination than in reality," finds a mirror in investing as well. Investors often panic due to imagined worst-case scenarios, which leads to selling off assets at a loss. A Stoic investor, on the other hand, would assess the situation objectively before making a decision.

Heraclitus' insight, "No man ever steps in the same river twice, for it's not the same river and he's not the same man," is a poignant reminder of the dynamic nature of investing. The financial landscape is ever-changing, and successful investors must continuously adapt their strategies.

Lastly, Aurelius's quote, "Waste no more time arguing about what a good man should be. Be one," can be seen as a call for investors to act according to their plans and strategies, rather than procrastinating and being swayed by market noise or the latest trends.

By applying Stoic wisdom, investors can cultivate a resilient mindset, navigate uncertainties more effectively, and make more informed decisions. Stoicism, thus, offers not just a philosophy for life, but valuable insights into the art of investing as well.

It's crucial to understand that if you can master the human side of investing, you can figure out the numbers. If you can't master the human side of investing, the numbers don't matter.

Crafting a Stoic Roadmap: The Importance of Intentional Planning

The stoic philosophy teaches us the importance of understanding our inner selves, of knowing what we can control and accepting what we cannot. It's about ensuring our emotions, thoughts, and actions are in harmony. This same essence of harmony, control, and understanding can be drawn upon when we transition from the realm of investing wisdom to crafting our financial roadmap.

Drawing a parallel from Stoicism, imagine your journey in the financial world as a Stoic's journey through life. Just as Stoicism guides us to start by understanding our internal compass, our 'purpose' in the financial journey must be our starting point. Marcus Aurelius once remarked, "Very little is needed to make a happy life; it is all within yourself, in your way of thinking." In investing terms, it means understanding your goals and motivations before taking any action.

Remember Epictetus's insight about controlling our thoughts and reactions? This speaks to the 'planning' stage. Before reacting to the volatility of financial markets or the allure of trending investments, one must have a robust plan in place, a kind of inner fortress, a stoic would say. Without this, you'd be allowing external events to dictate your actions, leading you astray from your true purpose.

Lastly, just as Stoics emphasise aligning actions with rational thoughts and proper intentions, the 'portfolio' should be constructed in alignment with the purpose and plan you've set forth. When Seneca pointed out that "We suffer more often in imagination than in reality," he could very well be speaking to the investors who, without a clear roadmap, act on unfounded fears, and speculative noise.

By integrating Stoic wisdom, we understand the importance of sequence: the internal reflection of 'purpose,' the thoughtful creation of a 'plan,' and the aligned actions of building a 'portfolio.' Just as Stoicism is a philosophy for life, it can guide us in the journey of financial planning, ensuring we don't drift aimlessly but move purposefully towards our goals.

Thus, as we transition into the art of crafting your financial roadmap, let's keep the Stoic's way at the heart of our approach: Purpose, Planning, Portfolio. Safe travels on your financial journey, with the Stoic stars guiding your path.

Creating Your Financial Roadmap: Purpose, Planning, Portfolio

One of the biggest mistakes novice investors make is pursuing "portfolio, plan, purpose" rather than "purpose, plan, portfolio." Constructing a portfolio first, without defined goals or a strategic plan, will send your investments veering dangerously off course.

The Common Misstep - Portfolio Before Purpose

Many investors mistakenly start by investing without any defined investment goals or time horizon in mind. This speculative approach is like setting sail without any destination - you will drift aimlessly. Always start by defining your purpose - your investment goals and time horizon.

The Detour - Portfolio Before Planning

Equally problematic is building a portfolio before crafting a strategic financial plan. This misguided approach is like embarking on a road trip without any map or GPS to guide you. You will get turned around and lost. Don't build your portfolio until you have a financial roadmap in place.

Correcting Course - Purpose, Then Planning, Then Portfolio

Beware the trap of "portfolio, plan, purpose" that ensnares many novice investors. To reach your desired investment destination, you must pursue things in the proper sequence:

Purpose - Define Goals

Planning - Create Roadmap

Portfolio - Construct Aligned Investments

By adhering to this order, you will stay on course towards your investment goals.

Bon Voyage! - Executing Your Plan

With your purpose, plan and portfolio prepared in the proper sequence, you are ready to set sail on your investment journey! Stay focused on your financial compass and goals, avoiding detours based on emotion or speculation. Calm seas ahead!

Chapter 6

Why on Earth Would Anyone Do This?

Mark Twain once said, “History doesn't repeat itself, but it often rhymes.” Similarly, Voltaire observed “Man tends to repeat his mistakes.” In the realm of investing, this rings especially true; we've navigated countless financial storms and apocalyptic scenarios before. This is especially evident in investing. Time and again, investors fall prey to the same pitfalls—be it the lure of quick riches, herd mentality, or failing to diversify. Past market downturns and bubbles have shown that lessons are often forgotten or ignored. The historical records serve as testament to repeated patterns of exuberance followed by regret. Wise investors recognise these patterns and strive not to repeat the errors of the past, understanding that human nature, in the dance of investing, often steps to the same old tune.

It has often been said that the market has drained many investors' funds over the years. The reality is that Investors have been responsible for their losses due to their decisions in the market.

Given that the market has multiplied 70X since 1960 (excluding dividends), it's a delusional to solely blame the market for financial losses. Historically, the market isn't the culprit — investors' choices are.

Before we go any further, let's shed light on two fundamental terminologies in investment parlance:

1. Bull Markets

"Bull markets are born on pessimism, grow on scepticism, mature on optimism, and die on euphoria." – John Templeton

When we talk about a bull market, we're referring to a season in the financial landscape where share prices and other investments generally trend upwards. Picture it as a sustained positive rally in the stock market. Confidence among investors during this period is typically high, fuelled by a sense of optimism about the economy's health and the enterprises they're investing in.

During a bull market, the hunger for stocks overshadows their availability. This heightened demand pushes prices upwards, creating an encouraging cycle. Investors hold the belief that their chosen companies are doing well or possess solid growth potential, thus prompting them to buy more shares. As this buying activity increases, prices continue to rise.

A multitude of factors can usher in a bull market. These include a booming economy, thriving businesses, and increased disposable income for investing. Positive reports about corporate profits, ground-breaking technologies, or supportive government policies can also stoke investor enthusiasm.

Amid a bull market, investors may witness the growth of their portfolios. It can be a golden window for long-term investors to generate profits or accumulate wealth. However, it's crucial to remember that bull markets aren't eternal. At some point, market conditions will shift, reversing the upward trend and potentially leading into a bear market.

2. Bear Markets

In contrast, a bear market represents a phase where stock prices and other investments generally slide downwards. Picture it as an extended downturn in the stock market. During a bear market, investor confidence often wanes, and there's a prevailing sense of gloom about the economy and the companies whose stocks are up for trade.

In a bear market scenario, the availability of stocks surpasses their demand. This surplus of supply and lack of demand trigger a downward cycle, driving prices lower. Investors grow apprehensive about economic conditions, company profitability, and other elements that could affect their investments. As more people offload their shares, it further exacerbates the price fall.

Various elements can precipitate a bear market. These include economic recessions, geopolitical uncertainties, dismal corporate profits, or even major events like a global pandemic, as witnessed with COVID-19. Such an event caused the S&P 500 to slump by 34% over three months at the onset of the pandemic, only to rebound rapidly as the world developed strategies to cope with it.

During a bear market, investors often witness their portfolios shrinking, which could lead to temporary losses. These periods can be trying for those heavily invested. However, bear markets don't last forever and can offer lucrative opportunities for investors.

Braving a bear market demands patience, discipline, and a long-term vision. History shows us that markets have a knack for bouncing back from downturns and ushering in new growth phases. Therefore, it's important for investors to avoid making impulsive decisions borne out of fear or panic. Instead, they should remain well-informed, adhere to their investment objectives, and be prepared to ride out the temporary turbulence.

It's key to remember that a bear market is part of the market cycle. While it can be testing, it also reveals opportunities for experienced investors who have seen these cycles unfold before. By staying alert, managing risks, and maintaining a diversified portfolio, investors can position themselves for potential future growth when market conditions inevitably swing back. Stock market prices have always gone up considerably more than they go down over time. If it were the other way round, there would be no companies left as we would have hit ground zero decades ago.

Bizarrely, the stock '*market*' is the only market on the planet where people run out of the store when everything is on sale. We all love a discount. When our favourite drink or food is priced attractively low, we fill up our carts. When that desired television set is discounted, we hurry to purchase it before the price rises again. But when stocks are 'on sale', novice investors wait until prices rise before investing. This approach is completely irrational.

Making financial choices based on immediate turmoil is unwise. History teaches us that upheavals, no matter how severe, are temporary blips in the grand timeline. From world wars and economic crises to pandemics and other significant events, all had an endpoint. This is precisely why the four most dangerous words in investing are "this time is different." It never is. It just feels this way at times. While some situations took longer to normalise than others, they all eventually subsided. Hence, basing long-term strategies on fleeting disruptions is irrational, no matter the scale of the present crisis. In the world of investing, unpredictability is a constant, with threats always seeming imminent. Yet, the essence of smart investing lies in trusting time's healing power. Patience is challenging but essential for success.

THERE'S ALWAYS A CRISIS

Human nature is indeed a failed investor. We just aren't hardwired to be good investors. It is a skill that must be learned.

Now, let me present a conundrum: "Would you rather excel during bull markets or bear markets?" A poll showed a preference of nearly two to one (63% vs. 37%) for performing better during a general market downturn (Bear market). This sheds light on the severe irrationality of human nature as it pertains to financial markets.

Bull markets last much longer than bear markets and result in far greater increases in equity values than the temporary reductions during bear markets. This is a straightforward fact that is clearly demonstrated by the 10% average annual compound return of mainstream equity markets over a hundred years.

Armed with this knowledge, a rational long-term investor would undoubtedly prefer to excel during the extended, higher climbs of a Bull market. To say that one prefers "outperforming in a bear market" is merely a euphemism for "losing less." This means: "I would rather my portfolio experience smaller losses during the market's periodic but short-lived and always transient downturns, even if it ultimately leads to a less profitable long-term outcome."

A truly rational investor—a real-world individual swayed by raw human nature but aided by a behavioural investment coach would not make this choice. However, understanding this flawed reasoning can offer insights into why individuals who could own large portfolios of persistently successful companies might prefer to lend to these companies.

In other words, you can understand the misguided logic that drives individuals to buy bonds (lending to businesses) instead of stocks (owning a piece of many businesses). To shed new light on the irrationality of bonds, we must disregard some of the most compelling facts. Among these is the fact that for about the last hundred years (1923 to 2023), the average annual compound total return from mainstream stocks has been six percent above inflation, while the return from bonds has been much less, at two to three percent above inflation.

Ignoring these persuasive facts is necessary because they are not convincing to human nature in its misled state. The superior return of stocks is achieved by simply weathering their temporary downturns.

Yet, these temporary downturns are precisely what human nature obsesses over. As Nobel laureate Richard Thaler points out, "The pain of losing money is twice as intense as the pleasure of gaining." Due to this self-induced "pain" human nature loses sight of the temporary nature of declines.

Howard Marks, an American investor, and author, posed and responded to an insightful question in his memo to investors from July 2023:

"Which is worse, buying at the top of the stock market or selling at the bottom of it? For me, the answer is easy: the latter. If you buy at what turns out to have been a market top, you'll suffer a downward fluctuation. But that isn't cause for concern if the long-term thesis remains intact. And anyway, the next top is usually higher than the last top, meaning you're likely to be ahead eventually. But if you sell at a market bottom, you render the downward fluctuation permanent, and, even more importantly, you get off the escalator of a rising economy and rising markets that has made so many long-term investors rich. This is why I describe selling at the bottom as the cardinal sin in investing."

I wholeheartedly agree with his reasoning. This is indeed the ultimate investor cardinal sin.

Despite this, the reality does not change, which is why our appeals to historical records are ineffective. Faith, patience, and discipline are the first victims of a temporary market decline, replaced by that fear: "This time is different." Thus, when given a choice, unaided human nature would prefer to do better during bear markets than bull markets by a ratio of two to one.

Certainly, in that statement, the standout term is unquestionably 'unaided'. A proficient adviser's support becomes the key determinant and is thus invaluable, because in its absence, the investor is bound to fail. After all, they are only human. However, we might possibly find another route to engage our latent potential for rationality in these issues. The strategy would be to halt discussions about abstracts and refrain from employing complex jargon like “stocks,” “bonds,” and “the stock market,” and instead bring the investor back to the pivotal decision: Is it, in the grand scheme of things, more beneficial for them to own diversified portfolios of successful businesses, or to provide loans to these companies?

Investing long-term in a broad collection of the world's biggest and most profitable companies remains the final fortress of rationality in an ever-risky world. Sensible companies will consistently strive to safeguard their capital and earn an excellent return on that capital. Acknowledging this, we then pose the question: “Why do established, robustly financed, consistently profitable businesses borrow funds?” Let's focus this question on the firms whose shares contribute to the Standard & Poor’s 500-Stock Index, and whose combined market worth is currently around $35 trillion as of July 2023.

The requirements for being listed in the Index are that the company must be based in the United States, its value must be at least $13.1 billion, its shares must be highly liquid with no less than 50% of the outstanding shares accessible for public trading, and the aggregate of its earnings for the past four quarters must be positive. We then ask again: not only why these firms would issue bonds, but why would they ever consider borrowing money in the grand scheme of things?

There can be only one primary response to this question, the logic of which must be clear: Because they believe that they can reinvest the borrowed capital at a considerably higher return than the cost of borrowing. If they were not convinced of this, they wouldn't borrow; it would be counterproductive. And who, it's reasonable to ask, will benefit from that extra return, after the interest is paid to the bond holders and the bonds are redeemed or refinanced? It's the business owners, of course. Owners of high-performing businesses—the shareholders—tend to earn considerably far more than those lending to the businesses— the bondholders.

In my professional life, I've met countless people who—due to their sadly misguided human nature—simply couldn't accept that stocks are safer long-term investments than bonds. However, I don't recall ever meeting someone who couldn't understand and even agree with the concept that the owners of a successful business earn more—often a great deal more—than the lenders to that business.

For the long-term investor, one who is goal-oriented and operates with a well-defined plan, the fluctuations of the equity market—whether it's in a phase of growth (a "bull market") or decline (a "bear market")—should hold little to no relevance. When the market is on an upward trend, which is predominantly the case, such an investor directly benefits. Conversely, during temporary downturns or bear markets, the investor's increasing dividends are reinvested to purchase even more shares at reduced prices. Throughout both scenarios, the wonders of equity compounding persist. It's crucial to understand that for the dedicated long-term investor, a bear market is merely a fleeting setback in the ongoing, enduring bull market. This is all we can know, and all we need to know.

Doing the Wrong Things at the Wrong Time for the Wrong Reasons

In the complex world of investment, a peculiar yet common pattern emerges among many investors. They often fall into a behavioural trap where their actions are misaligned with optimal investment strategies. This tendency manifests as a habit of making misguided decisions, frequently characterised by doing the wrong things.

What exacerbates this issue is not just the nature of their choices, but also the timing. These decisions are often made at inopportune moments, further compounding their adverse effects. Furthermore, the underlying reasons for these choices are typically flawed, driven by misconceptions, herd mentality, or emotional reactions rather than sound financial analysis. This pattern highlights a significant challenge in the investment world, where rational decision-making is often overshadowed by irrational tendencies.

Chapter 7

Unveiling Common Misconceptions: How First-Time Investors View the Stock Market

"The greatest enemy of knowledge is not ignorance; it is the illusion of knowledge."

Stephen Hawking

From my personal experience, I've had the opportunity to engage with first-time investors who share a myriad of thoughts and concerns about the stock market. While I haven't conducted a formal survey, these insightful interactions provide valuable insights into the perceptions and sentiments that commonly emerge from this group of individuals.

Understanding the apprehensions and misconceptions of first-time investors offers a unique window into the larger societal perspectives on finance. The backdrop against which these misconceptions emerge is crucial to address for a holistic understanding.

The following perceptions and factors are the M&M's I referred to earlier.

Risky and Volatile

First-time investors often voice apprehensions about the perceived risks and volatility associated with the stock market. Many fear the potential of losing all their hard-earned money, which makes them cautious about taking the plunge into the world of investing.

Uncertain and Unpredictable

Among these investors, a common sentiment is the perception of the stock market as an unpredictable and uncertain realm. They might feel overwhelmed by the dynamic nature of the markets and find it challenging to predict outcomes.

Reserved for the Wealthy

Some first-time investors may believe that the stock market is exclusively reserved for the wealthy elite, leading them to think that investing is beyond their reach.

Lack of Understanding

Many of these individuals openly admit to lacking a comprehensive understanding of the stock market. They may feel intimidated by the technical jargon and complexities, which can hinder their confidence in making investment decisions.

Market Crashes and Financial Stress

I have often heard concerns about the potential for market crashes and the resulting financial stress that investing might bring. Memories of past downturns can cast a shadow of doubt on their willingness to participate in the stock market.

Gambling and Speculation

Some first-time investors draw parallels between the stock market and gambling or speculative activities, associating it with luck-based outcomes rather than rational financial planning.

Lack of Expertise

I have heard many express a lack of confidence in their ability to navigate the stock market successfully. They might consider investing a domain reserved only for financial experts and professionals.

Long-Term Investment

Amidst the cautious sentiments, a few first-time investors recognise the potential of the stock market for long-term investment. They understand that while risks exist, there are also opportunities for growth and wealth-building over time.

Educational Gap

In my interactions with first-time investors, many have expressed a desire for accessible and comprehensive education on investing. They seek knowledge and tools that will enable them to make informed decisions in the stock market.

Information Overload

In the digital age, potential investors are bombarded with a plethora of news, both positive and negative, about the stock market. From stories of individuals amassing immense wealth overnight to tales of sudden market crashes leading to widespread losses, the information they receive is polarised. This constant barrage can both allure and deter first-time investors.

Cultural Dynamics

Historically, in many societies, discussions on finance, especially losses or setbacks, are considered private. This absence of open conversations can result in many myths getting perpetuated without correction. People might rely on anecdotes and opinions rather than hard data, which can lead to skewed perceptions.

Role Models

The portrayal of investors in media and popular culture can also influence perceptions. When successful investors are often showcased as exceptional geniuses or savants, it may create a belief among the general public that one needs exceptional skills or insider knowledge to succeed, which is far from the truth.

Technological Advancements

The emergence of user-friendly investing apps and online platforms has made the stock market more accessible than ever. While they democratise investing, they can also give a false impression of simplicity. Without proper guidance, a new investor might treat investing as just another online game, not fully grasping the implications of their actions.

The Generational Perspective

Older generations might have experienced economic downturns and stock market crashes firsthand. Their cautionary tales, though rooted in genuine concern, can add to the apprehension among younger potential investors. Conversely, younger generations, who are more exposed to overnight success stories via social media and other platforms, might be too eager, underestimating the risks involved.

While my observations and speculative analysis cannot replace the insights gained from a formal survey, they do provide an understanding of the common perceptions and concerns that first-time investors might have towards the stock market. Addressing these concerns and providing adequate educational resources can help empower individuals to make confident and informed decisions when entering the world of investing.

In conclusion, the intricate tapestry of perceptions that first-time investors hold about the stock market is woven from myriad threads of societal influences, personal experiences, and the modern information era's challenges. For a sustainable investing culture, it's vital to address not just the misconceptions but also the larger context that gives birth to them. By doing so, we can foster an environment where informed decision-making becomes the norm rather than the exception.

Part 3

Cultivating the Right Investor Mindset

Chapter 8

Nobody Ever Went Broke Saving Money

"It does not matter how slowly you go as long as you do not stop."

Confucius

I am frequently asked, "When is the ideal moment to begin saving and investing and is now a good time to invest?" My responses remain consistent: The best time to invest was 30 years ago. The next best time is now, and it is always a good time to invest. It's akin to the concept that the optimal time to plant a tree was thirty years ago, but the next best opportunity is to plant one today.

Before we get into this, I want to emphasise that I'm not comfortable with the idea of investing in the stock market for a period less than 5 years. Such a short timeframe may not be sufficient to weather the inevitable downturns that markets experience. Short-term investors might not have enough time to recover from temporary losses before needing to access their funds. It is crucial for investors to plan their withdrawals well in advance.

For instance, it's not ideal to inform your advisor that you need £10,000 for a wedding on Monday when the market has just experienced a 10% drop the previous Friday. If you have a fixed amount of money that you know you'll need on a specific date in the future, it's wise to request those funds several months in advance and place them into a secure and easily accessible cash account. This way, your funds will be protected from market volatility.

For short-term money and emergency funds, it is always advisable to keep them in low-risk, easily accessible accounts such as National Savings. This ensures that your funds are safe and readily available whenever you need them.

With that caveat out of the way, let's get back to when is a good time to invest.

Reflecting on wishing you'd started investing thirty years ago reminds us that time waits for no one. However, dwelling on the past does not alter the present. Embracing the current moment and acting is crucial. By initiating your savings and investment journey now, you pave the way for future financial growth and stability.

While it would have been advantageous to begin earlier, focusing on the present and making a commitment to save and invest is the key to progress. Regardless of your current age or financial situation, there is value in starting today. Every small step taken today can have a significant impact on your financial well-being tomorrow.

So, when considering the best time to save and invest, remember that the past cannot be changed. Instead, channel your energy into the present and seize the opportunity to sow the seeds of financial prosperity. Just as planting a tree today can bring future benefits, initiating your savings and investment journey now holds the potential to bear fruitful results in the years to come.

When we witness events unfolding beyond our control, it might not feel like the right time to invest. It may seem wise to hold off and wait for better days, keeping our financial resources safe. However, when we take a step back and look at the bigger picture, history shows that, in the long run, the value of the stock market (the great businesses of the world) tends to go up.

I am always astonished by the number of clients who hesitate to invest when markets have fallen in value, waiting for things to return to normal. However, in the realm of stock market-based investing, normalcy is an ever-elusive concept. Delaying the decision to save and invest can mean missed opportunities for growth and financial security. The longer you wait, the more you potentially sacrifice in terms of potential returns and the power of compounding. By starting today, you give yourself the advantage of time and the ability to nurture your financial future.

Waiting to invest until the stock market returns to its previous level is like seeing a car you've been eyeing for six months priced at £18,000, only to be told by the salesman that they've reduced the price to £15,000 due to new stock. Instead of jumping at the opportunity, you decide to wait until it goes back up to £18,000 before making the purchase. It may sound crazy, but many investors adopt a similar approach when they hold back from investing after a market decline.

It's like everyone loves a good sale, but strangely, the stock market is the only place where everyone seems to run away when prices drop. This behaviour is quite baffling. If your favourite items in a supermarket were on sale at an unprecedented price, you would likely fill your shopping trolley, right? But when the stock market goes on sale, most investors do the exact opposite. Undeniably, our brains have a peculiar way of functioning on certain occasions.

Dating back from 1870, the UK stock market has shown remarkable growth over the past 150 years, even in the face of upheavals and catastrophic events. Despite enduring tragedies and financial crises, major businesses have consistently thrived in the long term. While today's challenges exist, they are unlikely to be as devastating as past events such as the one, two punch of World War One and the Spanish Flu, the Great Depression, or World War Two.

Imagine traveling back in time to 1870 with Marty McFly's time-traveling DeLorean and investing £1. Fast forward to 2023, and that single pound would have multiplied to an impressive £2,728, representing extraordinary growth of 272,700%, just like Marty's adventures in 'Back to the Future', to achieve such remarkable returns, we must be willing to embrace risk, volatility, and uncertainty.

Over time, the market relentlessly progresses, leaving us behind, and we end up missing out on much of the upswing. However, when greed overpowers our fear, we are drawn back into the fray, as no one wants to pass up the chance to accumulate the wealth that awaits the patient investor.

Perils and obstacles relentlessly encircle us, akin to the tightening grip of a colossal cosmic vortex, pulling us into its abyss. However, living in such a manner is futile. On a personal level, it would mean shunning any form of transportation, avoiding relationships, and confining oneself indoors. Financially, it would mean evaluating your wealth based on hoarded resources rather than participating in the ever-changing stock market. To achieve substantial growth like the astonishing 272,700%, we must embrace risk and uncertainty. Staying the course requires focusing on the ultimate goal rather than being swayed by temporary setbacks.

One significant downturn in the UK stock market was a temporary -73% decline during the 32 months of hardship from 1972 to 1974. This decline was during the stagflation years of the 1970s. However, progress resumed after that period, just as it did after the Dotcom Bust (-44%) and the Global Financial Crisis of 2007-2008 (-43%). As difficult as it is to believe, even the recent Covid-19 pandemic crash appears as a blip when viewed in hindsight.

Investing is akin to navigating through a series of challenges, but historical trends indicate that the market tends to recover and advance over time. It's natural to be concerned about our current troubles and wonder if they may lead to another calamity, prompting some to consider a more cautious approach. However, throughout history, the world has always faced various troubles, and as time unfolds, the market's path ahead will become clearer.

Considering the unpredictable nature of the investment market—as evidenced by the 1970s stagflation in the UK, the Dotcom Bust, and the Global Financial Crisis—it's important to approach investing with a well-calibrated perspective. While history shows us that markets do recover, this doesn't negate the importance of individual planning and strategy. Given these ups and downs, you might wonder:

What Defines a Good Return and What Level of Return Can You Realistically Expect?

I am often asked by clients what I think a good investment return is or what should I expect. Investment returns, frequently expressed as a percentage, are a measure of the gains or losses made from an investment over a specified period. The key question many investors grapple with is: "What is a good investment return?" Is it 3%, 5%, 10%, or more?

The answer, in reality, is multi-faceted. A 'good' return is relative, varying from one individual to another based on several factors:

1. Risk and Volatility Tolerance: Some are comfortable with high-risk, high-reward ventures that could yield returns well above 10%. Others prefer the less volatile safety of a more conservative approach, satisfied with returns around 3% to 5%.

2. Inflation Rate: The real return on an investment is its nominal return minus the inflation rate. If inflation is 2% and you earn a 5% return, your real return is just 3%. Ideally, your return should always be above the prevailing inflation rate to ensure your money's purchasing power isn't eroding.

3. Investment Goals: A retiree might seek stable, consistent returns to maintain their current standard of living. In contrast, a younger individual with a higher risk appetite might pursue aggressive growth opportunities to maximise wealth.

4. Economic Environment: In a booming economy, expectations for returns might be higher. In a recession, even breaking even might be considered a good return.

5. Duration of Investment: Long-term investments might aim for compounded growth, where even a seemingly small annual return can grow substantially over time. Short-term investments might need higher annual returns to meet specific objectives.

Historically, the stock market has registered an average return of 10% annually. However, it seldom delivers a precise 10% in any given year. Life would be so much easier if it just did this year in and year out without fuss.

A Quick History Lesson

Historically, over the last century, the stock market has registered an average return of 10% annually. However, it seldom delivers a precise 10% in any given year. Life would be far simpler if the market consistently delivered a steady 10% annually, without the unpredictable ups and downs in between.

Because it doesn't, many investors face a dilemma here. They set their sights on a steady return "around 10% annually," only to be confronted with the reality of market fluctuations (+20%, +15%, -12%, +9%, -18%, +16%, +12%, etc…).

Such unpredictable shifts often lead to impulsive decisions. In the real world, the road to the promised land of 10% has always been messy. The compounding experience feels anything but smooth because there is nothing linear about how the market compounds our money.

We shouldn't shy away from this fact. The key is to better align our expectations with the unpredictable nature of the market. When markets soar to all-time highs, we must remember that downturns are inevitable, ensuring we're not caught off-guard when they occur.

Conversely, during market declines, it's crucial to remember that the world isn't ending and that there are overarching positive trends destined to drive returns in the future.

Ultimately, the essence of setting realistic expectations lies in balancing optimism and caution, ensuring neither extreme highs nor lows sway our investment strategies.

INVESTOR EXPECTATIONS VS INVESTMENT REALITY

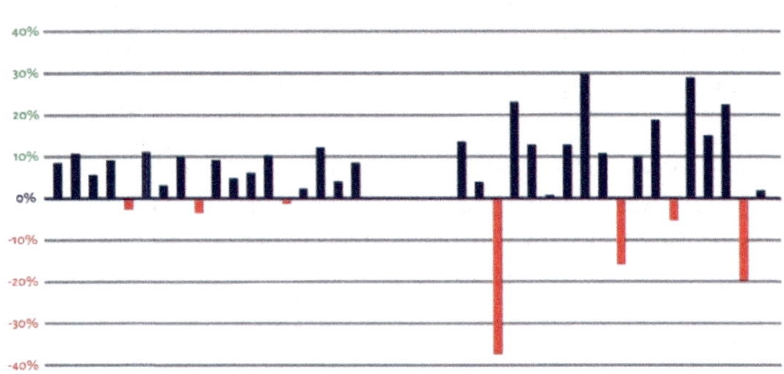

In my investing book, I take issue with a phrase that's tossed around far too casually in the advisory world: "Investments can fall as well as rise." Let's cut through the niceties—this statement grossly underplays the inevitable. I don't just hint or suggest to my long-term stock market investors; I assert unequivocally: your investments will absolutely fall in value from time to time. Believing in an incessant upward trajectory is akin to believing it will never rain again. It's pure fantasy. It's not just naive, it's dangerously misleading. Setting the right, unvarnished expectations for my clients isn't just good practice—it's an imperative.

Fundamentally, a good investment return is one that allows an investor to maintain their standard of living without the fear of ever running out of money. It's not solely about chasing the highest percentage. It's about understanding personal financial needs, goals, and the broader economic context.

As the saying goes, "It's not about timing the market, but time in the market." Investors would do well to remember that planning with prudence is critical and arguably more important than performance alone. It's not about hitting out of the park with every investment but ensuring a sustainable and secure financial future. Plan wisely, and let your personal circumstances guide your definition of a 'good' return.

Chapter 9

From Pain to Prosperity – The Investment Journey

"The gem cannot be polished without friction, nor man perfected without trials."

Chinese Proverb

In the world of investments, pain can be synonymous with gains. Some of the most significant opportunities arise following the market's most dramatic downturns and events. Prices soar when investors realise their previous reactions were exaggerated. However, seizing these moments demands upgrading our mental framework from the primitive fear and greed package.

Greed entices us during bull markets, similar to the 19th Century Gold Rush or the 21st Century Cryptocurrency Bubble, where we are drawn like moths to the flame. Yet, we end up getting burned. Fear takes over, compelling us to hold back and adopt a "wait and see" approach.

Inevitably, the market continues its march without us, and we miss out on most of the rally. Until, that is, greed overwhelms our fear again, pulling us back into action as nobody wants to miss the last opportunity to amass the riches that await us at Prosperity Heights. This is the primal rendition of the classic game - scissors, paper, stone. Greed triumphs over fear, while fear conquers greed. We swing back and forth in sync with the market's rhythm, but out of sync with the opportunities it presents.

Approaching the market in this manner only amplifies the risk of buying at high prices and selling at low ones. However, diving in when your instincts scream "Danger! Danger!" increases your chances of buying low and selling high. As Warren Buffett wisely advises, "be fearful when others are greedy and greedy when others are fearful."

Imagine two individuals at a party resisting a drink. The first declines, saying, "No thanks. I'm trying to cut back." In contrast, the second confidently says, "No thanks. I don't drink." Who's more likely to stay steadfast in their choice?

This small distinction mirrors our world of investing. Think of two investors during a bear market. The first hesitates, stating, "I want to remain invested, but the market's turbulence is daunting." Meanwhile, the second confidently affirms, "I'm a dedicated equity holder, with a plan, and committed for the long-term."

Who's more likely to stay the course? Who'll achieve more peace of mind and potentially better returns?

Humans instinctively avoid short-term pain. However, lasting rewards often come from enduring temporary discomfort. Good things come to those who wait. The saying "No pain, no gain" encapsulates this. Investor and entrepreneur Naval Ravikant offers a perspective: "If you're undecided on a challenging choice, opt for the short-term pain."

This principle applies both to wealth and health, especially in investing. It's distressing to witness a declining portfolio in the short run. Yet, this temporary instability paves the way for substantial long-term gains. Historical market charts demonstrate the immense value of enduring short-term hardships for long-term benefits. Even when markets tumble, it's irrational to assume they'll bottom out, as there's negligible historical support for such a view. It would take an apocalyptic event for thousands of great businesses to go bust.

Historical data suggests two things:

1. Choosing short-term ease in investing often leads to long-term regret.

2. Enduring short-term hardships has consistently resulted in long-term benefits.

In essence, while embracing short-term challenges might not be appealing, it's often necessary to achieve your long-term objectives.

Historical data suggests that a steadfast commitment to equities leads to favourable long-term results. Thus, embracing the identity of a "lifelong equity owner" might be the most effective approach in varied market climates. Remember, it's not the markets that lead to losses, but impulsive decisions.

As to whether now is a good time to invest, it's as good a time as any. For the majority of individuals, the key lies in the time spent in the market, not in attempting to time it perfectly.

Progress is not a guaranteed path, but we need not bemoan the absence of guarantees either. Uncertainty acts as the driving force behind our future returns. It is precisely due to the risk of potential losses that investors seek the promise of higher returns from equities.

The investment journey is much like the human experience in its entirety: filled with highs and lows, moments of doubt, periods of euphoria, and instances of rediscovery. As we navigate the labyrinthine paths of financial markets, it's vital to recognise some of the broader context and insights that shape our decisions.

Collective Memory: Just as our personal experiences influence our choices, the collective memory of financial history plays a vital role. Events like the Great Depression of the 1930s or the Financial Crisis of 2008 cast long shadows. They not only affect the generation that lived through them but also impact subsequent generations. These memories function as cautionary tales, reminders of the fragility of markets and the importance of prudence.

Emotional Intelligence: Financial literacy is undeniably essential, but so is emotional intelligence in investments. Recognising one's emotions, understanding their origins, and determining how best to act upon them is just as crucial as understanding market dynamics. It's often not the lack of knowledge but the inability to manage emotions that lead investors astray.

The Impact of Technology: In today's age, technology has fundamentally transformed investing. With real-time data, robo-advisors, and algorithmic trading, investors are both empowered and, at times, overwhelmed. The double-edged sword of technology can provide unparalleled insights, but it can also create an illusion of control, leading to overconfidence.

Globalisation: The interconnectedness of today's world means that an event in one corner of the globe can ripple through markets worldwide. Being attuned to global occurrences and understanding their potential implications is no longer optional. It's a necessity.

The Paradox of Choice: While having options is empowering, the sheer volume of investment choices available today can be paralysing. Mutual funds, ETFs, commodities, real estate, cryptocurrencies—the list goes on. Making informed choices in this sea of options requires clarity of purpose and a clear investment thesis. I will discuss buyer's paralysis further in the book.

Societal Values: Our investment choices are increasingly reflecting our societal values. The rise of ESG (Environmental, Social, and Governance) investing is a testament to this shift. Investors are now looking beyond mere financial returns, seeking investments that align with their ethical and moral values.

The Role of Advisors: In a complex financial landscape, the role of financial advisors has never been more critical. However, their role is evolving from mere investment guidance to one of holistic financial well-being, encompassing areas like financial education, emotional support during volatile times, and legacy planning.

Triumph Amidst Chaos: Why It's Important to Focus on the Destination and Not the Journey.

Imagine this scenario: You decide to stroll to a nearby restaurant for dinner with a friend. On your short walk, you come across a series of unexpected events:

A car accident.

A blazing house fire.

A child stranded up a tree.

Street performers asking for change.

An altercation unfolding in the middle of the street.

By the time you step into the restaurant, you're bursting with tales to recount. However, amidst detailing the chaos, you might overlook one crucial detail: you arrived at your destination safely, unscathed by the disturbances you observed. This journey mirrors the world of investing.

Throughout our investment journey, we are bound to face numerous challenges. Just consider the events since 1990 alone: The Gulf War, the tragedy of 9/11, Russia's invasion of the Ukraine, a global pandemic, and a record high inflation in four decades. This period also bore witness to two of the most devastating market crashes - the tech bubble burst and the Great Financial Crisis. And let's not forget the countless other headlines screaming the end is nigh.

Yet, here's a reality check: In 1990, the S&P began the year at 359 points. Fast forward to 2023, and it stands at a whopping 4,500. If one had reinvested their dividends, a mere £100,000 would have grown to an impressive £2.6 million.

It's evident that the majority of the pitfalls were due to individual investor choices rather than the market itself. History has shown us that crises, both genuine and perceived, will persist. As we've seen, the choice is yours: will you let them divert you from your path or remain focused on your long-term plan?

One of the reasons why the stock market can be so frustrating is because the returns are inconsistent and can be lumpy. They can be terrifying for extended periods. You could be underwater for years at a time.

In summary, the journey from pain to prosperity in investing is a multifaceted one, shaped by various external and internal factors. It's a journey that demands both knowledge and wisdom, introspection, and foresight and patience. As we stand at the intersection of history, technology, and evolving societal values, our investment choices will define not just our personal prosperity, but the kind of world we shape for future generations.

Remember, in investing, there are often challenges and uncertainties that can cause discomfort or pain, but staying focused on your goals and making informed decisions can lead to significant rewards over time. No one receives rewards for betting on a sure thing. Yet, investing in the continued progress of humanity and its primary engines of productivity has yielded fruitful results over the past 300 years. In the world of investments, embracing some pain may be the key to unlocking the ultimate gain.

Chapter 10

Balancing Act: The Moral Tightrope of Profiting from Corporate Success

"Greed's worst point is its ingratitude."

Seneca

In the world of investing, a curious paradox often arises, one that highlights the dichotomy between investor complaints about company profits and their simultaneous benefit from those very profits. On the surface, it may seem counterintuitive for investors to criticise the very thing that brings them financial gains, but a closer examination reveals a more nuanced picture of the relationship between investors and the companies they support.

When investors complain about the immense profits that certain companies generate, they often express concerns about income inequality, corporate greed, and the impact on societal welfare. They argue that excessive profits can lead to overpaid executives, neglect of employee welfare, and environmentally damaging practices. From this perspective, it may seem morally contradictory for investors to profit from what they deem as unjust or unethical practices.

However, the true essence of investing lies in the pursuit of financial gains, and this remains the driving force behind investors' decisions. Investors allocate their capital into profitable companies with the hope of reaping returns on their investments. They are, in essence, entrusting their resources to these companies in the expectation of earning dividends or seeing their stock values rise. Thus, while they may criticise the means through which profits are generated, their core motivation remains cantered on financial growth.

This apparent dichotomy points to a broader debate within the realm of finance and ethics. Investors face a constant balancing act between their financial goals and their ethical principles. Some may choose to align their investments with their values, seeking out companies that prioritise sustainability, social responsibility, and fair practices. However, for many investors, the bottom line takes precedence, and they prioritise the pursuit of financial success over ethical concerns.

Furthermore, this dichotomy also underscores the role of shareholders in shaping a company's direction. As part-owners of the organisation, investors wield a degree of influence over the company's decision-making processes. By expressing concerns and demanding greater accountability, investors can help steer companies towards more ethical practices. In this sense, their complaints serve as a mechanism for encouraging positive change within the corporate landscape.

To resolve this dichotomy, a new generation of investors has emerged – those who focus on impact investing. These individuals seek to achieve not only financial returns but also positive societal and environmental outcomes. By directing their investments towards companies that demonstrate a commitment to sustainability and social responsibility, they aim to align their financial goals with their ethical principles.

In the realm of investing, the age-old adage "conscience comes at a cost" resonates deeply, particularly in the context of ethical investing. While ethical investors prioritise principles and moral values in their financial decisions, they often find themselves making sacrifices in pursuit of higher ethical standards. One of the apparent costs of ethical investing is the potential trade-off in historic returns compared to those achieved through traditional, less ethically inclined investments in the general stock market.

Ethical investing involves actively seeking out companies that align with certain social, environmental, or governance criteria. These investors may avoid putting their money into industries that contribute to environmental degradation, exploit labour, or engage in controversial practices. While this approach brings a sense of fulfilment and peace of mind for staying true to one's values, it may also lead to missed opportunities for higher returns in sectors that might not uphold such stringent ethical standards.

The general stock market is characterised by its diversity, with companies spanning various industries, some of which may not prioritise ethical considerations. Historically, certain sectors have seen substantial growth and impressive returns on investment, attracting a significant share of conventional investors. Choosing to invest ethically might mean bypassing these potentially lucrative opportunities and instead directing funds towards companies that prioritise social responsibility and sustainability.

However, it is essential to consider the long-term impact of ethical investing beyond immediate financial gains. While historical data might indicate that non-ethical investments outperform ethical ones in certain periods, this trend is subject to change as society becomes more conscious of sustainable practices and as ethical companies demonstrate their resilience and adaptability to evolving market demands.

Moreover, the concept of "cost" in ethical investing is multifaceted. The financial sacrifice that ethical investors make in the short term could lead to larger societal benefits in the long run. By directing capital towards companies committed to positive change, ethical investors can play a pivotal role in shaping corporate behaviour and driving industries towards more sustainable and responsible practices. The resulting impact on the environment, labour rights, and community well-being can be far-reaching and might ultimately prove more valuable than any short-term financial gains foregone.

The price of conscience in ethical investing lies in the potential trade-off between historic returns and staying true to one's principles. While ethical investors may not always achieve the same financial gains as those pursuing conventional investment strategies, their commitment to sustainable, responsible practices can generate positive externalities that benefit society as a whole. As the world increasingly recognises the importance of ethical considerations, the value of such investments may extend beyond financial metrics, making conscience a potentially rewarding and transformative force in the world of finance.

In conclusion, the dichotomy of investor complaints about company profits while simultaneously benefiting from those profits reflects the complex nature of investing. It reveals the inherent tension between financial gains and ethical considerations. While some investors may criticise the means through which profits are generated, their core motive remains cantered on achieving financial success. However, this paradox also serves as a catalyst for change, encouraging investors to engage with companies and push for greater ethical accountability. Ultimately, investors have the power to shape the corporate landscape and drive progress towards a more sustainable and responsible future.

And whether you like it or not, equities have shown themselves to be the only asset class that fully captures human ingenuity.

Chapter 11

Behaving Yourself to Wealth

"We are what we repeatedly do. Excellence, then, is not an act, but a habit."

Aristotle

Our behavioural traits, both beneficial and detrimental, are developed throughout our lives. These traits mirror our beliefs, the information we consume, and our social circles. Essentially, our habits define us. Traditional wisdom underscores the idea that our beliefs, feelings, and attitudes are the precursors to how we behave, yet in the realm of investing, I've discovered the reverse is often true.

It suggests that what we think, and feel will naturally lead to corresponding behaviours. This viewpoint holds that if we harbour a certain attitude towards an endeavour, our actions will align with that perspective. For instance, if we have a positive attitude towards exercise, we are more likely to engage in physical activity.

However, the realm of investing presents an intriguing deviation from this commonly held belief. In the world of finance and investments, it's not always our attitudes that guide our actions, but rather our actions that can significantly influence our attitudes.

When someone begins investing, they might not have a well-formed perspective about the stock market, or about certain investment strategies. They might have apprehensions, uncertainties, or even misconceptions. However, once they take the plunge and start investing, their experiences - be they gains, losses, or lessons - will reshape their attitudes towards investing. A person who experiences early investment gains might develop a risk-seeking attitude. Conversely, someone who is faced with short term losses early on might become overly cautious.

This phenomenon in investing underscores the importance of experiential learning. Sometimes, we need to act in order to form or refine our attitudes, rather than waiting for our attitudes to dictate our actions. This reversal can be both enlightening and cautionary, as actions based on limited knowledge can lead to unintended consequences. But it also speaks to the human ability to adapt and learn from experience.

In the intricate realm of investing, inexperienced investors often approach the market coloured by their personal perceptions, which are influenced by the latest alarms and crises, both real and imagined. To the novice eye, every headline or piece of breaking news may seem like a potential market-moving event, leading them to react impulsively. Such perceptions, although not always grounded in the actual mechanics or realities of the market, can heavily drive investor behaviour. It's a classic case of perception superseding reality. Consequently, understanding this gap and its influence is essential. It underscores the importance of discernment and education in investment decisions, ensuring reactions are based on substance rather than mere shadows.

In essence, while many aspects of life seem to follow the formula of "attitude leading to action," investing often showcases the dynamic nature of the relationship between our beliefs and behaviours. It reminds us that while our attitudes can indeed influence our decisions, our direct experiences, and the actions we take play a pivotal role in shaping our perspectives and habits.

Each of our habits was cultivated over time; we weren't born with any of them. A birth certificate may entitle you to chase your dreams, but it doesn't equip you with the skills and habits needed to shape your life. These are formed, fostered, and developed progressively. The same can be said for how we view money.

Consider this, we weren't born with the habit of brushing our teeth. It's a routine we developed over time. Have you ever skipped a day of brushing? Most likely, no. This exemplifies the power of a habit. Now, let's examine some habits that could lead to wealth creation, as well as ones to avoid.

Many people who have poor money habits spend their entire time and energy earning money because they don't have it, desire it, and would do anything to obtain it. Unfortunately, when people pursue money, they often end up penniless. Have you ever heard the saying, "It's not about how much you make, but how much you keep"?

Conduct a quick calculation. How much money have you earned in the last 5, 10, 20 years? And how much of that do you still possess? I bet your figure was sobering and a little depressing. It is for most people. Living significantly below your means and prioritising saving is a fundamental principle in building wealth, but it's not a simple task. It requires substantial discipline and commitment.

In diving deeper into the intricacies of financial behaviour, it becomes evident that the way we interact with money transcends mere transactions; it's deeply intertwined with our identity, values, and vision for the future. Here are a few characteristics of detrimental financial habits:

Cultural Influences: Our cultural background and upbringing play a significant role in shaping our financial behaviours. Some cultures prioritise savings and are risk-averse, while others encourage spending and living in the moment. Understanding the cultural narratives that influence our financial behaviours can help in refining them.

Peer Pressure: The societal pressure to 'keep up with the Joneses' can divert many from their financial goals. This pressure to conform to certain lifestyles or purchasing decisions, even if they're beyond one's means, can lead to long-term financial ramifications. Recognising and resisting such pressures is vital.

Education's Role: Surprisingly, even well-educated individuals can be financially illiterate. Financial education, often not part of traditional curriculum, plays a pivotal role in fostering good money habits. Continuous learning and seeking knowledge about financial matters can set the foundation for sound financial decisions.

Emotional Spending: Money often becomes a tool to cope with emotions – be it stress, sadness, or even joy. Recognising when spending is driven by emotions rather than needs or genuine desires is crucial. Building alternative coping mechanisms can prevent financial decisions that are later regretted.

The Power of Automation: In the digital age, automating financial tasks, like savings or bill payments, can mitigate the chances of human error or oversight. It takes the emotional equation out of the picture and ensures consistent adherence to financial goals.

Mentorship: Just as in any other domain of life, having a financial mentor can be transformative. Learning from someone who has navigated the financial maze successfully can provide invaluable insights and shortcuts.

The Fluidity of Money: Money is fluid; it comes and goes. This fluid nature requires adaptability. Financial strategies that worked in one's 20s might not be applicable in their 40s. Regularly reassessing and recalibrating one's financial strategy is crucial to remain aligned with evolving life goals.

Purposeful Spending: Adopting a philosophy of purposeful spending, where each expenditure aligns with a clear intention or goal, can lead to greater financial satisfaction. It ensures that money is spent on things or experiences that genuinely add value to one's life. Warren Buffet astutely observed, "If you buy things, you do not need, soon you will have to sell things you need."

Giving Back: One's relationship with money also gets influenced by the act of giving. Philanthropy or even small acts of financial kindness can instil a sense of purpose and demonstrate the impact money can have beyond personal accumulation.

Let's pause here and establish a wholesome understanding of money. We all need income to survive, and it's either we control money, or money controls us. Money is neither evil nor the essence of life, it's merely a resource. Money simply amplifies your existing character traits. If you're a bad person, more money will exacerbate this, and if you're good, you can do better with increased resources.

Adopt a healthy mentality towards money. Instead of viewing money as a problem, start thinking of it as energy, a resource to be managed judiciously.

Contrary to popular belief, money is not the root of all evil; the love of money is. An overattachment to money can lead to a meaningless life. True wealth comes from financial security and the ability to make a difference and serve others.

Why do so many people struggle to modify their expenditure and savings habits?

I theorise that financial challenges often paralyse people into inaction and delay. Many people fail to transform their financial lives because they set expectations beyond their immediate reach. To avoid this pitfall, take small, incremental steps towards your goals and remain persistent. If you veer off course, or rather, when you veer off course... simply reset and restart.

In conclusion, the journey to financial enlightenment is not merely about accumulation but understanding. It's about introspecting on the myriad factors that influence our relationship with money and continually refining it to serve our higher goals. Through mindful engagement and informed decisions, one can harness the true power of wealth, which lies not just in its possession but in its purposeful utilisation. By altering our perspective and mindset about money, we can unlock opportunities we never knew were possible.

Part 4

Adopting an Effective Investing Strategy

Chapter 12

The Virtues of Simplicity and Low Costs

"Simplicity is the ultimate sophistication."

Leonardo da Vinci

When it comes to investing, the allure of complexity and high stakes is always present. We are tempted to chase the latest hot investment fad, employ complex strategies, and pay high fees for so-called expertise. But in my decades managing clients' investments, I've learned time and again that keeping things simple and sticking to low-cost investments is the smartest path for the individual investor.

Imagine you're playing a game of poker. The more skilful players at the table often make money not by brilliant plays, but by being patient and avoiding major mistakes. Similarly in investing, the best returns tend to go to those who stay in the game long term without fretting over daily market moves. To use a cricket analogy, don't swing for sixes. The secret is singles and doubles year after year.

Indexes like the S&P 500 are a simple way to benefit from the long-term growth of businesses without stock picking. Paying exorbitant fees to brokers or managers who promise dazzling gains often just lines their pockets while hampering your returns. Instead, investing in low-cost, globally diversified funds that track the overall market avoids layers of costs.

Of course, human nature makes us excited to try beating the market. But investing is not entertainment, it's a methodical process. Those who have the discipline to tune out speculation and stick to a buy-and-hold strategy with low expenses are usually rewarded in the long run.

The ambition of an everyday investor shouldn't be to identify the winners. They, nor their financial 'guides', are equipped to do that. Rather, their aim should be to own small pieces of a broad range of top-performing global businesses, which are expected to perform positively over a long period.

These financial 'guides' are often active fund managers and financial advisors, promising they can regularly outperform the market. However, I have strong reasons to doubt their potential for success. Low cost, globally diversified funds have historically beaten more expensive actively managed funds over the medium to long-term.

Costs can escalate significantly when substantial annual fees, and active trading costs are all factored into the active investor's calculation. There are numerous intelligent individuals involved in managing active funds. However, their efforts largely cancel each other out, and their intellect will not compensate for the costs they impose on investors. Investors will, on average and over the long term, fare better with a low-cost globally diversified fund than with a selection of actively managed funds.

This brings us to another timeless principle: "It's not what you make, but what you keep."

Economies, markets, and investment vehicles evolve, but one unchanging truth is the significance of expenses. Compound interest is often called the eighth wonder of the world, illustrating the profound effect time has on the growth of an investment. However, the same principle applies in reverse when it comes to costs. The cumulative impact of even a seemingly small fee can eat into returns considerably over a lengthy investment horizon.

In our digitally connected age, information abounds. While this has democratised knowledge to an extent, it's also paved the way for an overload of data and opinions. The investment landscape is no longer just about equities, bonds, or real estate. It encompasses a myriad of asset classes, each with its jargon, nuances, and so-called experts. For the individual investor, it's easy to feel like a child in a sweet shop, overwhelmed and enticed all at once. But just as in nutrition, where the basics of balanced eating trump the latest fad diets, in investing too, sticking to foundational principles is the key.

Furthermore, this barrage of information often prompts knee-jerk reactions, making investors churn their portfolios more often than necessary. Every buy or sell decision incurs a cost, not just in transaction fees but also potential tax implications. Simplicity advocates for fewer, well-considered moves. By reducing the noise and cutting through the clutter, investors can cultivate a more measured and long-term approach to wealth creation.

One might wonder, in the face of all this complexity, why the virtues of simplicity and low costs aren't more widely promoted? The answer, perhaps cynically, lies in the fact that simplicity doesn't sell. The finance industry, with its myriad products and solutions, often profits more from complexity. A narrative of high stakes, intricate strategies, and exclusive access is undoubtedly more enticing than a straightforward approach of consistent, low-cost investments. But as consumers of these financial products, individual investors would do well to remember that often, more is less.

Moreover, the concept of simplicity extends beyond just investment choices and costs. It encompasses one's entire financial life. From having a clear and concise financial plan to understanding one's risk appetite genuinely, embracing simplicity can lead to more transparent, stress-free, and ultimately, successful financial outcomes.

The long-term consequences of consistently overpaying are substantial. Such financial oversights might necessitate extended years in the workforce, constrain your capacity to assist your children financially, or diminish the opportunities and flexibility you envision for your lifestyle.

For those embarking on their investment journey or even seasoned investors feeling overwhelmed, remember this: at its core, investing is about allocating resources today for a better tomorrow. Strip away the jargon, the charts, and the noise, and this basic tenet remains. Focus on this, keep costs low, and the path to financial prosperity becomes a lot clearer.

I am convinced that the expensive endeavour to outdo the market leaves investors susceptible to a variety of counterproductive behaviours. I do all I can to keep the costs for investment, ongoing education, servicing, and advice as low as I can.

Investing successfully doesn't necessitate a degree, specialised training, insider connections, vast experience, or mastering an endless amount of skills. It's about mastering just a few fundamental practices and applying them consistently. As Bruce Lee famously said; “I fear not the man who has practised 10,000 kicks once, but I fear the man who has practised one kick 10,000 times”.

In conclusion, while the glitz and glamour of the financial world can be enticing, it often pays to remember Leonardo da Vinci's wise words. In the realm of investments, as in many aspects of life, simplicity truly is the pinnacle of sophistication.

Chapter 13

The Investment World's Best Kept Secret

"Investing should be more like watching paint dry or watching grass grow. If you want excitement, take $800 and go to Las Vegas."

Paul Samuelson

Let me let you in on a big investment secret. By simply putting your money in a medium to long-term, low-cost, globally diversified fund, even the know-nothing investor will probably achieve better results than many proclaimed 'investment gurus'. Paradoxically, when 'dumb' money acknowledges its limitations, it ceases to be dumb. It might sound harsh, but trust me, it's true. It's not really about being 'dumb', it's about being financially in the dark. The problem is that we don't know what we don't know. I don't fully understand cryptocurrency or the inner workings of how hedge funds work, and quite honestly, due to their complexity, extreme volatility, and the high level of risk attached, I am not particularly interested in learning more about them. I do however fully understand equities – companies that produce goods and services and sell them to billions of people globally for a profit and then share it with the owners.

As an owner, you get to participate in the company's growth and often will receive an income in the form of a dividend payment. You can become an owner through simple, transparent, and super low-cost investment funds. It's the simplest and most reliable way to create and grow your wealth.

You don't have to be a stock market investment wizard to thrive. "The stock market is a device for transferring money from the impatient to the patient." - Warren Buffett

Patience and calm, thus, are not just virtues, but prerequisites for successful investing.

Satisfactory investment returns don't require you to be an expert. If you aren't, it's essential to recognise your limitations and adopt a strategy that has proven to deliver reasonably good results. Embrace simplicity and avoid chasing unrealistic goals. Whenever a financial advisor promises instant guaranteed profits, swiftly decline their offer. And don't merely walk away from such proposals – RUN!

So, how does one navigate this intricate landscape of investing? The first step is acknowledging that chasing after the next shiny object or "hot tip" is rarely, if ever, a sustainable strategy. Instead, there's a profound wisdom in following the fundamentals, based on historic data and practical investment principles.

For those new to the investment landscape, the sheer volume of options can be daunting. From the cacophony of crypto enthusiasts promising astronomical returns, to niche start-ups purporting to be the next big thing, it's easy to get seduced by the siren song of quick riches. But remember the tale of the tortoise and the hare: steady and slow often wins the race.

Consider property, for instance. The UK's property market has always been viewed as a gold standard for investment. And while there's undeniable appeal in owning tangible assets like bricks and mortar, one must not ignore the hassle, unpredictability, taxes, and ongoing costs associated with property ownership. Additionally, property is an illiquid asset, making it challenging to convert bricks and mortar into immediate cash. Moreover, the initial capital outlay is immense. Conversely, equities offer an entry into the world of ownership without the responsibilities of direct management. This freedom and flexibility can't be understated.

Another area where investors often falter is by frequently checking the value of their investments. Daily, or even weekly, scrutinising can lead to unnecessary stress, especially given the natural volatility of the markets. This behaviour often results in emotional decisions, such as panic selling when the market takes a temporary dip. Instead, quarterly, or even bi-annual reviews are more than sufficient for most long-term investors. And remember, every dip in the market is an opportunity to buy more at a discount.

There's also a burgeoning industry of robo-advisors, offering automated investment solutions based on algorithms. While these can be a great starting point for novices, it's essential to understand that they operate on a set formula and often lack the nuanced understanding that human financial advisors bring to the table. Personalisation, based on your unique financial goals and risk appetite, can make a significant difference in outcomes over time.

Diversification, a term often bandied about in investment circles, is not just about spreading your money across different assets but also about geographic diversification. Global diversification ensures that when one market underperforms, another might be soaring. This balance is crucial for overall stability in your portfolio.

Economic cycles are a reality. Boom periods are followed by downturns, which are subsequently followed by recoveries. Historically, equities have not only weathered these storms but have also outpaced inflation over the long term, making them a sound investment choice. If you had invested in equities just before a market crash, as long as you didn't panic sell and remained invested, your patience would have been rewarded as markets invariably recover and then some.

If there's one narrative that's been perennially floated around in the world of finance, it's that of the "Investment Midas" - an individual with an uncanny ability to turn every investment into gold. Glossy magazine covers and prime-time TV slots often celebrate these rarities, and in doing so, perpetuate a dangerous myth: that to succeed in investing, one needs almost superhuman capabilities.

The reality, however, is diametrically opposite.

The Egalitarian Nature of the Market

One of the most appealing aspects of the financial markets is their inherent egalitarianism. Whether you're a hedge fund manager overseeing billions or a schoolteacher investing a portion of your monthly savings, the market does not discriminate. Everyone has access to the same shares, the same bonds, the same investment vehicles.

Fundamentals Over Flash

While there's no denying that certain investors have an exceptional knack for understanding market nuances, the bedrock of most investment success stories is a deep-rooted adherence to fundamentals. A solid grounding in the basics of investing — understanding risk and volatility, diversifying investments, having a clear financial goal, and above all, patience — often outperforms any fleeting 'genius' moves.

Volatility Is Not the Same as Risk

Volatility is a frequent topic in this book because the negative way most investors react to volatility is a primary reason for their failure. Esteemed investor and writer Howard Marks had insightful thoughts on this matter:

"I define risk as the probability of a bad outcome, and volatility is, at best, an indicator of the presence of risk. But volatility is not risk." - Howard Marks

It's important to note that a permanent loss of capital has historically been non-existent for those who diversify their investments. This points to behaviour and decision-making as the primary sources of risk. While this may be a difficult truth for many investors to accept, it remains an undeniable fact.

The Power of Consistency

While the investment world lionises the daredevils, the unsung heroes are the consistent performers. These are the individuals or institutions that, year on year, deliver steady returns, avoid the allure of speculative bubbles, and keep their eye firmly on long-term growth. Their strategies rarely make headlines because they're not 'exciting'. Yet, they epitomise the true essence of successful investing.

Learning From the Legends

Consider Warren Buffett. While many laud his uncanny ability to pick winners, what's less spoken about is his rigorous adherence to core investment principles. He isn't swayed by market euphoria nor despondent during downturns. He once quipped, "Our favourite holding period is forever." This mindset, devoid of frenetic trading and chasing short-term gains, is testament to the fact that genius lies not in extraordinary actions but in disciplined consistency.

In the grand tapestry of the investment world, while the flashes of brilliance of a few might capture our attention, it's the steady, unyielding progress of the many that truly defines success. You don't need to be the smartest person in the room to grow your wealth; you just need to avoid the major pitfalls, stay committed to the journey, and remember that sometimes, the genius move is to simply let time and consistent strategy do their work.

In conclusion, building wealth through investing doesn't require genius, secret strategies, or chasing after the latest fad. The true "secret" is rooted in basic, time-tested principles: understand what you're investing in, stay the course, remain patient, and be wary of anyone selling you a dream without a proven track record. As with many things in life, in the realm of investing, simplicity, consistency, and a dash of common sense go a long way.

Chapter 14

The Zero-Sum Game: Unravelling the Dynamics of Winners and Losers in the Financial Markets

"One man may be more cunning than another, but not more cunning than everybody else."

Benjamin Franklin

A pervasive myth has ensnared millions of investors, seduced by the notion that higher costs secure expertise and promise superior returns. It's as if they've forgotten the warning of Roger Daltrey of The Who, who famously sang, "We won't get fooled again." Yet, the allure of expensive promises persists. Drawn by slick marketing and the allure of exclusivity, many believe that by paying more, they're securing a seat in the upper echelon of investment returns.

Several studies have consistently shown that higher fees don't secure the supposed best in the business or guarantee better performance. In fact, many low-cost funds often outperform their pricier counterparts over the long run. Yet, the allure remains. The perceived value is misconstrued as actual value. Investors are lured by the promise of elite fund managers and exclusive strategies, thinking their higher fees will buy them market-beating results. This misconception is costly and can erode the potential growth of one's portfolio over time.

Can a Feline's Fluke Outfox a Financial Expert in Stock Picking?

In 2012, The UK's Observer newspaper was eager to find out. They set up an unusual competition, placing Orlando, a ginger cat, in a stock-picking face-off against three seasoned investment professionals and a team of high school students. With an imaginary £5,000 handed to each participant at the year's onset, the results at year's end were both amusing and enlightening. The student team's funds dwindled to £4,840, and the pros, though they managed a profit, landed at £5,176. Orlando, however, using a high-tech strategy of tossing a toy mouse onto a grid representing various companies, managed a princely sum of £5,542. While this experiment was more whimsy than empirical, it emphasises a theme echoed in academic finance for the past four decades (with contributions from Chicago Booth faculty): many professional stock-pickers who outperform are beneficiaries of luck rather than exceptional skill.

This revelation has been a driving force behind the surge in passive investing. From an investor's perspective, it matters little whether managers are skilled or not, because exorbitant fees often gobble up any excess returns from supposed expertise. And as for Orlando? Perhaps he was just paw-sitively in tune with the markets!

So, might there be a better way?

One strategy that aims to grow wealth, fulfil long-term financial goals, and avoid costly investing mistakes is passive investing. This approach, using so-called index funds, originated in the US over 40 years ago and has since spread to other countries, including the UK. The strategy is endorsed by Nobel Prize winners, investing legends like Warren Buffett, and even the UK's financial industry regulator, the Financial Conduct Authority.

It is my strong opinion that passive investing stands as the simplest and surest path to long-term investment success.

At its core, passive investing advocates for broad market diversification and minimal trading at a very low cost, in contrast to active investing strategies that attempt to outperform the market through narrower bets and higher trading turnover.

In contrast, active investing strategies are promoted to beat the market, but they often fall short due to higher costs and the zero-sum nature of active investing. Active investors try to outperform the market, but as a group, their returns are cancelled out by the winners and losers in the market.

In the past, there might have been a case for active investment managers having an edge over their peers due to access to exclusive information. However, in today's interconnected world with the internet and financial data platforms like Bloomberg, information dissemination is instantaneous and accessible to all investment firms simultaneously. This levelling of the playing field has transformed active investing into a zero-sum game.

Bloomberg provides financial news and data, including real-time and historical price data, financial statistics, trading news, and analyst coverage, across various mediums. This implies that every active investment manager receives identical information from the same source simultaneously. No one holds an advantage in this scenario. All active managers will interpret this information in their own way, creating a zero-sum game where everyone can't be right with their predictions.

In a zero-sum game, for one participant to win, another must lose an equal amount. In the realm of active investing, this means that if a fund manager or investment team consistently outperforms the market, there must be others who underperform by an equal margin. While some may experience occasional success, it becomes challenging to maintain a consistent edge over the market, given the immense amount of information continuously flooding the financial world.

In the digital era, billions of pieces of information are generated every second, with social media playing a pivotal role in shaping investor sentiment. Amid this information overload, it becomes increasingly unrealistic to believe that any fund manager and their team can consistently make the right calls and outperform the market consistently.

The expectations market is largely a product of the expectations of speculators, trying to guess what other investors will expect and how they will act as each new bit of information finds its way into the marketplace. The expectations market is about speculation. The real market is about investing. The stock market, then, is a giant distraction to the business of investing. Too often, the market causes investors to focus on transitory and volatile short-term expectations, rather than on what is really important- the gradual accumulation of the returns and by corporate businesses.

One of the significant dangers of active investing lies in the potential for investors to overpay for this strategy without any guarantee of outperformance. The costs associated with actively managed funds, such as research, analysis, marketing, and trading expenses, can be substantial. However, research shows that many active funds fail to outperform their benchmark indices consistently. Investors paying higher fees for these funds may find themselves earning lower returns in comparison to lower-cost passive index tracking funds.

On the other hand, passive index tracking funds provide a compelling alternative. By capturing the entire market, these funds aim to replicate the market's returns, offering a low-cost and diversified investment option. Historically, index tracking funds have shown impressive performance for long-term investors, without requiring frequent trading or trying to outguess the market.

For active funds to stay ahead, they must consistently outperform the market by a margin sufficient to cover the additional expenses incurred through active management. In reality, this task proves to be challenging and has led many investors to favour the simplicity and reliability of passive investing.

The era of the internet and social media has reshaped the investment landscape, turning active investing into a zero-sum game. While some fund managers may occasionally outperform, the odds of consistent market-beating performance are slim. Investors need to be cautious about overpaying for active management without a guarantee of better returns. Embracing low-cost index tracking funds provides a prudent and historically successful approach to long-term investing.

In spite of all these facts, many intelligent individuals embark on a journey to beat the market averages in investments – these are the active investors. Their counterparts, the passive investors, are destined, by nature, to perform at par with the market average. Their positions, when combined, will somewhat reflect those of a globally diversified, actively managed fund. Consequently, the remaining universe of investors - the active ones - must also perform around the market average. However, they tend to incur significantly higher costs, which means, after accounting for these costs, their net performance will be below that of the passive investors. Paying higher investment charges in no way guarantees you better returns, in fact, if long-term history is anything to go by, it has the opposite effect.

Active fund managers consistently demonstrate a dismal track record, and evidence further solidifies this fact. Standard & Poor's, an authoritative source in the financial industry, has diligently monitored the performance of active managers for over two decades. According to their 2022 report, even when accounting for fees and funds that dropped out due to poor performance, the results are shocking. After a five-year period, a staggering 84% of actively managed fund managers fail to surpass their benchmark, and this figure rises to 90% after ten years.

The extent of underperformance is so severe that Standard and Poor’s explicitly states in their report that active managers' results are "worse than would be expected from luck."

Can you think of any other industry or profession where the failure rate reaches such alarming levels, as high as 90%? Astonishingly, despite these abysmal outcomes, significant fees continue to be deducted from client's portfolios. Imagine gathering 100 people to flip a coin 10 times. Statistically, a few might see their coin land on heads all 10 times. This analogy is relevant to investing too. Thus, a very small percentage of fund managers can genuinely claim their market-beating performance is due to skill. Put another way, if someone told me I had a 93% chance of dying if I do ‘X’ I’m not doing it!

I am of the opinion that placing your financial future and investment decisions in the hands of individuals who face no consequences for being wrong, yet charge substantial fees for attempting to be right, is not only perilous but also remarkably foolish.

Any actively managed funds’ short-term successes are frequently followed by prolonged periods of underperformance. Over extended durations, very few active fund managers outpace market averages. Yet, they consistently levy substantial fees on their clients, often without delivering the expected returns. It's a rarity to encounter a fund manager who can consistently outperform the market. It's remarkable that academic luminaries and renowned investors like Warren Buffett and Charlie Munger, who themselves have bested the market, champion the benefits of low-cost, globally diversified funds such as index funds. May their wisdom and experience, possibly even more than my own, guide you to make more informed investment decisions.

In light of this overwhelming evidence, it becomes clear that every investor stands to gain from embracing low cost, globally diversified funds. Research consistently demonstrates that maintaining low costs is a key factor in achieving superior returns. My recommendation has consistently remained unchanged: Diversify. The old adage remains true; don't place all your eggs in one basket. This principle lies at the core of my investment philosophy.

For example, my most popular investment fund encompasses more than 29,000 businesses globally. Put simply, when you invest in these funds, you become a part-owner or lender to a vast array of companies and organisations worldwide. These portfolios cover the entire spectrum, from small enterprises to multinational corporations, across a wide range of industries including technology, healthcare, automotive, entertainment, banking, utilities, and travel.

From companies that manufacture raincoats during the rainy season and companies that produce sunglasses during the summer. In the unfortunate event of a single company encountering difficulties or going bust, its impact on the overall portfolio is significantly mitigated due to the power of diversification. The impact would be barely perceptible.

Buffett advises the public to use index trackers, emphasising that most institutional and individual investors are better off with minimal-fee index funds than trying to pick individual stocks or beat the market through active strategies.

While some may still consider active investing, the evidence suggests that the vast majority of active fund managers underperform the market over time. Ordinary investors are often outclassed by larger institutional investors with significant resources and capabilities.

In contrast, passive funds may not outperform the market, but they own the entire market, providing investors with broad market exposure and diversification. This collective investing approach allows passive funds to cheaply purchase shares of thousands of companies, ensuring investors consistently capture the average market return, minus minimal costs.

I frequently stress to my clients the significance of creating an "investment stronghold" by primarily allocating investments to low cost, globally diversified, and time-tested portfolios. By doing so, the financial markets can effectively generate the returns required, eliminating the need to rely heavily on any specific country, asset, stock, or the latest investment trend.

For investors without a compelling reason to believe they possess unique insights, passive investing offers an effective way to participate in the market's overall growth and achieve long-term financial success cost effectively.

So, why do so many persist in seeking market outperformance?

There are several reasons why many investors persist in seeking market outperformance despite the evidence that it is difficult to consistently beat the market:

Financial Incentives

The financial industry, including fund managers, brokers, and financial advisors, often have a vested interest in promoting the pursuit of market outperformance. They may receive higher fees or commissions based on the assets they manage or the products they sell. As a result, there is a financial incentive to attract investors with the promise of superior returns. Overcomplicating matters unnecessarily enables them to find justifications for the fees they charge their clients.

Overconfidence and Cognitive Biases

Many investors believe they possess superior skills or information that will allow them to outperform the market. Overconfidence can lead people to overestimate their abilities and underestimate the challenges and risks involved in beating the market consistently. Cognitive biases, such as confirmation bias (seeking information that confirms existing beliefs) or hindsight bias (believing past events were more predictable than they actually were), can also contribute to the persistence of seeking outperformance. I cover the main investor biases later in this book.

Emotional Factors

The desire for market outperformance can be driven by emotions such as greed and fear. Investors may be tempted by the potential for higher returns and the fear of missing out on lucrative investment opportunities. These emotions can override rational decision-making and lead investors to take on higher risks or engage in speculative behaviour.

Competition and Benchmarking

In some cases, institutional investors and professional fund managers are driven by the pressure to outperform their peers or benchmark indices. This pressure can stem from the need to attract and retain clients, justify their fees, or advance their careers. The fear of underperforming relative to others can lead to a persistent pursuit of market outperformance.

Lack of Awareness or Understanding

Some investors may simply be unaware of the challenges associated with beating the market consistently or may not fully understand the implications of fees, transaction costs, and taxes on investment returns. They may believe that actively managed funds or individual stock picking offer a better chance of superior returns without considering the evidence to the contrary.

It's important to note that while some investors may succeed in outperforming the market over short periods, it is challenging to do so consistently over the long term. The efficient market hypothesis suggests that stock prices reflect all available information, making it difficult to consistently identify mispriced securities and gain a sustainable edge in the market.

It's always advisable for investors to carefully consider their investment goals, risk tolerance, and time horizon, and to seek professional advice when making investment decisions. Diversification, asset allocation, and a long-term perspective are often more reliable strategies for building wealth over time than constantly seeking market outperformance. Most investors choose to invest in funds that hold thousands of companies. This way, if some companies in the fund are not performing well, the others can help balance it out.

In our personal lives, we are presented with numerous opportunities and decisions that necessitate careful evaluation. It is vital to assess the associated risks, examine potential outcomes, and consider the long-term implications.

When making decisions, it is crucial to consider both the potential benefits and drawbacks. While it is natural to pursue higher returns or be enticed by compelling ideas or sales pitches, we must bear in mind that in life, apart from death and taxes, there are no guarantees.

Overpaying for management fees for underperforming actively managed funds only serves to compound the losses and your misery.

Active fund management essentially involves the fund managers speculating on future trends - what's coming next, where it's coming from, when it's going to hit, and how long it will last before they switch strategies again. They often charge steep fees for their attempts to beat the global stock market's organic performance, even though there's no guarantee they will succeed.

In this scenario, investors should focus on two things:

Charges and Performance

There's one thing that's assured in this scenario...charges. The only fact an investor can be certain of from the beginning are the charges they'll need to pay to the fund manager. The performance of an investment can never be predicted or guaranteed.

I'm not a believer in fantastical thinking. Instead, I place my trust in numbers. William Sharpe, a Nobel laureate, illustrated that passive investors are likely to outperform active investors collectively because they bear lower costs.

In my opinion, individuals who invest in low-cost funds will generally yield better returns than those who choose funds with higher costs. This is simply because it's a matter of elementary mathematics. After three decades of advising clients, I firmly believe that active fund management can be a costly risk for investors, with no accountability for the fund manager beyond potentially losing your business.

Understanding the impact of fees on your savings can sometimes be challenging. If you're paying between 1% to 1.5% more than necessary in fees, it can severely deplete your savings over your investment timeframe. This essentially implies that the more expensive money manager must exceed the performance of less costly funds by this same percentage just to break even. If they fail to do so, you're essentially losing money compared to if you'd chosen a lower cost fund. Overpaying for underperformance is a double whammy suffered by millions of investors.

1% or 1.5% may not appear immediately noticeable but don't be fooled. Similar to the erosive impact of inflation on your investment, they can have a significant effect due to compounding. Compounding can work for you or against you.

So, ignore the noise, gimmicks, and the empty promises. Stay focused on owning a vast number of good companies for long periods while controlling costs. Patience and discipline will serve you far better than chasing hype. I'll conclude with a simple formula that has served my clients well:

Low Costs + Time = Investing Success

This isn't merely a debate between active and passive strategies. It's about choosing between a straightforward, cost-effective, and operationally efficient investment approach and one that's complex, costly, and operationally inefficient. It boils down to simplicity versus complexity, efficiency versus inefficiency, and high-probability outcomes versus low-probability ones. Investing already presents its challenges; there's no need to complicate it further with an intricate, inefficient, and costly approach. This is why the streamlined, affordable, and efficient high-probability model consistently comes out on top for the long-term investor.

It's essential for investors to look beyond the price tag and evaluate the actual value and performance, ensuring they're not merely paying a premium for a mirage. Keep it simple, think long-term, and let compounding work its magic. Follow those principles and you'll do fine as an investor.

Chapter 15

Investment Mistakes That Will Hurt Your Wallet.

"Time is your friend; impulse is your enemy."

John Bogle

Investors can, through their own actions, amplify the riskiness of their investments. Many indeed fall into this trap. Practices such as engaging in active investing to predict market fluctuations, not diversifying enough, paying exorbitant or needless fees to managers and advisors, and leveraging borrowed money can demolish the respectable returns that long-term ownership of the world's leading companies would usually offer.

This series of investment blunders isn't exclusive to the average individual investor. Large institutional investors, as a collective, have consistently fallen short of the returns achieved by the patient, low-cost investor who holds on to their investments for decades. One primary reason for this is fees: these institutions often pay considerable sums to consultants who subsequently recommend high-fee managers. That's a losing proposition.

I've met clients who have been paying more than 2% annually just for the privilege of being invested, with no ongoing support, advice, or education. To me, this is outrageous. In the investment world, a very rare thing exists; you get what you don’t pay for. You don’t have to pay sky high fees to get an inflation beating return. Long-term history has proven conclusively that the global stock market has happily delivered inflation beating returns over the long-term and at a very low cost. The more you minimise your investment fees, the greater amount of money you can allocate towards investments. This can have a huge effect over time.

Overpaying for Investment Fees: The Financial Placebo Effect

In the world of medicine, the placebo effect is a phenomenon where patients experience real benefits from a treatment that has no therapeutic value, simply because they believe it's effective. Similarly, in the financial realm, a parallel can be drawn with investors overpaying for investment fees in the belief that higher fees translate to superior returns. This can be aptly termed the 'Financial Placebo Effect'.

Here's a deep dive into this phenomenon and its implications.

The Perception of Value

A common notion among investors is that "you get what you pay for." This line of thinking suggests that higher fees should inevitably lead to better investment performance. After all, if a fund or a manager charges more, surely, they must be offering something extraordinary. This perception of value can mislead investors into believing that overpaying for services guarantees better results.

The Reality of Returns

Numerous studies have shown that higher fees do not necessarily correlate with higher returns. In fact, the opposite may be true. According to research conducted by Morningstar, lower-cost funds often outperform their more expensive counterparts over the long term. This is especially evident in the case of actively managed funds versus index funds. Index funds, which typically have lower fees, often outperform actively managed funds, especially after fees are taken into account.

The Psychological Comfort

Why would investors knowingly pay higher fees? The answer may lie in our psyche. Just as a placebo pill can make a patient feel better because they believe they are receiving actual medication, paying higher fees can offer investors a psychological comfort. They may feel they are getting a superior service, or they might believe that a higher-priced fund has access to better resources or expertise.

The Expensive Illusion

The financial placebo effect can be costly. Over time, even a small difference in fees can compound, leading to a significant difference in overall returns. If two funds offer the same return before fees, but one charges 1% more in fees, over a 30-year period, the difference in end wealth can be substantial.

Breaking the Illusion

Education is key. By being aware of the financial placebo effect, investors can make more informed decisions. Some strategies to consider include:

Research and Compare: Before choosing a fund or financial advisor, research and compare fees. Look beyond the marketing and focus on the numbers.

Understand Fee Structures: Different funds and advisors have different fee structures. Ensure you know how and for what you are being charged.

Focus on Long-term Impact: Consider using tools or calculators that show the long-term impact of fees on potential returns.

It's human nature to associate price with value. However, in the world of investing, this can lead to the financial placebo effect, where investors mistakenly believe that higher fees guarantee better returns. By being aware of this phenomenon, investors can make more informed choices and potentially save significant amounts over their investing lifetimes. Just as it's essential to question the efficacy of a treatment in medicine, it's equally crucial to scrutinise the value offered by investment services.

If you have the talent or can hire someone who does have a godlike ability, you might surpass the market. But the chances of maintaining this consistently are markedly low. Keep in mind, a single success doesn't constitute a trend. Here's a thing; if they could do it consistently, do you really think they'd be working for you?

Spotting stellar investment managers that can consistently outperform the market is nigh on impossible. If anyone could, they would be amongst the wealthiest people on the planet.

Sure, a few investment managers excel in their field though in the short run, it's difficult to determine whether a great record is due to luck, talent, or circumstance. Most advisors, on the other hand, excel more at accruing hefty fees than they do at generating high returns. Essentially, their prime skill is salesmanship. How else do you think these large companies with their multi-million-pound marketing budget make their money?

Active management may seem alluring, but it can be hard for those outside the sector to accept that trillions can be wasted on a futile endeavour. Large firms have deep pockets and spend millions every year on marketing to persuade you that they possess some special advantage or exclusive knowledge. Outside of well-known impartial consumer websites, it's best to avoid financial media. Their main goal is to sell you something or provoke you into hastily doing the for the wrong thing at the wrong time for the wrong reasons.

The stark reality is that most managers who try to beat the market will fail. The odds are also high that the person courting your investment won't be the exception who succeeds. Meanwhile, the unfortunate investor is shelling out more than necessary in the 'hope' of outdoing what the general market can accomplish on its own given the time.

Adding to the difficulty of finding that rare high-fee manager who earns their keep is the fact that some investment professionals, like some amateurs, will have a streak of luck over short periods. If 1,000 managers make a market prediction at the start of the year, it's highly likely that at least one will be correct for nine consecutive years. A thousand monkeys would have an equal chance of producing a seemingly all-knowing prophet. But one difference would persist: The lucky monkey wouldn't have a queue of people waiting to invest with them.

In essence, when trillions of pounds are entrusted to fund managers who levy high fees, it's typically the managers who gain substantial profits, not their clients. I firmly believe that investors, whether large-scale or small, should opt for low-cost funds diversified globally.

In Fred Schwed's renowned investment book titled "Where are the Customers' Yachts," a captivating story unfolds. The book, published in 1955, recounts the tale of a visitor to New York who marvels at the extravagant yachts owned by bankers and brokers. Of course, none of the customers could afford yachts, even though they dutifully followed the advice of their bankers and brokers. Today, some 70 years later, we can draw parallels by replacing the investment bankers with active investment managers.

Legendary investor and founder of Vanguard Investments, John Bogle once said, "Don't look for the needle in the haystack. Just buy the haystack." The quote suggests that instead of spending time and effort trying to consistently identify the best individual companies to invest in (the "needle" in the haystack), it is more prudent to invest in a diversified portfolio (the "haystack") that encompasses a wide range of great businesses. By doing so, an investor reduces the risk associated with individual investment choices and benefits from the overall performance of the market.

The world of investing is rife with traps that can ensnare both the naive newcomer and the seasoned veteran. Emotion, speculation, and a barrage of misleading information can distort one's perspective and lead to impulsive decisions. Some of the most significant blunders that investors make stem from allowing these emotional impulses to override reasoned judgment.

Another prevalent mistake is succumbing to the siren song of market timing, the notion that one can consistently predict when to buy low and sell high. It's a tantalising idea: jump into the market when it's poised to rise and leap out just before it plummets. However, even the most seasoned professionals cannot do this consistently. The reality is market timing requires being right twice — when to get in and when to get out. How likely is it that you'll get both decisions right every time? One misstep can result in missed opportunities or significant losses.

Timing the market involves predicting future market movements with a high degree of accuracy. For an investor to successfully time the market, they must accurately determine both when to enter and when to exit. However, achieving this consistently is extremely challenging for several reasons:

Inherent Uncertainty of the Market: Financial markets are influenced by a vast array of factors, ranging from economic data, geopolitical events, to psychological factors among investors. Predicting the interplay of these factors is complex.

Behavioural Biases: Humans are susceptible to a range of cognitive biases previously discussed such as overconfidence, herd behaviour, and loss aversion. These biases can often cloud judgement and lead to suboptimal decisions. For instance, during a market rally, the fear of missing out (FOMO) might push an investor to buy at a peak, only to regret it when the market corrects.

The Role of News and Events: Unforeseen news or global events can have immediate and drastic impacts on the market. Examples include sudden geopolitical conflicts, unexpected election outcomes, or unforeseen global health crises. These events are unpredictable and can rapidly change market sentiment.

Market Efficiency: The Efficient Market Hypothesis (EMH) suggests that at any given time, asset prices fully reflect all available information. If this is the case, then consistently outperforming the market through timing would be nearly impossible since all known information is already priced in.

Cost Implications: Regularly moving in and out of the market incurs transaction costs and create potential tax issues. Even if an investor could time the market with some degree of accuracy, the costs associated with frequent trading could erode the benefits.

Performance Pressure: The pressure to deliver consistent returns can lead investors to make impulsive decisions. Even seasoned professionals face the psychological pressure of past performance, which might affect their future decisions.

Historical Precedence: Many studies have shown that even professional fund managers, who have access to vast resources and research, struggle to consistently outperform the market over long periods.

In summary, while it's tempting to believe that one can master the art of market timing, the myriad of unpredictable variables combined with human behavioural tendencies make it nigh on impossible to achieve consistently. Often, a long-term investment strategy, based on solid fundamentals and periodic rebalancing, proves to be more effective than trying to time the market's every move.

Few people claim they're "timing the market." It might surprise you, but despite the frequent discussions about the dangers of trying to "time the market," can you recall anyone confessing they're doing just that?

I surely can't. I'd wager you can't either. Quite peculiar, isn't it?

Here's my theory:

People genuinely don't think they're attempting to "time the market" when they pull out of a plummeting market or dive headfirst into a surge. Instead, they genuinely perceive their actions as responsible investing. Can you spot the distinction?

Exiting a plummeting market, symbolically akin to fleeing a burning house, seems like a no-brainer. Joining in on a market frenzy often feels as if we're merely adapting to a transformed world, and we're just catching up.

Both moves are seen as acts of wisdom, rather than attempts to "time the market." In my view, steering clear of "market timing" is a breeze. The real challenge? Persuading individuals to refrain from moves that seem incredibly astute in real-time. Mistakes, when compounded, can haunt your finances indefinitely.

Such decisions inherently carry substantial risks. It's clear that our instinct to sell is sharpest when markets dip. However, historical data, notably from fund flows, underscores a recurring human error: many sell too close to market lows, often misjudging the timing.

Following a sell-off, deciding the right moment to re-enter is equally challenging. The market seldom offers a welcoming 'right' moment.

Even offloading during market highs can backfire, potentially sidelining you from substantial gains. Recall the mid-90s: many financial experts anticipated a market peak and liquidated their positions. Alan Greenspan's iconic "Irrational Exuberance" address was delivered in 1996. Yet, the market surged by another 100% before peaking.

Those who exited, even amidst bullish sentiments, inadvertently hampered their financial trajectory. The 90s aptly illustrate the adage, "The market can remain irrational longer than you can remain solvent."

A more pragmatic and less stressful investment approach? Weather the storm. The market will, at times, display bouts of irrationality, both in surges and plunges. However, the only guaranteed method to capture all market gains is to remain consistently invested. Never forget: the repercussions of being wrong can reverberate indefinitely.

A passive, long-term approach eliminates the need for this kind of predictive precision, insulating investors from the daily volatility of the markets.

Time Waits for No Investor

In the theatre of investment, there's a character we're all too familiar with: the Perpetual Waiter. This is the would-be investor who believes ardently in the concept of "perfect timing." They watch the market with a hawk's eye, waiting for that elusive moment when everything aligns - when stocks are at their lowest or the real estate bubble seems ripe for the piercing. They believe that there's a singular moment, a cosmic confluence, which if harnessed, will rain riches upon them.

But here's the tragedy of the Perpetual Waiter: while they're waiting for the planets of opportunity to align, time continues its relentless march forward. Days become weeks, weeks morph into months, and months roll into years. They study charts, analyse trends, and read forecasts. They discuss strategies at dinners and debate predictions with peers. But the actual act of investment remains a distant dream.

One day, they look over their shoulder and realise that the market never really offered the 'perfect' moment for which they were waiting. There were highs, there were lows, there were plateaus - but no single magical instant. Instead, the years have unfurled a tapestry of fluctuating opportunities, each with its own set of risks and rewards.

Ironically, those who stepped into the waters of investment, even hesitantly, even during less-than-ideal circumstances, now have a portfolio to show. Their assets might have weathered storms, experienced surges, or even trudged through sluggish phases, but they grew, changed, and most importantly, existed.

It Never Seems Like a Good Time to Buy

The Perpetual Waiter's quest for perfection rendered them paralysed. Their fears of the imperfect prevented them from seeing the broader panorama - that it's not about the 'perfect' time but rather about 'time in' the market. Investing is a journey, not a single leap, and sometimes the best time to start that journey is simply the moment the thought first crosses your mind.

Because in the vast chronicle of investment, time doesn't wait for the perfect moment. It just moves on, leaving behind tales of those who dared and those who merely dreamt.

Similarly, a lack of diversification can prove disastrous. Some investors chase past performance, pouring all their resources into a single asset class, sector, or stock that has been doing well. This is akin to putting all your eggs in one basket, which can be problematic if the specific investment or sector takes a downturn. Proper diversification ensures that if one area underperforms, other parts of your portfolio can compensate. It's vastly preferable to maintain a well-balanced portfolio.

Then there's the temptation of the latest "hot tip" or financial fad, a mistake that has burned many investors. Word of mouth, media hype, or simply the thrill of the 'next big thing' can sway investors into jumping onto a bandwagon without adequate due diligence. Such decisions, more often than not, are grounded in the Fear of Missing Out (FOMO) rather than solid financial logic. Later in the book, I explore the nuances of rebalancing a diversified portfolio and the pitfalls of trend-driven investing in greater detail.

Lastly, the very human tendency to let pride or fear dictate investment decisions can be detrimental. Some investors, unable to admit a mistake, hold onto underperforming assets for far too long, driven by the hope that they'll bounce back. Others might sell too soon, spurred by short-term market jitters or panic during downturns. Objectivity can be a scarce commodity in the face of fluctuating markets, but it is precisely during these times that it becomes invaluable.

To navigate the world of investing successfully, one must continuously educate oneself, maintain discipline, and stay the course even when faced with tempting shortcuts or daunting obstacles. While it's tempting to search for shortcuts or secret formulas, the reality is that the tried-and-true principles of patience, diversification, and low costs have withstood the test of time.

Indeed, as with many things in life, in the realm of investing, sometimes the hardest thing to do is to do nothing. Amid the clamour of stock tips, market predictions, and the endless stream of financial news, there's value in taking a step back, tuning out the noise, and simply letting the power of compounding work its magic.

In the end, it's worth remembering another pearl of wisdom from Bogle: "Investing is not nearly as difficult as it looks. Successful investing involves doing a few things right and avoiding serious mistakes." The path to investment success might be paved with pitfalls, but with a clear strategy and a disciplined mindset, it's a journey well within reach for every investor.

Never Let the Tax Tail Wag the Dog

I've played snooker competitively since I was 13. Imagine I am playing in a best of 9 frame final and I am 4 nil up and on the verge of winning. Yet, bizarrely, instead of sealing the victory, I ask my opponent if they want to extend the match to a best of 11 frames.

Sounds absurd, right? Why would I do this? What would be your reaction?

Yet, this odd behaviour mirrors a common conundrum in the investment sphere.

Investors often possess a stock, or an investment fund that has performed exceptionally well, becoming a significant chunk of their wealth.

Victory seems certain.

However, they hesitate to sell due to two prevailing fears:

The stock or fund might continue its upward trajectory, leading to potential FOMO (Fear of Missing Out).

Selling now might mean paying a hefty sum in capital gains taxes.

Let's delve deeper into these apprehensions.

Thought 1: Consider the alternative – the stock or fund nosedives, and you're left with huge losses. Is that a gamble you're willing to take?

One might argue the stock in question is a "safe bet." But history is littered with examples like Enron, and Goldman Sachs and others that were once deemed "safe." The pivotal question remains: is the perceived minimal risk worth the stakes?

Thought 2: A common misconception paints capital gains taxes as punitive. In reality, they signify a triumphant investment venture. In essence, owing capital gains tax means you've successfully profited. After all, weren't profits your ultimate goal?

The victory is yours; recognise it.

Whether it's holding on with crossed fingers, hoping the tide won't turn, or wishing for the stock price to dip to save on taxes – both scenarios sound equally irrational when said aloud. Ultimately, the decision rests in your hands, but it's vital to evaluate these aspects before choosing your next move.

Chapter 16

The Winning Formula: Low-Cost Funds and Global Giants

"Beware of little expenses; a small leak will sink a great ship."

Benjamin Franklin

Investing wisely is a key responsibility I hold as a financial advisor. Over the years, I have consistently guided my clients to invest in what has always worked - a strategy built on the pillars of patience, long-term vision, and the power of compounding.

The cornerstone of this approach lies in investing over a medium to long term in low-cost funds. These funds pool investments from numerous individuals and invest in a broad range of companies, comprising thousands of the largest and most profitable businesses worldwide. By doing so, we create a diversified portfolio that reduces risk and provides exposure to various sectors and industries.

The magic of compounding then takes centre stage. As the investments grow, the earnings from one year become a foundation for growth in the following year, generating a snowball effect that multiplies wealth over time. The longer we stay invested, the more time our money has to benefit from this mathematical wizardry, resulting in exponential growth potential.

This strategy aligns with the principle of "time in the market" rather than trying to "time the market." Attempting to predict short-term market movements is inherently risky and often leads to suboptimal results. Instead, we focus on staying committed to our investment strategy, allowing the global economy and the underlying businesses to do their work and deliver returns over time.

Central to the ethos of this investment approach is an appreciation for the inherent strength of global giants. These behemoths, often with multi-decade track records, have built their businesses on strong foundations, innovative strategies, and an ability to adapt to the changing dynamics of the global economy. Their scale, diversified revenue streams, and established market presence make them reliable contributors to portfolio growth.

However, a common mistake investors make is equating familiarity with safety. Just because a company is a household name doesn't necessarily mean it's a good investment. Herein lies the beauty of low-cost funds that focus on global giants: they undergo rigorous scrutiny and assessment by teams of professionals before being included in a fund or index. The companies that make the cut are not merely popular but have demonstrated robustness in their operations, profitability, and strategic vision. Thus, investors indirectly benefit from the expertise of professionals who ensure that these global giants are indeed the creme de la creme of the business world.

Furthermore, low-cost funds offer the added benefit of liquidity. Unlike some other investment vehicles, if an emergency arises or if an investor's financial circumstances change, these funds often allow for relatively easy and swift access to capital. This flexibility can be a lifesaver in unpredictable times, ensuring that investors don't find themselves in a bind.

Another often-overlooked advantage of investing in global giants through low-cost funds is the potential for dividend income. Many of the world's largest companies have a track record of paying dividends to their shareholders. These dividends, when reinvested, add another layer to the compounding effect, enhancing the growth potential of the investment. Over time, this can significantly boost the total returns for an investor.

It's essential to remember that investing is a journey, not a quick fix. The ups and downs of the market are normal, and maintaining a long-term perspective helps navigate through volatility. In the face of short-term fluctuations, the resilience of a well-constructed portfolio shines through, especially when invested in the world's most successful companies.

Finally, it's worth noting the educational aspect of such an investment strategy. As investors observe their portfolios over time, they gain insights into the global economic landscape, understanding which sectors thrive under certain conditions and the interplay of various industries. This not only refines their financial acumen but also breeds confidence in their investment decisions.

In summation, the combination of low-cost funds and global giants is not a trend or a fleeting investment fad. It's an enduring strategy grounded in the principles of diversification, resilience, and the undeniable power of compounding. As an advisor, it's a privilege to guide clients along this proven path, watching as they realise their aspirations and forge a legacy of financial stability.

Chapter 17

Auto Lane Assist for Your Investments: The Power of Portfolio Rebalancing

Rebalancing your investment portfolio is a lot like staying in your lane while driving. If you were to close your eyes while driving, I'll bet any amount of money that you wouldn't be able to keep them closed for more than a few seconds before you would start dangerously veering out of your lane.

Just as a vigilant driver relies on small course corrections to stay in their lane, a prudent investor must periodically reassess their portfolio's composition.

Small course corrections become necessary to steer you back into your lane and keep you on track. Many modern cars have auto lane assist systems which monitor the car's position on the road, detects if the driver is unintentionally leaving their lane and reacts to let you know to make the adjustment.

Similarly, a portfolio can drift from its target asset allocation over time as some investments outperform others. Rebalancing brings your portfolio back into alignment, just as small turns of the wheel keep your car in the correct lane.

REBALANCING: "BUYING LOW AND SELLING HIGH"

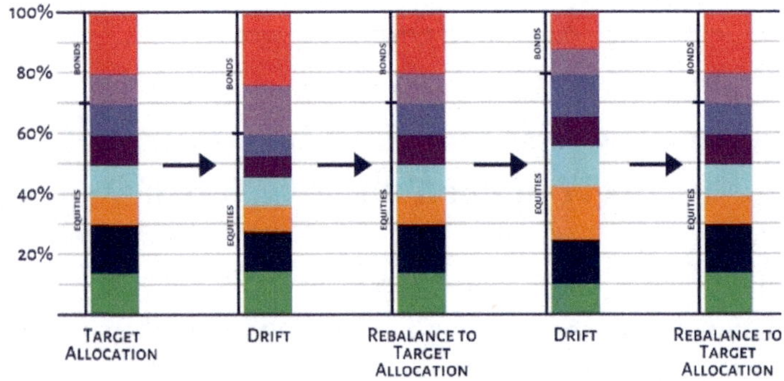

Here is an explanation of rebalancing a stock portfolio using percentages:

Imagine you want to allocate your stock portfolio with 60% in U.S. stocks and 40% in international stocks. But after a period of significant outperformance by U.S. stocks, your allocation shifts to 70% U.S. and 30% international. Your portfolio is now drifting out of lane.

Rebalancing in this case would involve selling some of the U.S. stocks that have grown to dominate your portfolio (trimming back the oversized allocation) and using the proceeds from selling U.S. stocks to buy more international stocks, which now make up a smaller portion of your portfolio.

This returns your stock portfolio back to the original 60/40 U.S./international mix and gets you back in lane. Rebalancing forces you to sell some U.S. stocks high after their growth and buy some international stocks that are now relatively "on sale."

For example, if your £100,000 portfolio was originally invested as £60,000 in U.S. stocks and £40,000 in international:

- After U.S. outperformance, it's now £70,000 U.S. and £30,000 international

- Rebalance by selling £10,000 of U.S. stocks and using that £10,000 to buy international stocks

- Portfolio is rebalanced back to £60,000 U.S. and £40,000 international

The percentages are restored to your target 60/40 allocation. This rebalancing discipline can improve returns over the long run by selling high and buying low. Sticking to your investment plan prevents emotion from creeping in during market swings.

Some clients ask, "Why sell the investments that are doing well to buy the ones lagging behind?" The reason is that markets are cyclical - sooner or later, today's winners may become tomorrow's laggards.

By rebalancing, we are taking some profits in the strong performers and buying more of the assets that haven't done as well but are now at lower prices. This discipline cashes in on cyclical rotations and may improve returns over long periods.

The trends don't last forever. What's hot now may cool off later. We rebalance to manage risk and keep a disciplined approach, not try to predict the future. Maintaining balance and allocation helps portfolios stay on track when market leadership eventually shifts.

Just like a vehicle alignment keeps your car driving straight, portfolio rebalancing keeps your investments headed toward your ultimate destination. Periodic rebalancing is essential for long-term success.

How often should you rebalance? For most investors, rebalancing once a year is probably fine, just like an annual vehicle safety inspection. For large portfolios, a quarterly or bi-annual review may be better, similar to checking your oil and tyre pressure more frequently.

Many modern investment funds have automatic rebalancing features, which take care of realigning the portfolio allocation, so investors don't have to do it themselves.

Easy, small adjustments maintain your original asset mix, just like minor course corrections when driving. Staying disciplined prevents you from drifting off track. Rebalancing keeps you in your lane on the road to financial success.

Part 5

Understanding Investment Risks and Returns

Chapter 18

Inflation's Creeping Constrictor: A Subtle Stranglehold on Our Financial Dreams

"Inflation is as violent as a mugger, as frightening as an armed robber and as deadly as a hit man."

Ronald Reagan

In the world of finance, there are obvious threats and then there are silent ones. Like a boa constrictor wrapping itself around its prey, inflation might not deliver an immediate lethal squeeze, but its effects are undeniable over time. The prey, in this case, are our dreams, aspirations, and the legacy we intend to leave behind. Inflation, unlike a sudden ambush, slowly encircles us much like a boa constrictor ensnaring its prey. The victim isn't just currency; it's our aspirations, our plans, and the legacy we hope to bequeath.

In popular culture, we often see figures that are relentless, unstoppable, and immune to reason. Take, for instance, the iconic Terminator from James Cameron's 1984 science fiction film. Much like the original Terminator who was an unstoppable machine, inflation, when unleashed, can be an equally unyielding force in the realm of economics. As a playful allusion to the movie, consider this: 'Listen, and understand. That inflation is out there. It can't be bargained with. It can't be reasoned with. It doesn't feel pity, or remorse, or fear. And it absolutely will not stop, ever, until your purchasing power is dead.' This analogy might sound dramatic, but the dangers and persistent nature of uncontrolled inflation cannot be understated.

For many retired couples, it's not uncommon for one partner to live another thirty years or so. Brace yourself, because in that timeframe, your yearly lifestyle cost could skyrocket, potentially tripling or more. Don't believe me? Financial planning isn't a game of exacts; it's a maze of unpredictability. If it's absolute certainty you yearn, die now.

Imagine stepping into retirement with a Lifestyle cost of £40,000 per year. Fast forward using trendline inflation, and you could be shelling out £100,000 or even more annually, just to keep your head above water and purchase the same exact items.

A Subtle Impact Over Time

Visualise a pot of water on a stove. At a low flame, it seems unaltered. But with time, it eventually boils and evaporates. Similarly, inflation, even in small doses, begins inconspicuously. Yet, as years roll on, it steadily eats away at the genuine worth of your savings.

One of the most profound tragedies about inflation is its insidious nature. It's like an odourless, but deadly gas. If someone were to reach into your bank account and take out a few pounds every month, you'd be outraged. But that's precisely what inflation does, albeit silently. Each year, your money loses a little bit of its purchasing power. Those sums that felt substantial a decade ago no longer have the same heft, and the lifestyle they promised grows more distant.

Funds that felt ample years ago slowly lose their strength, and associated dreams become distant mirages.

Real-World Implications of Inflation

It's not just about numbers on a screen, but tangible consequences. That dream of sending your child to a prestigious university, buying your dream home, or embarking on a luxurious retirement tour around Europe? They're all threatened by inflation's relentless squeeze.

Retirement, in particular, becomes a significant concern. Imagine having spent 40 years diligently saving, only to find out that the nest egg you've cultivated won't be sufficient for the retirement you envisioned. The longer we live, the more pronounced the effects of inflation become.

Moreover, the effects of inflation aren't always evenly spread. Certain sectors may experience price rises more acutely than others. For example, healthcare or education costs might rise faster than general inflation. For a parent aspiring to give their child the best education, or an elderly person needing frequent medical care, the effects of inflation can be disproportionately harsh.

The Consumer Society and Inflation

In our consumer-centric world, inflation's touch extends to daily life. Over time, essentials become pricier, and what were once considered luxuries, like a favourite coffee brand or annual holidays, start feeling like rare indulgences.

The Deception of Cash

In a world attracted to tangible assets, holding cash might feel safe, but it's a mirage. Like an ever-diminishing ice sculpture, the beauty and value of cash are fleeting. A sum of £100,000, with a 5% inflation rate, becomes merely £95,000 in a year, and almost halved in a decade. Meanwhile, investments, despite their short-term fluctuations, have historically not just matched but crushed inflation. That £100,000, if wisely invested, could potentially swell to £175,000 in the same period.

Why Hoarding Cash Can Be Financial Foolishness

Too Much Cash is Trash: When Your Savings Sink Instead of Soar

Ah, the comforting rustle of banknotes, the solid clang of coins, and the satisfaction of checking one's savings account. Cash! The old reliable. Or is it? Let's dive into the mirage of the cash comfort zone and the quicksand it actually might be.

The Illusion of Safety

Imagine a scene where you're carefully stacking bricks to build a wall of financial security. But instead of mortar, you're using wet sand. With every passing year, as inflation rates rise and the real value of money dwindles, those bricks become more and more unstable. This isn't just a one-year ordeal; the compounding effect of inflation means that year after year, your wall is inching closer to a collapse. That's what happens when you rely too much on cash.

Headline Savings Rates: The Magician's Misdirection

We've all seen the flashy headlines: "Savings Accounts Offering 5%!" But let's pull back the curtain for the big reveal. The actual savings rate is not as glamorous when you factor in the taxman's cut. Think of it like a cake where the government inevitably takes its (sometimes large) slice before you get to savour the rest.

For illustrative purposes, we'll stick with the headline rate you've seen advertised: "5% instant access." For ease of maths, let's assume you've plonked £100,000 into such an account. Over 12 months, you get £5,000 of interest before tax. As you glimpse that amount, a dark cloud starts to ominously appear; it's the taxman. But wait—there's a silver lining called the Personal Savings Allowance, where the government lets you keep the first £1,000 of interest tax-free. Beyond that? The remaining £4,000 is taxed at your marginal rate (let's assume 20%).

So, from that £4,000, 20% (or £800) goes straight to the taxman. This leaves you with £3,200. Add the initial tax-free £1,000, and you get a total interest of £4,200. Your end balance? £104,200.

Now, remember inflation? To just keep up with an 8.8% rate, your balance would need to be £108,800. When you do the maths, your savings, in real inflation-adjusted terms, sit at just over £95,000. Within a mere year, you've lost nearly £5,000 in purchasing power. Does that stash of cash still seem like a safe place?

And if you think that's a grim tale, the picture darkens for Higher Rate Taxpayers. Many are now finding themselves in this bracket as political and financial dynamics shift. For them, the interest of £5,000 trims down to just £3,200 post-tax. Here, your supposed "savings" of £103,200 are worth just over £94,000 in real terms.

As for Additional Rate Taxpayers, grab that dusty bottle of tequila, put on your comfiest crying pants, and take a moment to laugh (or sob) at the cosmic punchline that is your financial life!

Inflation: The Invisible Pickpocket

Inflation remains the ever-lurking shadow in this story. Like a thief in the night, it consistently erodes the buying power of your money. With a yearly inflation rate in 2023 at 8.8%, and with the compounding effect in play, this erosion is an unyielding menace. Newsflash! There isn't a bank account anywhere that pays anything like 8.8%.

Imagine you've bought a tub of ice cream, representing your savings, on a hot day, symbolising inflation. Initially, the ice cream seems perfectly intact, just as your savings appear unaffected in the early stages of inflation. This initial phase is deceptive, much like the quiet moments when you first put a kettle on the stove. The water (your savings) is there, seemingly stable.

However, as you leisurely search for a nice spot to sit and enjoy your ice cream, a subtle change begins. Slowly but surely, the heat (inflation) starts to affect the ice cream. This change is gradual, almost imperceptible at first, mirroring the initial, often unnoticed impact of inflation on your savings.

Just like how water in a kettle begins to warm up without immediate signs of boiling, your savings start to lose their value without immediate, visible impacts. By the time you settle down to enjoy your ice cream, you find that half of it has melted away. Similarly, in an inflationary environment, by the time you realise what's happening, a significant portion of your savings' purchasing power may have eroded. This slow, creeping effect of inflation is akin to the kettle finally reaching its boiling point, where the water starts to evaporate.

In both cases—whether it's your melting ice cream or the boiling kettle—what seemed stable and secure at first can gradually diminish to a point of significant loss, demonstrating the insidious and often underestimated power of inflation on your savings.

The Verdict: Cash Has Its Place, But Don't Make It The Throne

Cash is undoubtedly essential. It's the liquid buffer that comes to the rescue during emergencies, the cushion for when the financial seas get stormy. But as a long-term guardian of your wealth? That's like betting on a turtle in a horse race.

Remember, after adjusting for inflation, cash returns are largely negative. The allure of "safe" cash might be tempting, but in the vast theatre of finance, it might just set the stage for a tragic drama of dwindling purchasing power.

Just as we rely on net income rather than gross, it's inflation-adjusted returns that determine our true financial standing, not nominal cash returns. The real returns of cash are primarily negative and destroy wealth, impacting our purchasing power and the ability to maintain a certain lifestyle. Everything else it just noise.

The bottom line? Have some cash, by all means. But let's not place it on a pedestal. In the symphony of finance, cash is just one instrument, and often, not the most melodious one.

Gold vs. Stocks: A Long-Term Perspective

Many investors regard gold as the quintessential hedge against inflation. For millennia, it has served as a store of value, and its applications in jewellery and electronics lend it undeniable tangible worth. Moreover, in contrast to governmental regulated currencies, gold's supply is notably limited.

However, gold's efficacy as a hedge against inflation has been inconsistent. Let's delve deeper into the validity of gold as a reliable inflation safeguard.

The allure of gold as a prime long-term investment has grown amongst Americans, with 26% viewing it as the top choice this year (2023) compared to just 15% in 2022, as per a Gallup report from May 2023. Conversely, the stock market's charm dwindled, with preference dropping from 24% to 18%. Bonds, however, witnessed a subtle climb, going from 4% to 7%.

Historically, this pattern of preference shift is no stranger to periods when the stock market behaves bearishly. Such recalibrations by ordinary investors, influenced by past market behaviours, often go unnoticed by mainstream financial publications.

But let's delve deeper into the long-standing debate surrounding the merits of gold versus a diverse portfolio of quality companies for long-term investment.

To start, gold doesn't fit the typical profile of an investment. A genuine investment is anticipated to grow in value and yield a rising income over time. Gold neither yields a product nor offers returns on its own. It merely exists. While it may serve aesthetic purposes or function as a symbol of affluence, its primary financial role is that of an inflation hedge. But how efficient has it been in that role?

In January 1980, the Consumer Price Index (inflation) stood at 78. In 2023 it stands at 306. It's up nearly 4 times during this period. Casting our minds back, gold's price was capped at $35 an ounce from World War II until the U.S. ditched the gold standard in 1971. Subsequently, the 70s witnessed a surge, adjusting for two decades of inflation, peaking at $850 an ounce in January 1980.

Fast forward 44 years from that peak, and gold now stands at $1,965 an ounce. In this period, gold yielded no dividends or interest payments. For perspective, to merely keep pace with inflation since 1980, today's gold value should be around $3,200, but it's nowhere near that mark.

But wait, it gets much worse. If one had turned their gaze towards the S&P 500, they would have seen a meteoric rise. From a value of 115 in January 1980, the index now towers at 4,500 in September 2023. That's an astounding 39-fold growth, excluding dividends, something gold inherently lacks. With reinvested dividends, a mere $850 invested in the S&P 500 back in January 1980 would now be worth a staggering $101,057 today (2023). This equates to an annualised compound return of 11.61%.

Some argue gold's efficacy as an inflation hedge spans centuries. While the origins of this notion remain hazy, its relevance to today's "ordinary investor" worried about the stock market's volatility is questionable.

In summary, while gold has its unique allure, when viewed through the lens of historical data, a diversified stock portfolio considerably outshines its lustrous counterpart in the long-term investment arena. Remember, while past successes don't dictate future outcomes, historical data concerning inflation and investment returns is unequivocal. This isn't investment advice but an undeniable truth.

Chapter 19

From Incremental to Explosive: Harnessing the Full Potential of Compounding and Exponential Growth

"Compound interest is the eighth wonder of the world. He who understand it, earns it, he who doesn't, pays it.

Albert Einstein

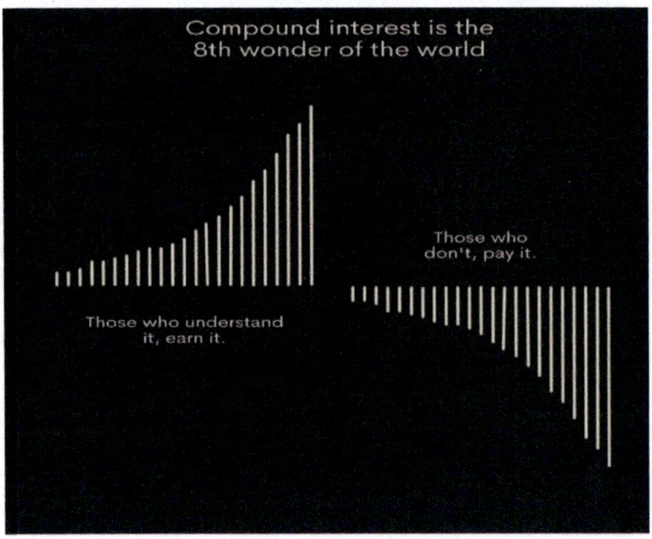

The Magic of Compound Growth – The 8th Wonder of the World

Compounding has been mentioned many times in this book so now let us take a real world look at just how powerful it can be. Compound growth is the snowball effect of reinvesting investment returns to generate additional earnings. As your investments grow, the returns they generate can be reinvested, leading to exponential growth over time. Starting early allows for a more extended period of compounding, magnifying the benefits significantly.

The Power of Starting Early

When it comes to building wealth and securing a financially stable future, few things are as crucial as starting to invest as early as possible. The secret lies in the remarkable phenomenon known as compound growth, which can work wonders over time. In this piece, we'll explore the significance of early investing and provide an illuminating example comparing two individuals—one who starts saving £100 per month from age 20 to 60 and another who invests £500 per month from age 40 to 60, both using an annual compound return of 7% for illustrative purposes.

Example 1: Investing from Age 20 to 40 with £100 per Month:

Let's consider an individual who diligently invests £100 per month from the age of 20 to 40, assuming for illustrative purposes an annual compound of 7% net of charges. By the time they reach 40, they will have invested £24,000 (£100 per month for 20 years). However, due to the power of compounding, their investment would have grown to an impressive £52,396. We will assume that this client never makes another contribution from this point. They just leave their investment growing to age 60. Using the same example investment net return of 7% per annum, their £52,396 that they had accumulated at age 40 will have grown to £216,613 at age 60.

Example 2: Investing from Age 40 to 60 with £400 per Month:

Now, let's examine another individual who starts investing later in life, beginning at age 40, but contributes a higher monthly amount of £400 to make up for lost ground. Over 20 years, their total investment would amount to £96,000. Considering the same annual compound return of 7%, their investment would have grown to £208,370 by the time they turn 60.

The Impact of Starting Early:

Comparing the two scenarios, we observe that despite the second individual contributing 4 times the monthly sum, they end up with a smaller investment value at age 60. This stark difference can be attributed to the compounding effect working in favour of the first individual who started investing earlier and then let their investment continue to grow until 60. Time, rather than the amount invested, becomes the most influential factor in harnessing its power.

The importance of starting to invest as early as possible cannot be overstated. By allowing your investments to benefit from the phenomenon of compound growth over an extended period, you position yourself for a more secure financial future. The examples provided demonstrate how even a modest monthly contribution can accumulate into a substantial nest egg when invested over several decades. Whether it's for retirement, education, or any other long-term goal, the sooner you begin, the more substantial the potential rewards. So, seize the opportunity to embark on your investment journey early, and let the magic of compounding work its wonders for your financial well-being.

It's important however to consider the negative effects of compounding when expensive charges are involved. Imagine you have £100,000 invested in an investment that experiences a 5% annual growth rate, but there is also an annual charge of 1.5% on the investment.

After the first year, your investment would grow by £5,000, bringing the total to £105,000. However, the 1.5% annual charge on the investment would be deducted, resulting in a charge of £1,575. So, your net total after the charge would be £103,425.

In the second year, the 5% growth rate would be calculated based on the new total (£103,425), resulting in growth of £5,171.25 taking the new total before charges to £108,596. However, the 1.5% annual charge would also be applied to the new total, resulting in a charge of £1,628. After deducting the charge, your net total for the second year would be £106,967.

This cycle continues, with the growth and charges being calculated each year. While the investment experiences compound growth, the charges also compound and have a detrimental effect on the overall growth of your investment.

It's important to be mindful of the impact of charges and consider them when evaluating the growth of your investment. Understanding the detrimental effects of compounding charges can help you make informed decisions and potentially mitigate their impact on your investment's growth.

It's crucial to highlight the significance of low-cost investments that have a minimal impact compared to investments with higher charges.

When it comes to investing, choosing low-cost investments can be beneficial. We all must pay to have our money invested, however, investments with lower charges, such as lower annual management fees have a smaller impact on your overall investment growth. This means that more of your investment's potential growth can be retained and compounded over time.

For example, if you have two investments with the same growth rate but different charges, the one with lower charges will naturally result in a higher net return over the long term. Even seemingly small differences in charges can have a significant impact on your investment's growth when compounded over many years.

By opting for low-cost investments, you can maximise the potential growth of your investment and mitigate the negative effects of compounding charges. It's important to carefully consider the costs associated with an investment and compare them to potential returns when making investment decisions.

The principle of compound interest can often be challenging to grasp. Here we look at the most common thing investors overlook regarding compound growth.

Quick example: Suppose the average investor has £100,000 to invest for 30-40 years and is offered two portfolio options:

Portfolio A: Less volatile, yet typically generates a 5% return on average.
Portfolio B: More volatile, but typically generates a 10% return on average.

If you then ask the average investor what they believe the difference in total return for these two portfolios will be at the end of the periods, what do you think they'll say? Most will tell you that portfolio B will outperform portfolio A by 2:1 as the expectation is that it will mirror the difference in the annual returns. This common assumption is grossly misguided, illustrating that the concept of compounding isn't as simple as it may seem.

In fact, the results are not even close to being 2:1.

Over a stretch of 30 years, portfolio B is projected to outpace portfolio A by a whopping 4X.

When extended to 40 years, portfolio B is predicted to overshadow portfolio A by a staggering nearly 7X.

It turns out that the avoidance of volatility is much riskier (and costly) than most people realise. Can you imagine knowingly giving up a 7X return just to avoid temporary volatility in the markets? It happens all the time, but not to my clients. But I have to wonder if people truly understood the ramifications of volatility avoidance, how many would still willingly choose to do so.

	5% Compound Return	10% Compound Return
10 YEARS	£162,889	£259,374
20 YEARS	£265,329	£672,749
30 YEARS	**£432,194**	**£1,744,940**
40 YEARS	**£703,998**	**£4,525,925**

In summary, selecting low-cost investments can be advantageous as they minimise the impact of charges and allow for more of your investment's growth to compound over time. Being mindful of charges and opting for highly diversified investments with lower costs can help you optimise the growth of your investment portfolio.

I often get asked about investment returns and how long it will take to double an amount invested. It's a common query, and while there are complex tools and calculators available, there's a simple rule that gives a quick estimate.

The Rule of 72 is a handy, straightforward formula used to estimate the number of years required to double the value of an investment at a fixed annual rate of compounded return or interest.

Explanation in Easy Terms: Imagine you have a magic doubling machine. You put something in, and in a certain amount of time, it doubles. The Rule of 72 helps you figure out how long that magic machine takes to double your money based on the interest rate.

Rule of 72 Formula: 72 ÷ interest rate = number of years to double your money.

Example: Let's say you have an investment (like a savings account) that earns an annual interest rate of 6%. You want to know how long it will take for your money to double.

Using the Rule of 72: 72 ÷ 6 = 12

So, at a 6% interest rate, your money will take roughly 12 years to double.

However, if you're earning a low rate of interest, like 0.5%, it would take a staggering 144 years to double your money! (72 ÷ 0.5 = 144) This highlights the perils of keeping cash on deposit long term. It could take multiple lifetimes to see significant growth, and that's before we even factor in the eroding effects of inflation, which will further diminish the value of your money over time.

If you want a quick idea of how long it'll take for your money to double, just divide 72 by your investment's annual interest rate. The result gives you an estimate of the years needed. But be wary: low interest rates can make your money stagnate, and inflation can further eat away at its real value. The larger the interest rate (the speedier the magic machine), the quicker your money doubles – but always be mindful of the hidden costs of inflation.

Similarly, the Rule of 114 is a rough guide tool to estimate how long it will take for your expenses or investment to treble (or triple) given a certain rate of inflation. To use this rule, you divide 114 by the annual inflation or growth rate. For instance, if you anticipate an annual inflation rate of 3%, it will take approximately 38 years (114 ÷ 3) for your expenses or investment to treble.

Throughout my career, people have sought my investment advice and knowledge about quirky tools such as the Rule of 72 and 114. Through these interactions, I've gained substantial insights into human behaviour. I have studied Behavioural Economics since 2012. It is a field of study that combines elements of psychology and economics to understand and explain how individuals make economic decisions. It seeks to uncover the cognitive, emotional, and social factors that influence human behaviour and decision making in economic contexts. Behavioural economics is an intriguing field that has empowered me to assist clients in making improved decisions and shield them from the pitfalls of common investor errors. My recurring advice has been to invest in low-cost, globally diversified funds and to keep things as simple as possible. However, I've observed that many wealthy individuals, institutions, or pension funds tend not to heed this advice.

From Hands-Width to the Heavens: The Magic of Exponential Growth

Here's a captivating concept about exponential growth that might sound surreal initially, perfect for sparking intriguing dinner party conversations. While your guests might find it hard to believe, they are indeed facts.

Imagine you have a regular A4 piece of paper, about 0.1mm thick. Imagine you could fold this paper on itself repeatedly. I know that physics doesn't allow it but imagine that you could keep folding this piece of paper in half. Each fold would double its thickness. How tall in inches, metres, or miles do you think the paper would be after an increasing number of folds?

Now, this is where the magic (and maths) happens:

After 10 folds: The paper would be around 102 mm or 10.24 centimetres thick—roughly the width of a hand.

After 20 folds: It's height would be around 105 meters, comparable to a 30-story building.

After 23 folds: Your paper would be taller than the tallest building in the world, the Burj Khalifa in Dubai, which is approximately 829 meters high.

After 30 folds: You're looking at a height of 107 kilometres, or well into space.

After 40 folds: The paper would stand at about 110,000 kilometres high, or about a third of the way to the moon.

After 42 folds: This unimaginably tall stack would have shot well past the moon at 440,000 kilometres.

After 50 folds: You are well on your way to the sun.

Consider this: every time you fold something in half, its thickness doubles. If that concept seems challenging to grasp, allow me to provide another illustration.

The Power of Exponential Growth: A Penny Doubled Daily

Imagine being presented with a unique employment proposition: I offer you a month's work, and at the end of it, you can choose your compensation method. The first option is a straightforward £1 million. It's tempting, right? A solid seven-figure amount handed to you after just one month. The second offer seems less appealing on the surface: I'll pay you a penny on the first day, but then I'll double that amount every subsequent day for the month. That means 1p on the first day, 2p on the second, 4p on the third, and so on. Which would you choose?

Let's break it down.

In the first week, the daily doubling doesn't seem impressive:

Day 1: £0.01

Day 2: £0.02

Day 3: £0.04

Day 4: £0.08

Day 5: £0.16

Day 6: £0.32

Day 7: £0.64 By the end of the first week, you've earned only £1.27 in total for your week's graft.

By the end of the second week:

Day 14: £81.92 Your total earnings by this point are £163.83. Still way off the £1 million mark.

But here's where things get wild.

By the end of the third week:

Day 21: £10,485.76 Your cumulative earnings are now £20,971.51. The power of exponential growth starts to shine through.

In the final ten days, the growth is astonishing:

Day 22: £20,971.52

Day 23: £41,943.04

Day 24: £83,886.08

Day 25: £167,772.16

Day 26: £335,544.32

Day 27: £671,088.64

Day 28: £1,342,177.28

Day 29: £2,684,354.56

Day 30: £5,368,709.12

Day 31: £10,737,418.24

By the end of the 31 days, your cumulative total would be an astounding £21,474,836.47. That's over twenty-one times the £1 million offer!

This illustrates the power of exponential growth. In the beginning, the results seem negligible, but over time, they compound into astonishing amounts. So, while a million pounds might seem like the smarter choice at first glance, the magic of doubling a penny daily for 31 days transforms that modest penny into a mountain of wealth.

The next time you're faced with a decision that pits immediate gain against potential long-term growth, remember the story of the doubled penny. It's a testament to the wonders of compound interest, patience, and the surprising power of seemingly small numbers growing exponentially.

This theoretical exercise underscores the incredible nature of exponential growth. While it's a fun thought experiment with paper, the principle has real-world applications. Consider the effect of compound interest on investments, and it gives you an appreciation for the small, consistent gains that can lead to astronomical results over time.

The key takeaway from all of this should be: start investing early and often. The biggest gains and returns always happen later in life. If you start investing today and earn a modest 6% return, that might not seem like a lot of money today.

But in 30 years? Earning a 6% return throughout your life, you'll start seeing huge returns later in life as you approach retirement.

Remember, investing is a long-term endeavour - you shouldn't be looking to double your money in 3-5 years. You should be looking to grow your money over time. I know the quickest way to double your money is to fold it in half, but remember, the Rule of 72 will guide in you in how long it will truly take to double your investment.

Chapter 20

But I Deserve More!

Affluent individuals often expect superior quality in all aspects of life due to their financial capacity. Whether it's food and drink, education, entertainment, housing, healthcare, or privileged VIP access, they believe their wealth should afford them a higher standard. In many instances, indeed, wealth can procure top-tier products or services.

Consequently, there is a reluctance among some financial elites to embrace financial products or services that are accessible to individuals with modest investment amounts. I recall attending a dinner party where affluent individuals proudly flaunted the exorbitant sums; they paid their investment managers. The words I heard were so astounding that I struggled to comprehend their sheer arrogance and blatant disregard for financial prudence. This wealthy hesitation persists even when the product in question is evidently the superior choice in terms of expected value. It's estimated that this quest for exceptional investment advice has cost the elites over £100 billion in the past decade. Perhaps stubbornness and arrogance play a part.

In the complex realm of investing, many are drawn to flashy strategies and promises of high returns, but they often overlook the impact of underlying costs. High fees are the silent killers of investment portfolios, steadily eroding potential gains without one realising it. It's reminiscent of the classic fable where, in the race for returns, the tortoise often beats the hare. This is especially true when the hare, representing hasty investment choices, is burdened by heavy fees. Making informed choices and being mindful of costs can make all the difference in the long run.

When it comes to wealthy individuals, stubbornness and arrogance can often influence their decision-making processes. Wealthy individuals may exhibit a higher degree of confidence in their own abilities and tend to be more resistant to changing their investment strategies or accepting alternative viewpoints. They may believe that their wealth affords them special privileges or insights, leading them to take on excessive risks or pursue expensive and speculative investment opportunities without fully considering potential downsides.

Moreover, the status and reputation that often accompany wealth can create a reinforcing cycle of stubbornness and arrogance. The societal perception of wealth as a measure of success may reinforce a wealthy individual's belief in their own infallibility, making it difficult for them to acknowledge mistakes or adjust their strategies when faced with unfavourable outcomes.

There have been numerous reported cases in which affluent individuals or high-profile figures have fallen victim to complex get-rich-quick schemes, resulting in substantial financial losses. It is my sincere hope that they come to the realisation that, given their existing wealth, simplicity, low cost, and tax efficiency should be their guiding principles.

Stubbornness and arrogance in investing can hinder wealthy individuals from seeking advice or considering alternative perspectives, limiting their ability to adapt to changing market conditions or recognise potential pitfalls. It is crucial for wealthy investors to remain open-minded, continually learn from others, and accept that even their success does not make them immune to the inherent uncertainties, behavioural biases, and risks of the financial markets.

By cultivating a mindset of humility and a willingness to consider different viewpoints, wealthy investors can mitigate the negative effects of stubbornness and arrogance, making more informed and balanced investment decisions that align with their long-term financial goals.

Human behaviour remains a constant barrier to successful investing and is unlikely to change because human nature is a failed investor. We are simply not hardwired to be good investors.

Wealthy individuals and institutions will continue to expect something 'extra' in investment advice. Advisors capitalising on these expectations will get rich at their clients' expense. This year, the allure might be cryptocurrency, next year, something different. The likely outcome of this procession of promises is encapsulated in the saying:

"When a person with money meets a person with experience, the one with experience ends up with the money and the one with money leaves with experience." - Warren Buffett

The psychology behind attempts to beat the market can be explained by these three factors:

1. Some people believe they deserve better.

2. Numerous financial professionals profit enormously from this belief.

3. They want to get rich quickly.

Jeff Bezos, the founder, chairman, CEO, and former president of Amazon, is indeed widely known as the one of the richest men in the world. During a meeting with Warren Buffett, one of America's most renowned investors, Jeff posed an intriguing question about Warren's investment thesis, noting its simplicity and yet its effectiveness has also made him one of the world's richest people. Jeff asked, "Your investment thesis is so simple. You're one of the richest guys in the world, and it's so simple. Why doesn't everyone just copy you?"

In response to Jeff's query, Warren Buffett offered an insightful perspective on why not everyone follows his approach. He said, "Because nobody wants to get rich slowly." This statement encapsulates an important aspect of human nature—the desire for quick and significant financial gains. Many individuals are attracted to the idea of getting rich quickly, seeking immediate wealth without the patience and discipline required for long-term wealth accumulation.

Buffett's response provides a profound insight into the nature of true wealth creation. It emphasises that genuine prosperity is typically achieved gradually and requires consistent, disciplined investing instead of seeking quick and speculative gains.

While the allure of shortcuts and rapid wealth accumulation may be tempting, it is crucial to recognise that sustainable financial success stems from a well-thought-out, long-term investment strategy.

His approach is rooted in the belief that enduring value lies in great businesses that have the potential to thrive over time. This perspective underscores the importance of patience and perseverance in the investment process. It requires an unwavering belief that exceptional companies will continue to innovate and prosper, generating substantial returns for long-term investors.

Time-Tested Tenacity: The Power of Staying the Course in Investing

Reading a physical book might seem like the most old-fashioned way to absorb knowledge. Yet, for depth and immersion, it outclasses its counterparts. Similarly, when it comes to investing, one might argue about newer strategies, trends, and quick-win tactics. However, 'buy and hold' or as I prefer, 'staying the course' through storms and sunny days alike, stands time-tested.

The undeniable truth is this: to secure a 100% return on the market's offering, one must remain invested 100% of the time. It's simple, yet many find it hard to digest. The unpredictability of the short-term is a given, a constant. But the long-term, fuelled by our collective drive for progress, holds a promise that's almost predictable.

Avoiding market turbulence might sound appealing, but more often than not, such avoidance jeopardises your long-term return. The mantra? Buy, hold, and steadfastly stay the course. It might seem like the most challenging strategy, but it surpasses all others in the end.

By cultivating a patient and long-term mindset, investors can position themselves to reap the rewards of sustained growth and financial stability.

Throughout my career, I've encountered numerous investors suffering from FOMO (Fear of Missing Out):

The novice investor who realistically acknowledges their limitations is likely to achieve better long-term results than the seasoned professional oblivious to their own weaknesses. I'm confident this strategy will persist in the future, as it has done for the past 200 years. The strategy is to invest through thick and thin and remain invested through thick and thin. Plan with prudence in mind, not performance.

Irrespective of its storage location, the primary purpose of money is to maintain its purchasing power. As long as your capital keeps pace with inflation, you will be able to sustainably afford the necessary goods and services as time goes on. On the other hand, if it fails to do so, your income effectively diminishes, necessitating certain sacrifices to cope. The world's leading companies, and therefore a broad portfolio of stocks, are almost certain to increase in value over time, given historical trends. Innovation, productivity improvements, entrepreneurial spirit, and ample capital will ensure this growth. Despite the constant naysayers profiting from their pessimistic forecasts, they're in trouble if they act on their own prophecies.

As an owner of a broad market fund, you are perfectly positioned to reap the benefits. And you should never panic or stop investing. The main risk is that novice or cautious investors will enter the market during a period of extreme optimism and then become discouraged when temporary losses occur. The total loss of capital from a low-cost, globally diversified investment plan is a distinctly human failure.

In my opinion, there are only two scenarios where a globally diversified investor could lose all their money:

- Global thermonuclear war. We'd all then have bigger problems!
- A massive meteorite striking the Earth having the same effect.

Barring these apocalyptic scenarios, subscribing to a vision where society could function without banks, retailers, fuel, technology, insurance companies, or utility companies is irrational. For an investor to lose all their money, all companies would need to vanish. This would be the doomsday scenario.

Chapter 21

Beyond the Hype: The Ineffectiveness of Following Media's Financial Pundits

"Those who have knowledge don't predict. Those who predict, don't have knowledge."

Lao Tzu – Chinese Philosopher

In today's fast-paced and ever-changing financial landscape, individuals are bombarded with a constant stream of advice and predictions from so-called financial experts in the media. These self-proclaimed gurus, armed with charts, graphs, and compelling narratives, often portray themselves as the key to unlocking financial success. However, a closer examination reveals a stark truth: if these experts were truly as accurate as they claim, they would have long retired to enjoy a life of leisure on a beach in the Bahamas. The fact that they continue to draft articles for a living raises questions about the value of their advice and the futility of relying on their guidance.

Morgan Housel, the writer behind the Psychology of Money, has spoken about the preoccupation with predicting future outcomes.

"The inability to forecast the past has no impact on our desire to forecast the future."

I think that's as true as it gets. We all want answers. The problem is there aren't any, especially about the short term. It doesn't matter what the fundamental or technical analysis says or what the analysts or pundits predict because anything is possible in the short term. This has always been the case and always will be, which is why timing the market is impossible. In the long term, it seems likely that the markets will generally follow earnings just as they've done for the last century. But in the short run, anything can happen.

FOCUS ON WHAT MATTERS

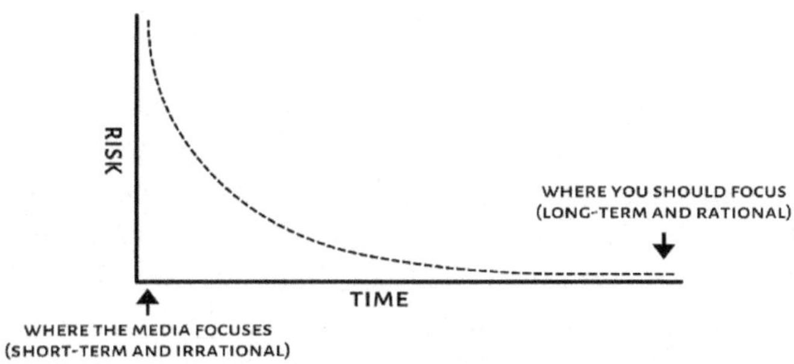

The media often presents these so-called experts as possessing almost mystical powers of prediction, able to foresee each fluctuation of the market with uncanny accuracy. Of course, the reality rarely lives up to the hype. More often than not, their prophecies are vague generalities or outright wrong. Yet this does not stop the constant parade of gurus making bold proclamations on business channels or finance sites. The savvy investor remains focused on what matters.

This overreliance on forecasts highlights a troubling trend - the desire for easy answers in an inherently complex system.

Investing successfully requires patience, discipline, and acceptance of uncertainty. It demands analysing economic fundamentals, understanding company valuations, and tuning out short-term noise. There are no shortcuts. But for many, the ambiguous science of investing proves unsatisfying. They instead seek financial astrology - the comfort of believing an expert can predict each twist and turn.

The irony is that true expertise leads to humility in forecasting. Seasoned investors know that markets are influenced by a confluence of hard-to-predict factors. They understand the folly of trying to time short-term fluctuations. Patience and discipline are the hallmarks of their approach. Rather than chasing predictions, they focus on what they can control - building diversified portfolios, rebalancing, minimising taxes. They accept uncertainty and avoid reactive moves based on speculation. In the end, this often generates better long-term results than lurching from one prognostication to the next.

The appeal of financial fortune-telling is unlikely to disappear. But for investors, the path to success lies not in futile short-term guesses but building a solid, long-term strategy. Tune out the predictions, focus on fundamentals, and accept that patience and discipline trump prophecy.

When it comes to market forecasters, there seem to be only two types - those who don't know and those who don't know they don't know. As the old saying goes, it's better to keep your mouth shut and be thought a fool than open it and remove all doubt.

Yet still the parade of self-assured gurus continues, armed with enough charts and technical babble to convince the gullible they possess powers beyond mere mortals to glimpse the unknowable future. One imagines them huddled around crystal balls rather than computers, divining the mystical shapes in candlestick charts rather than acknowledging the overwhelming evidence that such fortune-telling is folly.

Perhaps these financial astrologers should take a lesson from their cousins reading palms and tarot cards - at least they have the honesty to operate at the fringes rather than masquerading as experts on business channels. As renowned economist John Kenneth Galbraith quipped, "The only function of economic forecasting is to make astrology look respectable."

Warren Buffett, the esteemed "Sage of Omaha," astutely remarked, "Forecasts may reveal much about the forecaster, but they tell us nothing about the future."

So, for investors fed up with speculative prophecies that are about as reliable as horoscopes, the path forward is clear - tune out the self-appointed oracles and focus on an investment strategy grounded in humility, discipline, and acceptance of uncertainty. The financial future is yours to build, not for media pundits to predict.

Chapter 22

The Illusion of Expertise – Don't Believe the Hype

"If you don't read the newspaper, you're uninformed. If you read the newspaper, you're mis-informed."

Mark Twain

Financial experts in the media often project an aura of unwavering confidence, but their track records tell a different story. While they may boast about a few successful predictions, their overall accuracy remains highly questionable. Markets are inherently unpredictable, influenced by a multitude of complex factors that even seasoned experts struggle to fully comprehend. The truth is, no one can consistently predict the future with absolute certainty, not even those who spend their lives analysing financial data.

Understanding the inherent challenges faced by these experts in accurately forecasting market movements becomes clearer when examining specific instances. The following examples underscore just how challenging it can be for even the most seasoned financial professionals to regularly call the market correctly:

Conflicting Opinions and Market Noise: One only needs to tune into financial news channels or read prominent financial publications to encounter a cacophony of conflicting opinions. One expert may advise investing heavily in a particular sector, while another warns of an imminent market crash. These contradictory viewpoints leave investors perplexed, unsure of whose advice to follow. The truth is financial experts often have divergent opinions based on their unique perspectives, biases, and incentives. Their motivations may include attracting viewership, promoting their own services, or catering to the interests of their sponsors. In such a crowded marketplace of ideas, it becomes challenging to distinguish between sound financial advice and mere speculation. There are many reasons for this.

Chasing Past Performance: Many financial experts often refer to their past successes to bolster their credibility. They proudly highlight their accurate predictions and profitable investments. However, relying on past performance as an indicator of future success is a flawed approach. Financial markets are dynamic, and what worked in the past may not necessarily work in the future. Moreover, the very act of broadcasting their recommendations can influence market behaviour, making it difficult to replicate the same results. Investing based solely on historical performance can lead to disappointment and financial losses. I will add that very few investment companies show past performance beyond 5 years. They never seem to be able to boast consistent outperformance over 10 years or more. Why do you think this is so? It is because only a fraction of the thousands of investment funds have consistently outperformed the market over the long-term.

The Role of Luck: In the realm of finance, luck plays a significant role, often overshadowing genuine expertise.

Experts who claim to possess a secret formula for success often fail to acknowledge the element of luck in their achievements. They conveniently ignore the countless times their predictions missed the mark, or their investments went awry. It is important to recognise that even the most knowledgeable and experienced experts are not immune to the whims of chance.

Let's say you toss a coin, and I successfully predict it landing on "heads." Your probable reaction might be, "That was a lucky guess." I doubt you'd consider me some sort of coin-flip genius based on that single prediction. However, if you were to toss that coin 20 times, and I accurately predicted each outcome, you could start speculating that I possess a unique skill for this.

We inhabit a world where the media routinely parades forecasters who had one accurate prediction, often referencing major events like the 2008 crisis, and labels them as infallible experts. But, what about the countless predictions they got completely wrong? Why else would they be continuously referencing an event that happened years ago? Remember the adage, "even a broken clock is right twice a day."

The worrying reality is that there appears to be a negative relationship between a forecaster's popularity and their accuracy. In other words, the more well-known an expert is, the less precise their predictions tend to be.

So, who are the people typically interviewed by the media? Prominent figures who attract large viewerships, which, unfortunately, often come with inaccurate forecasts. Therefore, when you hear a prediction about the future, bear in mind that the person making it may have only been right once by chance and is probably no more accurate overall than a broken clock that randomly displays the correct time twice a day. Most crucially, remember that relying on a prediction introduces risk rather than mitigating it.

Alternative Incentives and Conflicts of Interest: Financial experts in the media operate within a broader ecosystem that includes advertisers, sponsors, and affiliations. Their advice may be influenced by various conflicts of interest, consciously or unconsciously. It is essential to remain aware that they may have ulterior motives for promoting specific investment products or strategies. Their financial gain may not align with the best interests of individual investors seeking unbiased advice.

Human psychology is influenced by what we are consistently exposed to, leading us to perceive it as normal, appropriate, and rational. If we regularly watch the financial news, we may develop the belief that predicting the future and timing the market are possible.

Although not explicitly stated, this notion is subtly suggested due to the overwhelming information overload that is deliberately designed to affect us. As the American novelist Gertrude Stein once observed, everybody gets so much information all day long that they lose their common sense.

What Drives Market Returns

Many external factors may seem important in driving investment returns, but they are often unpredictable noise. The media obsess over various external influences that may impact investment returns, such as politics, headlines, interest rates, earnings reports, and pundit opinions. They discuss these topics endlessly, while giving little attention to the more crucial factors that significantly drive future investment returns. These essential drivers include aspects like time, behaviour, average returns, faith in future growth, patience, planning, and the ability to ignore media frenzies.

In reality, trying to time the market or reacting to daily noise pales in comparison to the impact of these fundamental elements on long-term returns. Wise investors recognise the importance of focusing on these core factors rather than getting swept up in the latest predictions and market buzz. By creating highly diversified portfolios aligned with their risk appetite and volatility tolerance, and having the discipline to stay invested, investors can harness the power of time and compounding returns to their advantage rather than getting distracted by media hysteria or attempts to time the market. A planned, diversified portfolio focused on long-term compounding matters more than reacting to unpredictable external factors.

Heed the wisdom of investing titan Charlie Munger: "Take a simple idea and take it seriously." In essence, save more, invest in outstanding global companies, and practice patience. All other information is merely navel gazing.

While financial experts in the media may possess knowledge and experience in their field, it is crucial to approach their advice with scepticism and critical thinking. The futility of relying solely on their recommendations is evident in the fact that these pundits continue appearing in the media rather than being retired on a beach in the Bahamas. Markets are complex, and there are no guarantees when it comes to investing. Instead of blindly following the advice of self-proclaimed gurus, individuals should focus on developing their own financial literacy, diversifying their investments, and seeking guidance from trusted professionals who prioritise their clients' best interests. Ultimately, one's own due diligence and careful decision-making are key to navigating the unpredictable world of finance.

The Rarity of Long-Term Outperformance

When evaluating investment funds, most advertise their track records over relatively short time periods of 5 years or less. It is exceptionally rare to find funds with consistent market-beating returns over 10 years or longer on a level cost and risk related basis. This begs the question - why is persistent outperformance so uncommon? There are a few key reasons:

Competing in Efficient Markets:

What is the Efficient Market Theory?

Imagine yourself as a young child who likes trading toys with friends to make money. You buy cheap toys and sell them later at higher prices. A great business!

Now imagine overnight the toy market becomes perfectly efficient. All toys are instantly priced exactly right. No underpriced toys exist anymore. Your business stops working because you can't buy cheap and sell high when prices are always "fair".

This efficient toy market is like the stock market according to the Efficient Market Theory. It says stock prices fully reflect available information at all times. Just like the toy prices, stocks are always fairly valued, not under or overpriced.

In an efficient market, consistently beating the market is impossible. Stocks can't be bought low and sold high when their prices are "right". The stock market approaches this efficient state. Simple market-outperforming strategies tend not to work long-term. In a nutshell, the Efficient Market Theory says market prices are always reasonable in the present, so exploiting mispricings is very difficult.

The markets have become increasingly efficient over time as more participants enter the arena. Any new investing strategy that works will quickly diffuse across the industry as other managers seek to capitalise on its success. This dilution effect makes it difficult to maintain an edge for long periods. To sustain outperformance requires continually innovating with new insights before others can catch on. Many funds find it challenging to reinvent themselves beyond past strategies that brought them initial success. In this ever evolving and competitive landscape, there is one constant that affects all market participants equally: investment fees.

Ask Not For Whom The Fees Toll, For The Fees Toll For Thee.

This aphorism underscores the universality of investment fees—an inescapable reality for both novice investors and seasoned professionals alike. It emphasises that fees are an inherent part of the financial landscape, impacting every participant on their journey toward financial goals.

The Toll of Fees

Actively managed funds are invariably more expensive to run than passive index-tracking funds. This means that the active fund must outperform the tracker fund to justify its higher fees. If the active fund fails to sufficiently outperform the index after fees, the investor would have been better off in the low-cost index fund. Even small differences in fees can become substantial over long time periods due to the effects of compounding. Over decades, higher fees act as a significant drag on net returns to investors in actively managed funds relative to lower-cost index funds. While the fee difference may seem minor annually, the long-run impact can be dramatic. This underscores the importance of paying close attention to fees rather than solely focusing on past returns, which are not predictive of future performance.

The Odds are Stacked Against Most

With thousands of investment managers out there, simple mathematics dictates that only a very small subset will manage to outperform over decade-plus timespans. Some funds can post impressive short-term returns through happenstance, market factors, or temporary strategies. But few have the innovative and adaptable DNA required to stay ahead of the market's evolving efficiency across periods of 10, 20, or 30 years.

In summary, the rarity of long-term outperformance underscores just why investors should be wary of funds boasting impressive short-term returns. It also highlights the merits of low-cost, diversified strategies aligned with the investor's time horizon. Past performance alone provides little indication of future results.

When people inquire about my predictions for the stock market, my response remains consistent: it will fluctuate. I can't predict the future. Nobody can. But one thing's for sure - over time, we will see a steady upward trend despite various hiccups along the way. The global stock market (the great businesses of the world) will suffer from setbacks, but the thing to remember is that the declines are temporary, but the advances are permanent. The stock market has and always will behave this way. Pay no attention to any financial adviser who tells you that your investments can fall as well as rise. This is complete nonsense. They should be telling you that your investments categorically will fall in value from time to time.

It is wholly unrealistic to anticipate that the global stock market will perpetually increase in value without ever experiencing any downturns. Expecting daily, weekly, monthly, and yearly growth without any setbacks is simply unreasonable. As part of my role, a crucial aspect involves managing client expectations with utmost honesty. Don't be alarmed by the market's occasional downswing.

Investing is much like walking up a flight of stairs with a yo-yo in your hand. It will have ups and downs, but the long-term trajectory is always upwards. It's simply part of the larger scheme.

Remember, these fluctuations will recur in the future. Yet, in the face of these yo-yo-like dips and dives, we continue to climb the staircase of growth. This growth is fuelled by the relentless rise in revenue, innovation, and profits of the global economy and the greatest businesses in the world, continually boosting the market's value.

Investing with a long-term perspective and holding onto your investments is the key to benefiting from this powerful wealth generation mechanism!

The remedy to poor market timing is long-term share accumulation and maintaining investments even in the face of adverse news and low stock valuations. Never to sell when the news is bad, and stocks are well off their highs because it will probably be the biggest financial mistake you will ever make, and you are unlikely to ever recover from it. Adhering to these principles, the 'novice' investor who diversifies and minimises costs is almost guaranteed to achieve reasonable returns over time. This has been a constant since the inception of the markets over two and a half centuries ago.

Think of investing like sailing with the wind of global growth in your sail.

My perennial advice is a low-cost, globally diversified fund. The rationale is that the world's significant businesses are expected to thrive over an extended period. We must accept that consistently identifying winners and profitable investment periods or successfully timing market entries and exits is beyond anyone's capabilities.

I frequently reference Warren Buffett's wisdom in this book, and with good cause. The "Oracle of Omaha" stands as a monumental figure in the investment realm. Since making his first investment at the tender age of 11 in 1942, he's amassed an incredible 81 years of investment experience by 2023. His track record, spanning over eight decades, exemplifies his unique ability to consistently identify promising investments. Under Buffett's guidance, Berkshire

Hathaway metamorphosed from a struggling textile firm into a global powerhouse, underlining his strategic prowess. Given the financial world's almost reverential regard for him, and countless investors devouring his annual letters for pearls of wisdom, I recognise that I may not have the time to gain all the knowledge or benefit from his vast experience. However, who am I to dispute his invaluable advice? After all, delving into his insights provides an express route to grasping the complexities of investing successfully.

Given Buffett's monumental influence, his investment recommendations carry significant weight. He has frequently lauded the merits of low-cost S&P 500 index tracking funds. In fact, in his 2013 letter to Berkshire Hathaway shareholders, he provided a glimpse into the posthumous financial advice he's left for his wife's inheritance: 90% invested in a low-cost S&P 500 index fund and the remaining 10% in short-term government bonds. This counsel highlights his firm conviction in the long-term benefits of such index funds for a majority of investors. It's important to note that this advice was specific to his wife's situation and may not be suitable for all investors, as individual financial goals and circumstances vary. Nonetheless, it demonstrates Buffett's preference for a straightforward and cost-effective investment strategy for those who do not wish to actively manage their investments.

It's crucial for every investor to assess their personal financial circumstances and consult with professionals before finalising investment choices.

Chapter 23

The Danger of Sensationalist Financial Headlines: Putting Perspective into Context

"Many a small thing has been made large by the right kind of advertising."

Mark Twain

Mark Twain also said, "Never let the truth get in the way of a good story." The press and the media take this to the extreme. In today's fast-paced media landscape, financial headlines and clickbait have become increasingly sensationalist, aiming to grab attention and generate clicks. Unfortunately, this approach often neglects to provide the necessary context, leading to a distorted understanding of market events and their implications.

For instance, in October 2021, Bloomberg ran a headline proclaiming: "Zuckerberg Loses $6 Billion in Hours as Facebook Plunges." As readers delved into the article, it elaborated that Zuckerberg's personal wealth had "fallen" by more than $6 billion. However, there's a stark distinction between "losing" and "falling." The former implies a definitive loss, while the latter suggests a potential for recovery. In truth, Zuckerberg didn't "lose" anything unless he decided to liquidate his stock right at that moment of decreased value. This instance highlights the media's penchant for crafting attention-grabbing headlines, often prioritising sensation over nuanced context.

This sensationalist presentation can have severe repercussions, particularly for the novice investor who, driven by fear, might act hastily, leading to regrettable decisions. To me, such scaremongering financial headlines are not just misleading but downright irresponsible. They seem crafted to induce sheer panic. In a candid phrase, I describe it as financial porn. And to put it bluntly, when you multiply bullshit with bullshit, you don't just get a bit more bullshit, you get bullshit squared!

As if this wasn't concerning enough, there's the undeniable influence of the hefty marketing arms of investment firms and financial media establishments. They wield significant power and resources, fashioning narratives that benefit them—often at the expense of the average investor. Their main game? Not education, but attention. Not clarity, but sales. Their agenda? Profit.

Consider the headline: "The stock market fell 15% today!" While this may sound alarming at first, it fails to paint a complete picture of the situation. Headlines that stir fear seldom follow up with, "If you have extra funds you won't need for the next 5 to 10 years, now might be an opportune moment to invest as the stock market is essentially on sale." Instead, the narrative typically leans heavily into the ominous and dire.

The media highlights a market downturn with far more fervour than a 10% increase. This can be traced back to the "caveman investor" theory I mentioned in the beginning of this book, suggesting humans prioritise threats over opportunities. However, the motivation extends beyond that. The media's primary objective is to captivate and retain their audience.

Such statements omit crucial details, such as the composition of an investor's portfolio or its level of diversification. For instance, an individual with a diversified 60/40 portfolio, with 60% allocated to stocks and 40% to bonds, would generally only be directly impacted by the temporary market decline in relation to their stock holdings. So, they would not suffer a 15% loss on their entire portfolio. It would be a 15% temporary loss on 60% of their portfolio (the stocks element only). This equates to an actual reduction of 9% overall. By excluding this important information, the sensationalist headline needlessly frightens investors who may not understand the nuances of their own investments.

However, it's important to note that this diversification does not guarantee complete insulation from market downturns, as all asset classes can be affected during extreme market conditions.

Furthermore, these sensationalist headlines rarely provide historical context. They often fail to mention what the market was valued at a few years ago or how markets have consistently reached new highs over time or that the Standard & Poor's 500 index (the 500 largest companies in the US) has achieved an average annual return of approximately 10% over the last 100 years. By neglecting these crucial points, the media perpetuates a sense of doom and gloom, obscuring the reality that market fluctuations are a normal part of investing. Investors who are unaware of this historical perspective may succumb to panic and hastily make decisions that could harm their long-term financial goals.

These 500 companies cover every major sector of the world's most powerful economy. You can own a slice of all of these companies along with thousands of rest of the world's other great businesses at very low cost. Your chances of picking a single stock, or an actively managed fund, which will outperform the S&P 500 in the long run are very small. And remember, people have a vested interest in making investing far more complicated and expensive than it needs to be.

It is crucial for investors to educate themselves and seek out reputable sources of information that provide a balanced and contextualised view of market events. By understanding the long-term nature of investing, the benefits of diversification, and the historical resilience of financial markets, investors can make informed decisions that align with their financial objectives. Avoiding knee-jerk reactions driven by sensationalist headlines is vital to maintaining a steady course towards long-term financial success.

WHAT GETS ATTENTION IS RARELY VALUABLE

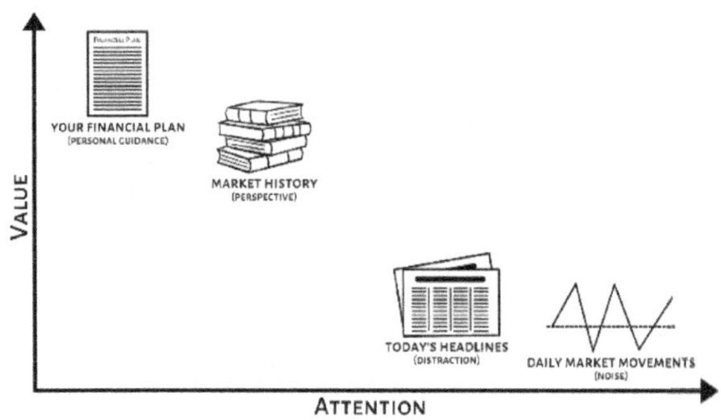

Sensationalist financial headlines without proper context can be dangerous, particularly for inexperienced investors. By distorting the reality of market events and neglecting historical perspective, these headlines generate unnecessary fear and pressure individuals into making rash decisions. It is crucial for investors to seek out reliable information and develop a comprehensive understanding of investing principles, enabling them to navigate the market with confidence and avoid regrets in the future.

The media often zeroes in on two primary focuses:

They dissect today's market occurrences and delve into the reasons behind them (captured in flashy headlines). But just how insightful is this information? At its best, it's just background noise. At its worst, it shifts attention away from the core issues. What truly carries weight and relevance as you strive for your goals?

Two things stand out: your bespoke financial plan and a grasp of market history.

Your individualised financial plan is tailored guidance designed for your unique financial situation. While understanding market history offers the much-needed backdrop to today's happenings, it allows you to make well-informed investment choices.

Tuning into financial broadcasts without a clear view of your plan or the lens of market history is akin to sailing a ship in dense fog without a compass or map. It's perilous. You need a destination. You need a navigational chart to guide your voyage. Plus, you need context, so you aren't thrown off course by every wave or gust of wind.

In conclusion, in the midst of the constant chatter and market noise, it's essential to remember that your financial journey is unique, and it requires a clear plan and historical context to stay on course. While the media may provide headlines and fleeting insights, the foundation of your financial success lies in your individualised financial plan and a deep understanding of market history. Together, they serve as your compass and chart, ensuring you navigate the financial seas with confidence and purpose, ultimately working towards your financial goals.

This is where a solid financial plan and knowledge of market history become invaluable. And that's the guidance I aim to deliver to my clients.

Chapter 24

The Investor's Dilemma – DIY or Working with a Trusted Professional

"If you think it's expensive to hire a professional to do the job, wait until you hire an amateur."

Red Adair

One of the most important aspects of a financial plan is planning on your plan not going to plan. Just like a GPS navigation system that navigates through roadblocks, you too must be adaptable because changes are likely to occur during your investment journey. In the medical world it might involve changing medication from time to time. Investing is a critical aspect of financial planning, and individuals are faced with the decision of whether to manage their investments and financial plan themselves or seek the guidance of a trusted professional.

The initial choice is to personally assume full responsibility and accountability for your decision making and actions. It involves investing considerable time and effort into developing the skills necessary to become a proficient investor who prioritises extensive research trying to maximise anticipated returns. By opting for this route, you'll be taking charge of your investments without relying on an experienced advisor.

Pursuing DIY investing without proper knowledge and guidance can be risky. Like you wouldn't self-diagnose a medical issue, it's wise to seek professional support when managing your finances.

If you are thinking of managing your own money in retirement, I have one question: why would you want to do this? Managing your finances is like getting a haircut - it looks easy, but it requires skill and experience.

I've been getting monthly haircuts for over 50 years. That's at least 600 haircuts I've sat through, watching intently in the mirror as the barber cuts my hair. But do you think observing all those haircuts qualifies me to cut my own hair? Of course not.

Just like cutting hair, properly managing investments takes training and expertise. One wrong slip of the scissors could lead to disaster. Similarly, one wrong financial move could devastate your retirement savings. With over three decades of experience advising clients, I've witnessed firsthand the disastrous consequences that can occur when retirees try to manage complex financial affairs on their own. Without proper guidance, even the most capable individuals can make costly mistakes navigating changing tax laws, volatile markets, and convoluted distribution rules. An advisor's role is to serve as an experienced guide so their clients can relax and enjoy retirement, rather than stress over financial decisions they weren't prepared to make. With so much at stake, it's critical to have an expert advisor you can trust - your retirement depends on it.

This is your financial future we're talking about. You've worked hard to save this money - why risk losing it through avoidable mistakes? Don't make the mistake of thinking you can do this yourself just because you've "watched" someone else do it for years.

Losing your car keys might cost £100 to replace. But making mistakes with your retirement savings could cost far, far more. I suggest you do not take that risk. Get professional help so you can relax and enjoy retirement, rather than stressing over DIY financial management. Your free time and peace of mind are too valuable to waste worrying over finances. After 30 years advising clients on retirement planning, I've learned that retirees should spend their time focused on what matters most - connecting with loved ones and creating lifelong memories. Retirement is meant to be enjoyed, not spent buried in spreadsheets and statements. With time being our most precious resource, retirees deserve to make the most of the chapters ahead without getting bogged down in ever-changing tax rules. Time is precious and life is not a rehearsal.

However, if you still want to spend your golden years self-managing you and your family's financial future, here are some of the key things DIY investors need to know to achieve successful outcomes and avoid pitfalls:

Becoming a qualified financial advisor requires years of study, exams, and experience. Grasping complex topics like taxes, investments, software, and potential bumps in the road typically necessitates formal training, exams, and continuing development.

It's critical to understand how taxes and inflation can impede wealth accumulation. Can you confidently calculate the numbers for your situation? Similarly, you need in-depth investment knowledge to choose suitable options. Cutting edge software helps validate assumptions and figures.

Watch out for the three big investing hurdles: distinguishing volatility from permanent capital loss, wrestling with inflation's erosive impact, and overcoming behavioural biases. Staying current on legislative and tax rule changes through professional resources is also important.

In short, DIY investing is filled with traps for the underprepared. Seeking trusted professional guidance maximises your likelihood of successful outcomes and avoids easily overlooked risks. Like your health, your finances deserve experienced care.

On the other hand, if you prefer a more hands-off approach and value the freedom and time to pursue other endeavours, you can engage with an experienced advisor. This entails working with a professional who will craft a financial plan based on what you want to achieve and utilise diversified and tax-efficient investment vehicles that require very little involvement on your part. Working with a professional also provides access to experience, guidance, and behavioural support. By doing so, you can aim for a more relaxed approach, freeing up your time and mental space to concentrate on other aspects of your life that bring you fulfilment rather than trying to do all this yourself.

Selecting the right financial advisor is crucial. You want someone who shows genuine interest in understanding you by asking questions like:

- What are your dreams and aspirations for the future?
- How do you envision your ideal lifestyle and how does it align with your financial goals?
- What are your top priorities when it comes to your personal and family life?
- How do you handle financial decisions in times of uncertainty or major life changes?
- Are there any specific life events or milestones you are planning for in the near future?
- What are the things that bring you the most joy and fulfilment in life?
- Have you thought about what you want your legacy to be and how you'd like to be remembered?
- Are there any experiences or adventures you've always wanted to pursue but haven't yet?
- How do you approach giving back or supporting causes that are meaningful to you?
- What is your philosophy on balancing financial security with living life to the fullest?

An advisor focused just on impressing you with stats and numbers isn't listening. The right one seeks to grasp your lifestyle dreams, relationships, hopes, concerns, and passions.

Look beyond only finance and consider how health, relationships, purpose, and lifestyle intersect with money for a more holistic view. Financial security enables life goals. See the advisor relationship as comprehensive, more therapist and life coach than just financial planner. Talk aspirations, struggles.

The core idea is to approach financial planning with an open, curious, interdisciplinary mindset rather than just narrow financial models. Bringing in diverse perspectives sparks creativity and innovation.

Look for an advisor who helps craft a financial roadmap for your most fulfilling life. Beware those pitching products over perspective. You want someone providing a life well-lived, not just well-invested. Get an advocate who cares about fully understanding you as a person, not just assets on a statement.

The invaluable services that Behavioural Investment Counsellors provide, which warrant fees far beyond their quoted rates, include intricate planning on a level that clients alone may not be capable of, as well as behavioural intervention to circumvent a client's most destructive human instincts. In my assessment, these two aspects respectively contribute 20% and 80% to the value of my fee. I assign no explicit value to excellent service and availability, as this is expected as standard.

The counsel provided by experienced financial planners and particularly those who study behavioural investment economics often proves to be accurate in the long run. This advice can be encapsulated as follows:

- Establish goals: Being specific about the timeline and the amount improves clarity, but regardless, the key is to set goals.

- Formulate a strategy to achieve these goals. Document this plan.

- Support the plan with a largely equity-based portfolio, bolstered by substantial cash reserves (recommendation: a year's living expenses for those accumulating wealth, and two years' worth for retirees who are drawing down their savings).

- Practice broad diversification; perform annual rebalancing.

- Entirely disregard the macroeconomy and pay no attention to market fluctuations in either direction. Avoid unnecessary interruptions to the compounding process.

- Given that neither the economy nor the market can be predicted, it stands to reason that the best time to purchase equities is when you have the funds, and the optimal time to sell them is when you require the funds.

Throughout an investing lifetime, there will undoubtedly be moments — both real and imagined, whether they are terrifying or exhilarating — when one or more of these principles appear to have been invalidated. Such occurrences are always deceptive, though it might take some time for this illusion to be revealed.

Unreasonable panic when superior businesses become bargains is not essentially different from abandoning diversification to pursue a popular trend: both are expressions of fear, just different types. One fear stems from the dread of losing all your money, the other from the fear of everyone else becoming wealthy except you. Nonetheless, both are forms of fear, and both lead to the erosion not just of wealth but of hope as well.

In the intricate world of financial planning, clients aren't just seeking someone with a sharp acumen for numbers; they yearn for an advisor who truly understands their aspirations, fears, and dreams. The pivotal traits that clients value in a financial advisor reflect this deeply personal aspect of financial guidance:

- **Availability:** Money matters can be unpredictable. When questions or concerns arise, clients want to know their advisor is accessible and responsive.

- **Likeability:** A personal connection makes discussions about money easier. It's human nature to gravitate towards people we like and feel comfortable with.

- **Knowledge:** Given that clients entrust advisors with their hard-earned money, they naturally expect them to be knowledgeable about markets, products, and strategies.

- **Listens:** Truly listening means understanding the client's goals, fears, and aspirations. An advisor who listens can tailor advice to the individual, rather than offering generic solutions.

- **Talks in Easy-to-Understand Language:** Finance can be complex. Clients appreciate when advisors can distil this complexity into language that's clear and relatable.

- **Above all, Trustworthiness:** Money is more than just currency; it's intertwined with hopes, dreams, and future plans. Trusting someone with one's financial future is a profound act. If that trust is broken, the impact can be devastating both financially and emotionally. To quote an old Caribbean proverb: "Trust grows at the speed of a coconut tree and falls at the speed of a coconut." Just as it takes years for the tree to mature and bear fruit, building trust is a slow process. But once trust is compromised, it can be shattered instantaneously, much like a coconut falling from its branch.

In sum, clients aren't simply hiring a financial expert. They're seeking a trusted ally who is available, relatable, knowledgeable, and most importantly, someone in whom they can confide.

Whether you choose the DIY planning route or engage with a trusted, experienced advisor, be sure to keep your complete financial picture and long-term goals in mind. It's completely understandable that many people want to try to manage their own financial affairs. After all, in an age of information accessibility, who wants to pay for sound advice? Yet, in most cases when it comes to money, opting for the DIY approach can be a false economy. The adage, "The bitterness of poor quality remains long after the sweetness of low price is forgotten," rings particularly true here. Saving fees here and there can easily be overshadowed by financial missteps along the investor's journey. Do you really want to be spending your quality time navigating the intricacies of financial planning, market fluctuations, and tax strategies?

A trusted advisor, who genuinely cares about you, serves as the best safeguard against an investor's most impulsive tendencies. They intervene at pivotal moments, advising, "You really shouldn’t de doing this.”

This piece isn't meant to scare anyone into seeking professional guidance but rather to humbly remind them of the potential pitfalls of trying to manage everything solo. The fee a client pays their advisor won't change the advisor's life. But the advice and reassurance provided to the client might very well change theirs.

Part 6

Recognising and Overcoming Investor Biases

Chapter 25

Navigating the Investor Mind: Unveiling the Biases that Shape Financial Decisions

"I can calculate the motion of heavenly bodies, but not the madness of people."

Isaac Newton

As humans, we possess a remarkable ability to analyse information and make decisions. However, this cognitive prowess comes with certain inherent quirks that can affect our judgment, especially when it comes to investing. Known as investor biases, these psychological tendencies can lead us to make irrational choices and impact our financial outcomes.

Investor behavioural biases are common in human behaviour and can have a significant impact on financial choices. These biases can affect anyone, from seasoned investors to newcomers in the world of finance. It's crucial to recognise that we all have these biases and understanding them can help us become better investors.

In this brief exploration, we'll delve into some of the main investor behavioural biases explained in layman's terms. By gaining insights into these behavioural tendencies, we can equip ourselves with the knowledge to navigate the complexities of financial decision-making more effectively.

Let's uncover the fascinating aspects of human psychology that influence our investment decisions and learn how to make more rational and informed choices in managing our investmcnts.

Overconfidence:

This bias occurs when investors believe they are better at predicting the future and making investment decisions than they actually are. They may take excessive risks, thinking they can beat the market consistently.

Loss Aversion:

As previously mentioned, people tend to feel the pain of losses more strongly than the joy of gains. As investors, they may hold onto losing investments too long, hoping they'll turn around, rather than selling and accepting the loss.

Confirmation Bias:

This bias happens when investors seek out information that supports their existing beliefs and ignore or downplay contradictory evidence. It can lead to a one-sided view of an investment's potential.

Herding:

Investors often tend to follow the crowd and do what everyone else is doing, even if it may not be the best strategy. This can lead to asset bubbles and market volatility.

Anchoring:

Anchoring occurs when investors fixate on a specific piece of information, such as the purchase price of an investment, and use it as a reference point for all future decisions. They may be reluctant to sell an investment if it hasn't reached a certain price, regardless of its current value.

Familiarity Bias:

Investors may prefer to invest in familiar companies or industries, even if other opportunities may have better potential returns. This can lead to an overly concentrated portfolio or putting all your eggs in one basket.

Sunk Cost Fallacy:

When investors hold onto a losing investment because they've already put a lot of money into it and don't want to admit their mistake. They focus on the past costs rather than the future potential.

Gambler's Fallacy:

This is the belief that past performance influences future outcomes in unpredictable events, like gambling or stock market movements. Investors may expect a streak of good or bad performance to continue indefinitely.

Emotional Bias:

Emotions like fear and greed can cloud judgement and lead to impulsive decisions. Fear can cause investors to sell during market downturns, while greed may push them to take excessive risks.

Understanding these biases can help investors become more aware of their potential influence and make more rational decisions when managing their investments. It's essential to stay informed, diversify your portfolio, and have a long-term investment plan to avoid falling victim to these biases.

Recency Bias:

In the intricate world of investing, these cognitive biases often play an insidious role, shaping decisions in ways that aren't always in an investor's best interest. Among these, recency bias stands out as particularly hazardous. But why?

Recency bias is the tendency to weigh recent events more heavily than those in the distant past. In the context of investing, it means giving disproportionate importance to recent market performance when making decisions about the future.

Similarly, to recency bias, the WYSIATI phenomenon can warp an investor's judgment. "What You See Is All There Is" suggests that people lean heavily on the immediate information in front of them, often overlooking potential nuances or additional data. In investment decisions, this might translate to an investor placing undue emphasis on a current news headline or a recent analyst's report without considering the broader context. Both recency bias and WYSIATI highlight the importance of holistic analysis and caution against letting a narrow slice of information guide one's entire investment strategy.

Here's why this is treacherous:

Short-Term Noise vs Long-Term Signal: Stock markets are inherently volatile in the short term. By reacting too much to recent market movements, investors might be responding to noise rather than true, long-term signals. This can lead to hasty and ill-informed decisions, like selling a fundamentally strong asset due to a temporary market downturn.

Amplifying Market Bubbles and Crashes: If a large number of investors are influenced by recency bias, it can exacerbate market bubbles and crashes. When markets are on a bull run, the bias might lead to overoptimism and overbuying. Conversely, during downturns, it can induce panic selling.

Distorted Risk Perception: Investors under the sway of recency bias may misjudge risk. If the recent past has been calm, they might underestimate risk, exposing themselves to nasty surprises. On the flip side, if the recent past has been tumultuous, they may overestimate risk and miss out on potential returns.

Picture this: You have a pet goldfish. Each time you sprinkle a pellet into its bowl, it dashes over with a zest as though it's witnessing food for the first time. Ten minutes later? Introduce another pellet and, lo and behold, you're greeted with the same lively response. It's as if the earlier morsel never existed. It's endearing in a goldfish, but for an investor, not quite the ideal.

Now consider the human investor: unquestionably more intricate than our aquatic companion, yet occasionally just as oblivious. We are frequently swayed by recent events in all aspects of our lives. This recency bias phenomenon can be catastrophic for an investor. A stock's surge last week? Suddenly, it dictates this week's investment tactic. But much like our goldfish's fleeting memory of the prior pellet, we might overlook the stock's long-term trajectory.

Factor in the "availability heuristic" to this mix. This jargon essentially implies that we're predominantly influenced by the most accessible information, such as the bold headlines declaring an abrupt market downturn or the skyrocketing debut of a new stock. Before we know it, we're mirroring our goldfish, captivated by the latest titbit of information, while overlooking the expansive reservoir of data that should be shaping our choices.

So, the next time you're on the verge of making a hasty decision based on recent buzz or a trending tip, conjure the image of our petite goldfish and its ever-fascinating "new" treat. Delve deeper, embrace the broader perspective, and strive to outwit our bowl-dwelling friends. They might win hearts with their brief recalls, but our investments, well they warrant a more visionary approach.

In essence, recency bias blinds investors to the bigger picture, making them susceptible to making long term decisions based on a limited, often misleading, snapshot of reality. Recognising and countering this bias is crucial for any investor aiming for sustainable success in the financial markets.

Chapter 26

The Performance Illusion

"The eye sees only what the mind is prepared to comprehend."

Robertson Davies

The performance illusion is one of the most common mistakes investors make. Our brains instinctively look for shortcuts to solve problems using heuristics - quick solutions that allow us to move on rapidly. When reviewing annual investment statements, most people instantly check the figure at the bottom right of their statement to see if the value is up or down from the previous year. This reveals two facets of the performance illusion.

Firstly, statements represent a snapshot in time. The date chosen could coincide with a temporary market reversal that skews perception. A day earlier or later could show drastically different results. One day out of 365 cannot convey the full story. Market timing can benefit or penalise you.

This is where a financial planner provides value, helping you understand biases and temper expectations. They add perspective when emotions run high. The second facet of the illusion is more dangerous. For instance, when we see our investment increase by a certain monetary value, we might feel elated. However, if this gain is only a small percentage compared to the market average or our investment's potential, we're not really getting ahead. It's like celebrating a £5,000 gain on a £500,000 investment, when in reality, this only equates to a 1% growth – akin to what you'd earn in a risk-free savings account. The danger lies in overlooking crucial details such as growth rates, fees, and how our investment performs relative to benchmarks. Over time, even small underperformances can lead to significant missed opportunities. Thus, it's essential to analyse our investments critically, keeping this illusion in mind, to ensure we're genuinely maximising our returns and not just getting swayed by nominal gains.

Many clients overlook low growth rates and excessive fees for years because they focus on absolute monetary gains rather than relative performance. Their investments substantially underperform the broader market while they remain unaware, falling victim to the illusion. Even savvy investors make this mistake when busy lives prevent close oversight.

Our brains gravitate toward seemingly simple upward trends, glossing over rigorous analysis. By reviewing actual returns versus benchmarks, the reality becomes clear - the performance illusion causes lagging outcomes. Staying vigilant requires scrutinising results, not just superficial growth.

I often see investors earn 2-3% returns when markets generate 5-7% in the same period. High management fees further erode results. Only through education and transparency can these pitfalls be avoided. I make benchmarking analysis a cornerstone with every client.

The implications of underperformance compound massively over time. Even a 1-2% return gap annually becomes dramatic when extrapolated over decades. This can meaningfully impact lifestyle, retirement options, and legacy planning. It represents an opportunity cost many fail to fully grasp.

An advisor's mission should be to maximise clients' potential by avoiding common psychological traps like the performance illusion. Achieving this requires an investigative mindset and accountability. I believe in equipping clients with knowledge and resources so we can have informed, productive discussions about strategy and results.

Long-term investing success depends on vigour, patience, perspective, and partnership. By regularly reviewing performance with a critical yet constructive eye, investors can achieve better alignment between expectations and outcomes. I count it a privilege to help guide clients through the inherent complexities and fluctuations of the market to reach their financial goals.

The performance illusion is sadly one of many blind spots even seasoned investors can fall prey to. Behavioural finance reveals the power of cognitive biases to distort our decision-making. By being aware of these tendencies, we can counteract them through education, transparency, and disciplined analysis. I consider it a key responsibility to shed light on areas of potential misperception.

Ongoing success requires acknowledging our subjective limitations. My aim is to serve as an objective, trusted advisor who confronts illusions with facts. By maintaining high standards of insight and communication, clients gain an accurate perspective for structuring their financial lives. The rewards of long-term investing come to those who confront realities over mirages.

Ensuring my clients truly understand the nuances of their investments is paramount. By managing their expectations effectively, I strive to prevent any misconceptions rooted in the performance illusion. My commitment goes beyond just securing returns; it's about fostering a transparent, informed partnership where clients can navigate the financial landscape with clarity and confidence.

Chapter 27

Demystifying Risk - Understanding its True Nature in Investing

"Risk comes from not knowing what you're doing."

Warren Buffett

Risk is a term frequently heard and discussed in various contexts, and in the realm of investing, it holds particular significance. However, the true definition of risk is often misunderstood or inaccurately defined. By understanding the true nature of risk, investors can make informed decisions to achieve their long-term financial goals.

In the world of investments, risk can be attributed to two main factors. Firstly, it involves the possibility of a permanent loss of capital. This is undeniably the most feared aspect of risk, as certain investment scenarios, like putting all of one's eggs in one basket, carry the genuine risk of a complete loss.

Secondly, risk encompasses any decision that moves an investor further away from their financial goals. For example, adopting overly conservative investment strategies might lower the potential for higher returns, ultimately decreasing the likelihood of achieving financial goals.

It is crucial to differentiate between risk and volatility, as they are not interchangeable terms. Volatility refers to price fluctuations around a trendline and does not inherently equate to risk. Unfortunately, the media often confuses the two, leading to temporary market volatility being mistaken for a permanent loss of capital. The biggest mistake investors make is confusing volatility with the permanent loss of capital. These are two very different things. As investors, understanding this distinction is key to making well-informed decisions.

I cannot emphasise enough how essential it is to recognise that risk is not a simplistic, one-dimensional concept perpetuated by the media. It is a multifaceted and complex topic that requires proper definition and understanding to make informed decisions and achieve long-term financial goals. The "stay the course" approach is a vital component in navigating these risks effectively.

Historical data provides valuable insights into the relationship between risk and market performance. Despite temporary market volatility, the stock market has demonstrated remarkable growth over time. For instance, from 1960 to 2022, the market experienced an impressive 78X increase, excluding dividends. Moreover, £100,000 invested in 1990 with dividends reinvested would have grown to more than £2.2 million in 2021, representing a 22X return.

These figures highlight that the market has been a significant force for wealth expansion, and its risks have often been exaggerated. However, it is essential to acknowledge that there are risks in investing, and prudent decision-making and a disciplined approach are vital to navigate potential pitfalls.

I ask clients which is more important to them: keeping what they have or making more? Most clients say both, but you can't do both with equal emphasis. Every attempt to make more introduces the possibility of not having any more of what you have today.

In essence, the decision between preserving what one has and making more is a dynamic process that requires careful consideration of personal circumstances, risk tolerance, and financial goals. It's rarely a black-and-white choice and often involves finding a middle ground that aligns with an individual's unique situation. A skilled financial advisor can help clients navigate this delicate balance by crafting a customised strategy that strives to satisfy both objectives to the best extent possible.

At the planning level, portfolio decisions that introduce risk often appear counterintuitive and surprising. For instance, some investors believe that adopting a conservative approach with their portfolios is wise, assuming it will safeguard against the painful, albeit temporary, market volatility—the media's synonymous portrayal of risk.

While this conservative strategy may initially seem prudent, it can lead to a lower long-term return and reduce the likelihood of achieving financial goals. In fact, it may increase the risk to the investor's financial plan, as it moves them further from, rather than closer to, their objectives. Regrettably, the secondary effects of such popular strategies are often overlooked or ignored.

It is noteworthy that risk at the planning level can often be masked as prudence, making it all the more alluring and misleading to investors.

Shifting our focus to the behavioural level, we can identify several ways in which risk is introduced. For instance, selling during a bear market due to fear, succumbing to investment fads, chasing the best-performing stocks or funds, and acting on market forecasts are all examples of behavioural decisions that can be detrimental to long-term financial success.

In normal market conditions, few investors feel susceptible to these errors. However, prolonged exposure to irrational markets can lead to regrettable decisions. Hence, another way to view these behavioural choices is as "any decision that your future self may come to regret."

The key question then becomes: How can we identify and avoid these decisions in advance?

Considering market history, it becomes evident that investors are most likely to regret any decision that deviates from staying the course. The market's impressive growth of 78 times since 1960 was achieved by simply owning the market and staying the course. Therefore, any alternative decision, at the very least, introduced the possibility of interrupting that growth—this is the essence of risk.

To mitigate risk in investing, investors should avoid making impulsive decisions based on short-term market movements. Fear-driven selling during a bear market or chasing trends are examples of such pitfalls that can hinder long-term financial success. Instead, staying the course and adhering to a disciplined, long-term investment strategy is more likely to yield favourable outcomes.

This underscores the importance of adhering to the simple mantra of "stay the course." While uncomfortable at times, it remains the most effective strategy for mitigating various behavioural risks over the long term.

Understanding the true nature of risk in investing is paramount for making sound financial decisions. Risk should be recognised as the possibility of a permanent loss of capital or any decision moving one further from their financial goals. Volatility, on the other hand, may cause temporary fluctuations but should not be equated with risk. Historical evidence demonstrates that disciplined and patient investors have reaped significant benefits from the market over time, dispelling the myth that it is inherently risky.

By adopting a clear understanding of risk and making informed choices, investors can navigate the dynamic world of investing with confidence, leading to greater success in achieving their long-term financial objectives.

Chapter 28

The Stock Market Paradox: Unveiling the Peculiar Aversion to Investing in Great Businesses

"The trouble with the world is that the stupid are cocksure and the intelligent are full of doubt."

Bertrand Russell

From my earliest encounters with the stock market, I found myself deeply intrigued by the widespread belief that it carries a deep inherent risk. This fascination prompted me to delve into the subject, determined to elucidate its true essence and debunk the prevailing myths surrounding it. In my pursuit, I have crafted an explanation designed to shed light on the reality of the stock market, presenting it in a way that leaves no room for ambiguity. I can only hope that my efforts have borne fruit and that my elucidation proves both comprehensible and eye-opening to all who come across it.

When given a choice between high or low investment risk, nearly everyone opts for low risk. But when the choice is a high or low return, people's answers often differ. This dichotomy reveals an inconsistency in how we approach investment decisions. We shun risk yet crave return. As we plan our financial futures, goals should steer us more than generic risk ratings. Rather than focusing narrowly on a 1-

10 risk score, our priorities and desired outcomes should drive investment selection. A retirement plan centred on funding a comfortable lifestyle will likely demand bolder choices than one content with preserving wealth. Defining objectives first brings our true risk tolerance into clearer focus. What we want to achieve gives meaning to risk, not the other way around. With purpose as the compass, we can navigate the investment terrain and select a wise path forward.

For novice investors, investing in the 'stock market' is perceived as "volatile and risky". But it isn't in the way you might think it is when you understand what the stock market is and how it works.

Consider a hypothetical conversation about investments. You might ask me how I invest my money. In response to your query, I might suggest that my fundamental strategy is "to possess a diverse collection of shares in nearly 30,000 of the largest, most reputable, financially stable, profitable, and innovative companies on the planet. Companies we engage with daily without a second thought."

If I'm not mistaken, you'd likely find this strategy appealing, sensible, enticing, and perhaps even reassuring. Now, what if I had responded to your identical question simply by stating, "I invest in the stock market?"

I suspect your immediate reaction might lean towards, "That seems excessively risky, particularly for someone who isn't particularly young." In the first scenario, I was indirectly referring to owning a number of globally diversified index tracking fund such as the Standard & Poor's 500-Stock Index (comprising 500 of the largest US companies).

As already alluded to, the collective value of the 500 companies comprising the S&P 500 reached approximately $35 trillion in 2023, which accounted for around 83% of the total value of all publicly traded companies in the US. In essence, both responses yield nearly identical outcomes. Through owning portions of its 500 largest and most stable constituents, I would be investing in virtually the entire stock market. Furthermore, by investing in nearly 30,000 companies, I am also gaining a stake in other great businesses worldwide.

I have no problem whatsoever sharing with you that my portfolio consists entirely of equities. Yes, you did read that correctly; 100% of my money is invested in a huge collection of the greatest businesses on the planet. When I tell people this, I typically get one of two reactions:

1. That sounds really risky.

2. It's because you're young, right?

But believe me, it's neither about my appetite for risk or volatility, nor my age. For the record, I am 57 at the time of writing this book. It's about my 30 plus years in the business and my understanding of how this stock market investing game works. I guess you could say I’ve been around the block a few times.

I recognise that incorporating assets that could potentially lower my expected future returns will delay my financial goals or require additional savings. Given this mindset, I see an all-equities portfolio as a purely rational investment approach.

For those of you still sceptical about the long-term wealth potential of investing in thousands of the world's top businesses, I urge you to carefully examine this graphic showing the performance of the S&P 500 index:

EQUITIES: GROWTH AND INCOME

SINCE 1960:		
S&P PRICE	DIVIDENDS	INFLATION
↑ 68X	↑ 30X	↑ 11X

SINCE 1990:		
S&P PRICE	DIVIDENDS	INFLATION
↑ 12X	↑ 5X	↑ 2X

Having observed the S&P 500 performance graphic spanning over six decades, the evidence is palpable. This time-tested index, representing some of the most influential businesses globally, showcases the inherent strength and resilience of diversified investing. Not only has it demonstrated a consistent upward trend over the long run, but it has also significantly trounced inflation, preserving and enhancing the purchasing power of its investors.

It's not about isolated years or short-term fluctuations, but the overarching trend, which has consistently moved upwards over the long run. For any long-term investor, this graphic should serve as both a confirmation of the power of persistent investing and a reassuring testament to the potential of building wealth when anchored in such proven market pillars.

Here's a simplified breakdown of my investment strategy:

For long-term objectives - lean on long-term assets (equities) For short-term needs - opt for short-term assets (bonds/cash). Apart from keeping a healthy cash emergency fund, I don't have any short-term goals, so why would I hold any short-term assets? It wouldn't make any sense and would only dilute my potential returns over the long haul, especially considering the typically lower yields of these assets compared to equities over extended periods. I do however hold a cash buffer for emergencies and unforeseen events.

The most effective trick in successful investing is seeing yourself as a Forever Equity Holder. When you adopt the mindset of a Forever Equity Holder, external media chatter diminishes.

You transition from reacting to acting.

From a trader's stance to an owner's.

From a doubtful view to a hopeful one.

Headlines merely become side notes.

The power to tune out distractions comes from one potent concept: Forever. As a forever holder, you understand that daily, weekly, or yearly events are trivial in the grand scheme of things. Because, over an extended period, the majority of things perceived as crucial lose their significance. What truly matters is time. Being a forever holder grants you the greatest gift: ample time to let scenarios unfold naturally. This viewpoint aligns with historical accuracy. Instead of attempting to outmanoeuvre or surpass the market, focus on mastering your behavioural instincts.

Embracing the forever holder mindset safeguards us from the behavioural pitfalls that often disrupt investment strategies.

It is an undeniable truth that the businesses surrounding us shape our daily lives. From banks and insurance companies handling our financial matters, to utility providers keeping our homes running smoothly, and technology companies revolutionising the way we connect and interact. The influence of these corporations is omnipresent. Despite our significant reliance on these entities, there exists an astonishing aversion among many individuals towards investing in the stock market—the very platform that fuels the growth of these great businesses. But why is this the case?

They might not have taken the time to contemplate the true nature of the stock market, which is likely why they hold such a perspective.

The Money Trail

"Arithmetic is the first of the sciences and the mother of safety." – Louis D. Brandeis. American lawyer

Let us embark on a thought experiment. Take a moment to glance at your recent bank statement. Where does the lion's share of your hard-earned money go? It likely flows towards banks, insurance, shopping, utility companies, fuel, technology, and food providers. Most of your remaining expenses are likely to be allocated to discretionary activities such as purchasing from online retailers like Amazon, subscribing to streaming services like Netflix, enjoying television services like Sky TV, and indulging in holiday experiences.

Now, pause and ponder: Who benefits the most from this financial exchange, you, or the companies from which you are purchasing? Undoubtedly, it is the companies. They thrive because of our continuous reliance on their products and services. Yet, despite this reality, many of us hesitate when it comes to investing in these very same companies—the ones that billions of consumers use effortlessly in their everyday lives.

The fundamental principles of investing arithmetic are incredibly straightforward. What's intriguing, however, is that many investors struggle to acknowledge what is glaringly evident, right within their field of vision. Alternatively, it seems even more prevalent that they intentionally overlook reality because it contradicts their ingrained beliefs, biases, excessive self-assurance, and unquestioning adherence to the conventional functioning of financial markets, which appears to have persisted for an eternity.

So, let's walk through a day in the life of a typical UK consumer and how this translates to investing. Picture yourself or your neighbour in this narrative.

Your alarm goes off from you Apple or Samsung smartphone and you will probably check for any calls or messages. If you are on social media, you will almost certainly check your Facebook and Twitter accounts and might take the time to look at a mildly amusing video of a cat on YouTube that a friend has sent you. You're far from alone in this, with over 2.2 billion iPhones sold by Apple and 1 billion by Samsung globally.

Your provider might be Vodafone, a giant in the telecom industry, servicing millions of customers who pay them monthly.

Perhaps the first thing you do is adjust the thermostat in your bedroom. Odds are, this thermostat is produced by Honeywell, the world's leading thermostat manufacturer. Their thermostats are a common sight in many households and you're tapping into British Gas.

As part of your routine, you might set off on your morning run, lacing up your Nike trainers. As reported by Matt Powell, an industry analyst at The NPD Group, Nike sells an impressive 25 pairs of shoes every second. You might jog alongside your neighbour, who happens to work for IBM, a multinational company employing hundreds of thousands globally.

After your run, you prepare for the day. You might use a Gillette razor, shower with Dove soap, and use Head and Shoulders shampoo. Brushing your teeth with Colgate, you're one of the billions of consumers purchasing Unilever and Colgate-Palmolive products daily.

Dressing for work, you switch on Sky news to find out what is going on in the world, where you are bombarded with advertisements from a multitude of other household name brands that you use regularly. A commercial with a well-known sports personality discusses the benefits of Humira

(AbbVie), a drug used by thousands globally to combat arthritis.

Your using electric to brew your Nescafé coffee and you have a bowl of Kellogg’s Cornflakes.

On your way to work, you stop for petrol at your local BP station, a multinational oil and gas company headquartered in the UK.

There's some roadwork happening, and you wait while a JCB digger is unloaded from a lorry. JCB is a world-renowned manufacturer of construction equipment.

Before you go into work, you get your latte from one of the 33,833 Starbucks stores.

Arriving at work, you boot up your computer running on a Microsoft Windows operating system, used by over a billion people worldwide. The computer's processor is likely manufactured by Intel, the world's largest semiconductor manufacturer.

Your company's networking system might be manufactured by Cisco, a global leader in networking for the internet.

An email comes in from your insurance broker about your buildings and contents renewal policy with Aviva. Aviva operates in 16 countries, serving over 33 million customers. They're also contacting you with information about a Bupa healthcare policy, a leading private healthcare provider in the UK.

Lunchtime arrives, and you might grab a meal from McDonald's, joining the millions who purchase meals there every day. You might also enjoy a Coca-Cola, with 1.9 billion cokes served daily worldwide.

Post-lunch, you withdraw cash from an HSBC ATM. HSBC is one of the world's largest banking and financial services organisations.

You stop at Boots to pick up a few essentials. Boots has thousands of stores in the UK, visited by millions of customers every day. While you are in there you might buy some Scotchgard Spot Remover, Post-It Notes, and Scotch Tape, all produced by 3M. It's a fun fact that Post-It Notes were invented by accident. You might also grab some plasters, a Johnson & Johnson product. This iconic brand's logo has been used for over a century. At Boots, you also fill a prescription for a cholesterol medication like Lipitor, made by Pfizer. Pfizer is one of the largest pharmaceutical companies in the world, employing over 90,000 people worldwide.

You initially planned to pay cash but decide to conserve your notes and instead use your credit card - either your Visa or Mastercard. Visa is a widely used credit card network globally, while Mastercard has over 290 million cards issued. These credit cards are being used by consumers every day paying for goods and services and lining the pockets of businesses all over the world.

On the drive home, you decide to finish the patio project you started two weeks ago. So, you swing by B&Q to pick up some necessary supplies. B&Q is the biggest home improvement retailer in the UK. They are owned by

Kingfisher plc, an international home improvements company with over 1,900 stores.

You look forward to finishing the project before your sister and her husband fly in on a British Airways flight over the weekend. British Airways is one of the UK's largest airlines.

Your final stop before heading home is at Tesco. This multinational grocery and general merchandise retailer are one of the largest in the UK, with millions of customers visiting its stores every day.

After loading up your car, you grab a pizza for family night. The plan is to watch a film on Netflix or Amazon Prime. These streaming services are used by millions worldwide. Something catches your eye and you hit the pause button to order it from your smartphone on Amazon.

As you unwind from the day, I want you to remember that the companies you interact with daily, from Apple to B&Q, are not just businesses you buy from, but also potential investments. So how many of these great companies did you and everyone else use today? Most people easily engage with 20 to 30 through both necessity and choice. Now multiply that by the billions of consumers on planet earth. And yet many people still think the stock market is very risky. I beg to differ. The companies we've discussed today are familiar to us all, represent the strength of the global economy, and continue to operate regardless of market fluctuations.

They continually strive to innovate and increase their profits year after year. So, as the global economy experiences tough times, I encourage you to have faith in these corporations.

Holding a share in these formidable businesses is not akin to gambling with a lottery ticket - it signifies part-ownership of the company. Provided our foundational analysis of these businesses remains steady, doesn't it seem logical to own a stake in the companies we utilise daily, often without a second thought, and stay invested in them even during challenging times?

Owning a Piece of Greatness

Consider the sheer magnitude of the corporations we interact with daily. They span across various sectors, ensuring that even during challenging economic times, some businesses flourish while others endure temporary setbacks. Investing in the stock market should not be seen as a risky endeavour, but rather as an opportunity to own a small piece of hundreds, if not thousands, of the greatest businesses on the planet. By becoming an investor, you are effectively claiming a stake in these enterprises and participating in their success.

Diversification and Resilience

One of the fundamental principles of investing is diversification—spreading your investments across multiple companies and sectors. This strategy safeguards your portfolio from the volatile nature of individual businesses and allows you to benefit from the collective resilience of the market as a whole. While certain sectors may experience turbulence, others may thrive, creating a balancing effect that can mitigate risks and provide stability to your investment journey.

As we navigate through our daily lives, we often overlook the powerful tapestry of industries and brands that support our routines. These companies, with their expansive global presence, are not just products or services we casually engage with; they're the backbone of the modern economy and a testament to the potential of long-term investing.

Next time you sip your morning coffee or tune into your favourite show, remember: you're not just a consumer, but a potential shareholder in a grand global narrative. It's time to think beyond the purchase and see the bigger picture – the vast world of investment opportunities that's interwoven with our everyday lives.

Part 7

Achieving Long-Term Investing Success

Chapter 29

Decoding the Risk Levels: Unravelling the True Risks of Everyday Asset Classes

"In investing, what is comfortable is rarely profitable."

Robert Arnot

Investors are often introduced to the typical 1 to 10 risk scale ladder, an attitude to risk tool designed to gauge their tolerance for investment risk. However, this scale can be dangerously misleading if misunderstood, leading to misconceptions and potentially detrimental investment choices. I'd like to briefly address it here, but I'll delve deeper into it in chapter 31.

Many investors erroneously believe that climbing this risk ladder necessarily means moving into inherently riskier asset classes, such as startup companies, commodity futures, and cryptocurrencies. While high-risk investments exist, most people tend to invest in funds that mitigate these risks. These common investment funds typically consist of a diverse range of thousands of the top companies in the world. As a result, they seldom include any of the aforementioned high-risk assets. In reality, the risk ladder is less about the nature of the investment and more about the level of exposure to market volatility.

Many investors fear volatility due to the uncertainty and risk it introduces to their investments. Fluctuations in market prices can lead to potential losses, and this fear of losing money can be significantly distressing. Additionally, volatility can be challenging to predict and manage, creating a sense of unease or lack of control. This fear can be amplified for those who are heavily reliant on their investments for future plans, such as retirement, as volatility could jeopardise these goals.

Furthermore, high volatility often coincides with economic uncertainty or downturns, which can further increase investor anxiety.

Accepting volatility is about embracing the inherent nature of the market and developing strategies to navigate it effectively. Here are several strategies that can help:

Education: Understanding the nature of markets, including the fact that volatility is a normal part of investing, can help alleviate fear. Knowledge about historical market patterns can also offer some comfort, showing that markets have always experienced periods of volatility followed by recovery and then progression to new highs.

Long-Term Perspective: Short-term market movements can be erratic and unnerving, but over the long term, markets have generally trended upward. By focusing on long-term goals and maintaining a consistent investment strategy, one can weather short-term volatility.

Diversification: Having a well-diversified portfolio can help manage and reduce the risk associated with volatility.

Different assets respond to market changes in different ways, so having a mix of assets can smooth out returns.

Risk Tolerance: Identifying your risk tolerance is crucial. If you're more risk-averse, you might want to create a more conservative portfolio that could potentially be less affected by market volatility.

Emotional Discipline: It's important not to let fear drive investment decisions. Being patient and avoiding panic selling during market downturns can help maintain your investment strategy and potentially lead to better long-term results.

Professional Advice: Working with a financial advisor can be beneficial. They can offer personalised advice and help design a portfolio and strategy that aligns with your risk and volatility tolerance and financial goals.

Remember, volatility isn't always negative - it can create opportunities for investors to buy quality investments at lower prices. In the end, becoming comfortable with volatility often comes down to education, planning, and maintaining emotional discipline. So, what is your volatility composure level?

The Vision of an Investor: Days, Years, or Decades?

In the ever-fluctuating world of investments, perspective is key. When you glance at the financial charts, where does your eye land? On the zigzags of days, the calmer undulations of years, or the steady ascent of decades? For the short-sighted, the daily bumps and troughs of the stock market might provoke anxiety or exuberance. They see each jolt as a potential crisis or opportunity, reacting with every twist and turn. It's a rollercoaster ride, exhilarating but exhausting.

Those who stretch their vision a bit further, focusing on years, witness fewer highs and lows. They perceive a broader picture, riding out short-term turbulence with the understanding that the market has a rhythm, with both ups and downs.

Yet, the savviest investors, those with their sights set on the long horizon, appreciate the beauty of decades. They recognise that, while daily fluctuations and yearly cycles are a part of the journey, it's the long run that truly matters. Over decades, many of the momentary disruptions fade away, rendering a smoother and more predictable path of growth. What do you fixate on?

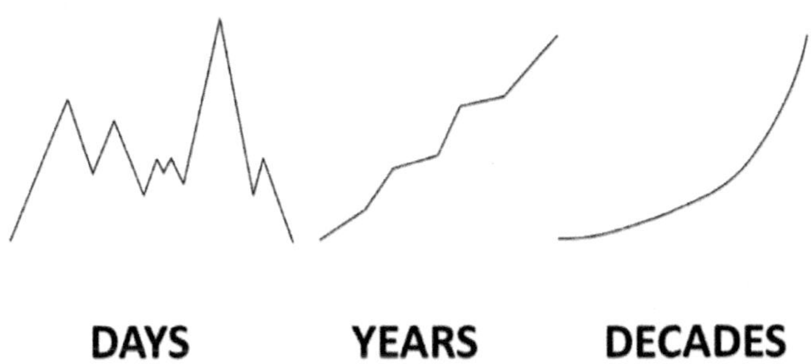

Such investors don't get lost in the noise of the present; instead, they're attuned to the harmonious song of the future. Their investments are not reactions to today's headlines, but decisions grounded in long-term visions and goals. The time horizon you choose to fixate on will significantly influence your investment outcomes. So, as you ponder upon your investment journey, ask yourself: Are you a sprinter, reacting to every ripple? A marathoner, gauging the years? Or a visionary, with an unerring focus on the horizon of decades?

Remember, volatility is but a momentary cloud in the vast sky of financial growth. Let your focus, determination, and goals dictate your path, and you might just find that the journey, spread over decades, is not only smoother but also more rewarding.

Gaining the proper perspective on volatility is a journey unique to each investor. A financial advisor's role is to serve as an experienced guide, drawing on historical insights and client-specific considerations. By taking the time to understand an investor's situation holistically, advisors can help determine an optimal risk profile that stays true to their objectives. This bespoke process considers both rational metrics and emotional factors integral to long-term success. Volatility may be inevitable, but preparation and partnership with an advisor can transform unease into opportunity. With the right framework tailored to their needs, fluctuating markets can become a navigable terrain on the path to an investor's financial destinations. The risk ladder is merely the first step of a rewarding expedition ahead.

The image clearly illustrates how volatility smooths over longer time horizons. Daily fluctuations appear erratic and frightening when viewed in isolation. But when compounded over years and decades, a steady upward trajectory emerges. Short-term volatility dissipates into long-term growth.

This visualisation provides an important perspective - while daily market swings garner attention, they are not the most useful metric for long-term investors to concentrate on. Becoming preoccupied with day-to-day volatility can be detrimental, tempting one to make impulsive moves out of fear. But by focusing on the years and decades ahead, the daily noise fades to the background.

It takes discipline to maintain this long view amidst near-term turbulence. But historical data shows extending your gaze smooths short-term volatility into long-term opportunity. The most successful investors concentrate on horizons of 10, 20 or 30 years, not days or weeks. They see daily ups and downs as expected noise on the path to real wealth creation.

So, while dramatic short-term market movements understandably capture investor attention and concern, it is crucial to see them in context. The years and decades ahead reveal a clearer trajectory not distorted by daily distractions. Concentrate on the long-term climb, stay invested based on goals, and let time work its compounding wonders. The texture transforms from volatility to visibility when the proper perspective is applied.

Chapter 30

Volatility Composure

"Be fearful when others are greedy and greedy when others are fearful."

Warren Buffett

Volatility composure is best described as a combination of previous experiences and behavioural tendencies, highlighting how an investor tends to respond to shifts in the market value of their investments and overall stock market fluctuations. The key aspect is how they actually react, not just how they think they will, when the stock market encounters turbulence. It questions how emotional responses of individual investors influence their actions. During periods of market volatility, those with high volatility composure are likely to disregard market news, maintaining their stance regardless of daily events, while investors with low volatility composure are more prone to actively seeking information (such as seeking reassurance from their advisor or frequently monitoring the market) and acting, potentially deviating from their long-term financial plans.

Components shaping volatility composure include the ability to adhere to a long-term strategy (a form of discipline), maintain calm amid chaos (another discipline form), and prevent excessive anxiety when their financial situation seems uncertain. Volatility composure positively correlates with traditional "risk tolerance" measures and negatively associates with perceptions of financial loss (the "personalisation of loss").

However, it also stands as a distinct element separate from other aspects of an individual's experiences and personality that might shape investor behaviour (like judgment, risk personality, preferences). Volatility composure differs from investment preferences or judgment. For instance, you might favour risky penny stocks while lacking the composure to see its value diminish. Similarly, you might exhibit high composure but focus excessively on short-term profits and losses.

Rather than concentrating on specific cognitive or behavioural biases, the behavioural-guidance aspect of investment management can significantly boost annual portfolio returns. In simpler terms, guidance from a trusted advisor can assist investors in making improved decisions and adopting more beneficial behaviours concerning their investments. By comprehending our usual reactions to market instability, we can develop a strategy to mitigate and ultimately enhance these behaviours.

Setting aside the topic of volatility for a moment, if a prospective investor understands and accepts that a low-cost, globally diversified portfolio has been the best-performing asset class over the past century, then the question posed by the risk ladder changes. Instead of asking "How much risk am I willing to take on?", the question becomes "How much of my capital am I prepared to invest in the asset class that has historically produced the best returns?" The larger the proportion of your capital invested in this sector, the greater the volatility you must be willing to withstand to achieve the desired returns.

As an illustration, suppose an investor scores a 7 out of 10 on a standard risk attitude questionnaire commonly employed by financial advisors. This score effectively signifies their willingness to allocate around 70% of their portfolio to investments that have historically exhibited strong long-term performance within the primary asset classes commonly chosen by most individuals. In this scenario, it could involve investing in a diverse portfolio of the world's most successful businesses, as this is essentially what the stock market represents.

The remaining balance of their investment, in this example 30%, can then be allocated to lower-risk, lower-reward, and less volatile assets. These could include corporate or government bonds, commercial property, or fixed income. It's crucial to keep in mind the impact of inflation on investments with low yields, as it can gradually erode their value over time. Many clients, however, misunderstand this, assuming that a higher position on the risk ladder translates to riskier investments. In reality, the underlying asset class remains the same and its inherent risk level does not change.

What does change is the investor's exposure to volatility, not underlying risk. The larger your investment in a vast portfolio of the world's leading businesses, the greater volatility you must be prepared to endure. Market returns and volatility are inseparable companions; one cannot expect the former without the latter. However, throughout history, those who have been able to embrace greater volatility have often been rewarded for their willingness to do so.

The "riskiest" asset allocation is that which has the smallest margin for error over the course of the planning period. The "least risky" asset allocation is that which has the largest margin for error over the course of the planning period. This perspective changes everything.

However, it is crucial to remember that while these lower risk and volatility investments may offer a sense of security, they are also more susceptible to the erosive effects of inflation. Over time, inflation can diminish the real value of these investments, impacting the overall purchasing power of the returns.

Embracing volatility rather than fearing it is crucial for investors for several reasons. Firstly, volatility provides opportunities for potential higher returns. Market fluctuations can create undervalued assets, enabling investors to buy stocks or other investments at lower prices and potentially sell them at higher prices when the market recovers.

Secondly, volatility allows for portfolio diversification. Different asset classes and sectors can perform differently during market swings. By diversifying their investments across a range of assets, investors can mitigate risk and potentially minimise losses during turbulent periods.

Furthermore, volatility tests an investor's long-term perspective and discipline. By staying focused on their investment goals and maintaining a long-term mindset, investors can avoid making rash decisions based on short-term market fluctuations. Volatility can serve as a reminder to stick to an investment strategy rather than succumbing to emotional reactions.

Embracing volatility helps investors build resilience and adaptability. Financial markets are inherently unpredictable, and volatility is a natural part of the investment journey. By understanding that volatility is a normal part of the investment landscape, investors can develop the mental fortitude needed to navigate through challenging periods and make informed decisions.

In conclusion, embracing volatility allows investors to seize opportunities, diversify portfolios, maintain discipline, and build resilience. By reframing volatility as a potential ally rather than a foe, investors can approach the market with a more confident and strategic mindset.

Chapter 31

Redefining Risk

"There are no gains without pains. He that would catch fish, must venture his bait."

Benjamin Franklin

Snakes and Ladders: The Stock Market Edition

The timeless game of Snakes and Ladders provides an apt analogy for the intricacies of stock market investing. Just as in the game, investors aim to climb the ladder, steadily building their wealth through informed choices, diversification, and adherence to long-term strategies. The well-constructed ladders in our investing game represent stable, high-performing assets, like global equities. These ladders are the instruments of steady, sustainable growth.

However, just as we find in the game, there are snakes lurking. These pitfalls are not always obvious, and they can derail even the most experienced investors. They embody the perils of media noise, a tumultuous whirlwind of opinions, speculations, and sometimes baseless predictions that can lead an investor astray. Investing based on emotions or the latest media buzz is akin to landing on the snake's head, with a rapid slide down, away from one's financial goals.

Another snake is our very own behavioural biases. These intrinsic patterns of decision-making can push us to act on impulse, favouring short-term gains over long-term stability, or making decisions based on past experiences rather than current data. Such biases can be a silent saboteur, waiting to send an investor tumbling back down.

It's worth noting that while the stock market isn't a game, understanding its Snakes and Ladders nature can equip investors with a perspective that emphasises patience, resilience, and continuous learning. And just like the game, with the right strategy and a bit of luck, the ultimate prize—a robust financial future—is within reach. But always remember, a wise player knows when to sidestep the snakes and when to take the next step up a ladder.

A Tale of Two Risk Ladders

The investment risk ladder should not be viewed as a mere measure of inherent risk, but rather as a reflection of an investor's tolerance for volatility within the historically top-performing asset class: the global stock market. Recognising this can empower investors to align their investment strategy more closely with their personal financial goals, risk appetite, and volatility tolerance.

Yet, there's a prevailing misconception about what the investment risk ladder entails. Many perceive it as a transition from what investors perceive to be safe investments into inherently riskier ones, such as investing in Brazilian teak farms, Dubai car parks, and cryptocurrencies. It's crucial to understand that these are indeed riskier ventures, laden with dangers including currency risks.

Moreover, many of these speculative investments aren't regulated and lack any protective measures for the investor.

In contrast, the mainstream investment risk ladder is more about asset allocation between historically proven entities. Here, the "steps" on the ladder indicate the portfolio allocation between stocks, bonds, and cash. Climbing higher on this ladder means increasing stock holdings and reducing bonds or cash. The underlying investment remains the same wherever you are on the ladder, the only difference is the allocation ratios between cash, bonds, and equities. At its essence, it asks the investor: "How much of my money am I willing to allocate to the global stock market?"—which translates to owning a slice of thousands of the world's most successful businesses. This approach, grounded in history and performance, offers a more structured and potentially rewarding avenue for long-term investors.

Understanding investment risk is a critical aspect of any investing strategy. However, a common misconception is found amongst investors, particularly those focused on medium to long term investments. Many investors view the investment risk spectrum in a particular order, moving from what they perceive as the 'least risky' to the 'most risky'.

This traditional viewpoint from low risk upwards typically goes as follows: cash deposits, government bonds, corporate bonds, physical property, commodities/alternatives, current market trends or fads, global equities (the great businesses of the world), emerging markets, single large companies, and finally, single small or start-up companies.

Nonetheless, this perception is flawed when you consider three key factors: volatility, inflation, and loss of capital.

Taking these critical elements into account, the spectrum of investment risk becomes markedly different. Starting with the lowest risk and progressing to the highest, the reality is that for the informed long-term investor it looks more like this: global equities, physical property, emerging markets, commodities/alternatives, corporate bonds, government bonds, cash deposits, single large companies, single small companies, and finally, what's making money now or fads.

Starting from the 'lowest risk', it might seem counterintuitive to some to place 'global equities'/the great businesses of the world at the beginning of the list. This adjustment comes down to their ability to manage volatility effectively. Large, successful companies are generally well funded and often have robust strategies for managing market fluctuations and maintaining their value over time, making them relatively less volatile and thus, lower risk. These businesses are constantly innovating and evolving.

Taking this a step further, the more companies across different sectors you are invested in, the higher the diversification and lower the risk. Ideally, you should be invested in many hundreds if not thousands of these great businesses.

Following global equities, we have physical property. The reason property ranks lower in risk is due to its innate resilience against inflation. Unlike cash or bonds, physical property can retain its value and even appreciate during inflationary periods, providing a natural hedge against inflation.

Emerging markets, commodities/alternatives, corporate bonds, and government bonds follow suit. Each holds a greater degree of risk than the previous, largely owing to factors such as inflation and economic instability. However, asset types such as emerging markets, commodities, and alternatives can offer the potential for higher returns, which can be attractive for those willing to shoulder the increased risk.

To put this in context:

Since 1960, with dividends reinvested, the S&P 500 (as a proxy for stocks) has returned a compounded average annual return of 10%. Bonds have returned closer to 5-6% on average.

However, inflation has averaged around 4% over this period if you combine the US and UK.

Accounting for inflation, the real return on stocks has been around 6% (10% nominal minus 4% inflation). For bonds, it's been around 2% (6% nominal minus 4% inflation).

So historically, stocks have dramatically outperformed bonds and cash after inflation. However, there is a trade-off for seeking those higher returns. The trade-off is the being able to stomach greater volatility. That's because a significant portion of the investment is placed in areas more prone to fluctuations: the stock market.

Many investors fail to consider these important historical inflation-adjusted return facts.

Surprisingly, cash deposits, often viewed as the safest of safe havens, sit in the middle of the pack. They are certainly low in volatility, but they come with a serious drawback:

inflation risk. Cash deposits can lose value over time as the purchasing power of the pound in your pocket decreases due to inflation. This loss of purchasing power, particularly over the long term, poses a genuinely devastating risk to investors.

Single company investments, whether large or small, carry a high degree of risk due to the potential loss of capital. Investing in a single company, regardless of its size, means placing all your eggs in one basket. If that company performs poorly, you could face significant losses. This is also known as ‘concentration risk’.

Finally, at the riskiest end of the spectrum, we find 'what's making money now/herd mentality' or fads. These are often speculative, trendy investments that could offer quick high returns but come with significant volatility and a real possibility of total loss of capital. This category typically includes investments that are in vogue or popular at a particular point in time but may not have a solid foundation for long-term success.

But Here's the Twist: The Stock and Bond Ladder

Now, think of a different ladder. This one isn’t about diversifying into riskier asset classes, but rather about how much of your investment is in just one class: the global stock market (great businesses of the world).

The key distinction is that the underlying assets (stocks and bonds) remain the same as you go up the ladder - you are just adjusting the mix between them. This is vastly different than getting into fundamentally riskier asset classes like speculative investments such as cryptocurrency.

In summary, there are different risk ladders. One involves asset classes with different inherent risk levels. The other is about adjusting stock vs bond exposure. Know which ladder you're on, and don't assume climbing always means more risk. It may just mean turning up the volume on investing in the stock market to seek higher real returns over time, while accepting and tolerating the inevitable increase in volatility.

This graphic clearly illustrates what most investors believe to be true regarding different asset classes, accurately factoring in the relative impact of volatility, inflation and the potential loss of capital, along with the reality.

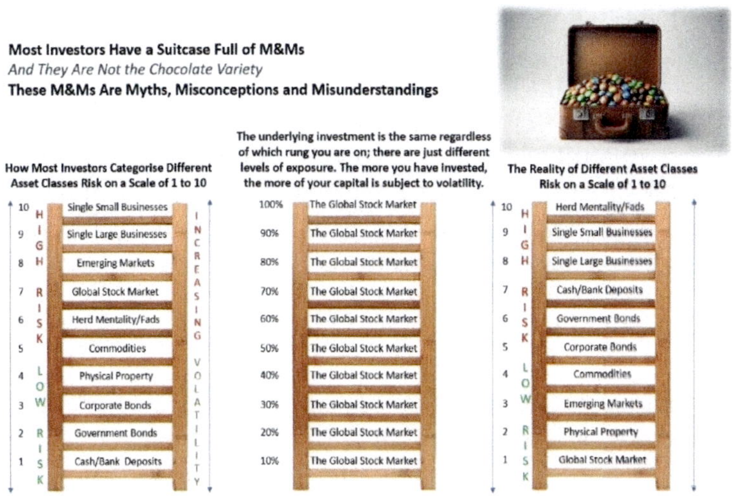

When investors allocate funds to the global stock market, which comprises the leading businesses of the world, the portion of their portfolio not invested in this sector often shifts toward options perceived to be of lower risk, lower reward, and less volatility, such as bonds and cash.

Working with a trusted adviser is of paramount importance when it comes to making sense of investment risk ladders. Such an adviser acts as a knowledgeable guide, providing valuable insights about risk that can significantly impact investment outcomes. They possess a deep understanding of the subject matter and can offer objective perspectives and analysis.

By collaborating with an advisor, investors gain access to information enabling them to consider more options and potential consequences. This partnership fosters an environment to expand knowledge, enhance critical thinking, and develop a comprehensive understanding of asset class risks.

Re-evaluating our understanding of investment risk is crucial, particularly for long-term investors. It's not just about volatility - we must also consider inflation and loss of capital threats. A nuanced understanding of risk can help build a balanced, resilient portfolio better equipped to deliver sustained returns over time.

A Paradigm Shift

To overcome the aversion towards investing in the stock market, it is essential to shift our perspective. Instead of fixating on the idea of investing in the market, we should focus on owning a small fraction of numerous exceptional businesses which operate globally 24 hours a day.

By embracing this mindset, we align ourselves with the very enterprises we rely on daily, becoming active participants in their growth and prosperity.

The aversion to investing in the stock market despite our profound dependence on the companies it encompasses is indeed perplexing. Recognising that these businesses flourish precisely because of our constant patronage should motivate us to consider the immense benefits of becoming investors. By diversifying our investments across various sectors, we can not only safeguard our finances but also enjoy the collective success of countless remarkable enterprises. It's time to overcome our aversion, broaden our horizons, and embrace the opportunity to own a slice of the greatest businesses on the planet.

Chapter 32

The Relentless Healing Power of the Stock Market

"Bull markets are born on pessimism, grow on scepticism, mature on optimism, and die on euphoria."

Sir John Templeton

Templeton's quote emphasises the cyclical nature of markets and the progression of investor sentiment. It suggests that the best opportunities arise in times of pessimism, making a case for optimism even in the face of adversity.

When it comes to investing, optimism is the only realism. This belief is supported by the facts and historical evidence. If we don't embrace optimism and acknowledge the positive trajectory of human history, we would need an alternative explanation that goes against these established facts. It's evident to me that in an often-irrational world, capital behaves rationally. If capital is dissatisfied with its current situation, it retreats and waits for better opportunities. This explains why, despite the chaos in the world, the value of good companies, their earnings, dividends, and overall worth have continued to rise.

In my view, pessimism can be likened to a mental illness. It goes against intuition when we consider the numerous catastrophes we've experienced and yet observe the positive numbers in the market. For instance, in 1975, the S&P 500 index was valued at 90, whereas in July 2023, it's approaching 4,500—a fiftyfold increase. Inflation has only increased tenfold during the same period, meaning markets have outperformed the cost of living by a factor of 5 to 1.

A negative outlook on the future doesn't resonate with historical perspectives.

While one might see the present as heralding doom, this perspective challenges the entire tapestry of human existence and the essence of our nature. Throughout time, advancements have always emerged amidst looming crises. It's been consistent in the past, and it will be in the future.

However, what you seek is often what you find, and your returns will likely reflect that belief.

Over the long run, capital has proven to be rational. However, companies may make grave mistakes driven by excessive optimism at the top of market cycles or excessive pessimism at the bottom. Additionally, human beings are prone to other flaws. Yet, if capital is rational, eventually, equities will correct themselves of any excesses in pessimism or optimism. The survival of the fittest principle also applies, leading to the disappearance of poorly performing companies.

Irrationality is inherent in the free market and human nature. Just as you can't attribute periods of market contraction or excessive optimism to irrationalism, you shouldn't ignore the fact that these are manifestations of human nature. Capital, like any other aspect of human nature, can go to extremes during good or bad periods, resulting in volatility. However, focusing on volatility alone causes investors to miss the bigger picture.

Volatility has never permanently halted a rising trendline. While it may temporarily impede progress, the upward trajectory continues inexorably. Every successful investor I've encountered has concentrated on this rising trendline, while failed investors inevitably fixate on irrational excesses that ruin their portfolios and retirement plans.

While the daily turbulence of the markets provokes strong reactions in the short-term, a look at history reveals the unrelenting upward march of human progress. The stock market is no different. Despite periodic corrections, crashes, and manias, over time equities continue their ascent, driven by the ingenuity and productivity of businesses.

Consider the last century - two world wars, the Great Depression, stagflation in the 70s, the dot-com bubble, the housing crisis. Each catastrophic in their own right, with markets plummeting dramatically. Yet looking back, these proved mere blips on the charts compared to the relentless growth in corporate earnings and shareholder value over decades.

The market's resilience stems from its rational pricing of future expectations rather than present troubles. With each crisis, no matter how severe, investors eventually recognise that human creativity and innovation will overcome and thrive again. The market reprices accordingly, reflecting this indestructible optimism.

Viewed through this lens, volatility and downturns are less causes for panic than opportunities to reassess and rebalance.

By focusing on fundamentals rather than reacting reflexively to daily swings, investors positioned in high-quality companies can ride out storms and benefit from the inexorable recovery.

Patience and discipline are key. Making drastic portfolio changes based on short-term noise often backfires. But maintaining exposure appropriate for one's time horizon and risk tolerance allows compounding to work its magic.

Of course, prudence demands a cash reserve on hand for near-term needs. But equities must play a central role for long-term investors to outpace inflation. There is simply no substitute for the wealth generation of productively deployed capital in well-run enterprises.

By tuning out provocative headlines and pundit pronouncements and focusing on this long arc of progress, investors can calm anxieties and continue steadily accumulating shares in the companies powering the future. Market volatility cannot alter the fundamental trajectory of human achievement.

Balancing risk is akin to a tightrope walk. Naturally, there's a desire to shield our savings from the unpredictable short-term whims of the stock market. Yet, we owe it to our future selves to ensure our savings not only keep pace but ideally outpace the inevitable rise in future costs.

It's always tempting to chase the allure of short-term guaranteed returns on "safe" investments, but such pursuits can often sidetrack a balanced, long-term strategy. While having a robust cash reserve for immediate needs is always wise, holding excess cash in anticipation of the market's next move can backfire. By adopting a steady, long-term (some might even call it mundane?) investment strategy, you stand a better chance of setting both your present and future self on a secure financial footing, come what may.

Successful investors continuously stick to their plan. Unsuccessful investors continually react to the media headlines and markets.

The Upward Trajectory of the Stock Market Explained

The stock market, when observed over extended periods, has historically showcased an upward trajectory. There are several logical reasons for this trend:

Economic Growth: At its core, the stock market reflects the health and productivity of the economy. As economies grow, producing more goods and services, businesses expand and become more profitable. This growth is reflected in their stock prices.

Innovation and Adaptation: Over time, companies and economies innovate, develop new technologies, and adapt to changing circumstances. This dynamic evolution often leads to increased efficiency, opening up new markets and revenue streams, ultimately boosting stock values.

Inflation: A certain degree of inflation is typical in most economies, which means that the absolute value of money decreases over time. As a result, nominal stock prices tend to rise even if the real value (adjusted for inflation) remains somewhat stable.

Reinvestment of Dividends: When investors earn dividends, many choose to reinvest them, purchasing more shares. This act of reinvestment can push stock prices higher.

Long-Term Investor Mentality: Many investors have a long-term horizon, understanding that while the market may experience short-term volatility, the long-term trend has historically been upwards. This collective mindset promotes stability.

Now, consider a hypothetical scenario where the stock market went down more often than it went up. If that were the case, we would indeed have approached a "ground zero" situation many decades ago, where stock values become virtually nil. Such a catastrophic decline would suggest not just failing companies but failing economies, collapsing governance, and societal breakdowns. Essentially, for stock values to consistently plummet to such depths, the very fabric of organised society and commerce as we understand it would need to unravel.

In essence, the upward trend of the stock market isn't just a result of financial mechanics but is also indicative of human progress, societal resilience, and our innate drive to adapt, grow, and thrive.

Chapter 33

Diversification, Asset Allocation and the Danger of Fixed Income

"Investing isn't about beating others at their game. It's about controlling yourself at your own game."

Benjamin Graham

I am of the opinion that a fixed income investment strategy over what can easily be a 30-year retirement of rising costs is financial suicide. I am a huge advocate of diversification. I'm not a big fan of asset allocation. There is a critical distinction.

The difference is there's enormous potential and necessity for diversification within an equity portfolio. That's what I call a portfolio. That's what I call diversification. Typically, asset allocation is stocks, bonds, and cash. And for a long term, multi decade, multi-generational investor, it's prudent to reconsider the allocation of assets in bonds and cash. My scepticism towards an overabundance of these assets stems from their fundamental trade-off. Frankly, it involves sacrificing a significant portion of the permanent return offered by equities in order to protect against their temporary volatility. This, in my opinion, is an irrational activity bordering on madness for the long-term investor.

Add in a temporary market downturn of say 25% on what could be described as a low risk and reward portfolio and the problem becomes much bigger, with the portfolio potentially losing a quarter of its value before rebounding.

This can lead to significant problems especially when they reach the income phase in retirement and must rely on their portfolio for living expenses. For instance, it's one thing if you are in the accumulation, pre-retirement phase as market declines don't matter as much. However, once in retirement, withdrawing say £20,000 or £30,000 annually from a portfolio that has just lost 25% of its value can be devastating. Suddenly you are taking income from 25% less capital while the risk of depleting your funds prematurely increases dramatically.

So, while human behaviour may not affect investing abilities as much during accumulation, it becomes a major issue in retirement when market declines have real impacts on annual income. Opting to withdraw less can be a choice, but it comes with its own set of risks, and who would really want to choose that path? Overall, human behaviour and life realities make investing difficult, especially in retirement when market volatility directly reduces the income individuals rely on. Addressing this will require strategies that account for human limitations and retirement income needs during periods of market turbulence.

So, how can we tackle this problem for individuals who are in the income-earning phase of their lives?

The answer is relatively simple: Enter retirement with a cash fund equivalent to two years' worth of living expenses. If you don’t have this amount in savings, then transfer this amount within your pension fund to a cash account. This is easily arranged. Then if the need arises, either financially or psychologically, to halt withdrawals, one can tap into that cash fund and live off it for two years, much like how a camel lives off its hump. After two years, the skies will most likely have either completely cleared or largely cleared, but one certainly wouldn't have depleted their funds. At that point, one can consider setting aside another two years of expenses in preparation for the next inevitable but temporary market decline. This is an area where seeking guidance from a trusted advisor can be extremely valuable, as they can provide advice and help formulate contingency plans.

Investors need a clear strategy. Without direction, reaching your investment goals becomes a challenge. Often, I'll receive a call from a concerned client declaring, "This time, it's different." This sentiment is the recurring refrain of the unsettled investor. Historical trends and the trajectory of capital suggest persistence. Yet, many investors, swayed by emotions and current events, feel the present situation is unprecedented. When such doubts arise, I remind my clients: this too shall pass. Ultimately, the market will rebound. The only true long-term risk is succumbing to transient fears.

Harry S. Truman once insightfully observed, "There is nothing new in the world except the history you do not know." In the realm of investing, this rings especially true; we've navigated countless financial storms and apocalyptic scenarios before.

Indeed, I've noticed that investors who view crises with the mindset "This too shall pass" generally have a track record of being correct more frequently than those who panic, thinking "This time it's different", and rush to exit.

In my view, adopting a fixed income investment strategy throughout a 30-year retirement period characterised by rising costs is financial suicide. I strongly advocate for diversification, while I'm not particularly fond of asset allocation. It's crucial to understand the distinction between the two.

THE REAL RISK

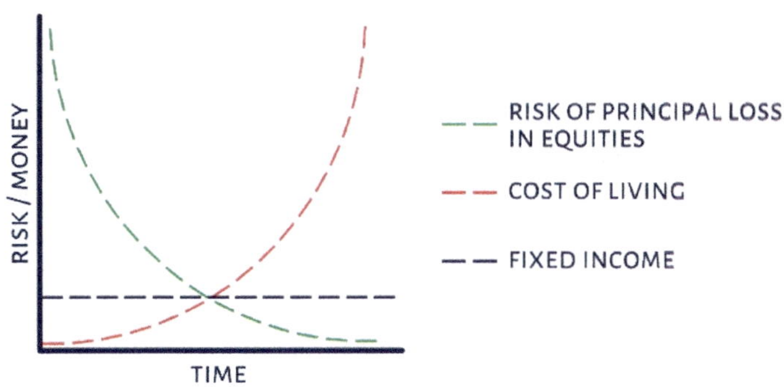

Since World War Two, the stock market has experienced an average decline of 30% roughly every five years. The crucial factor differentiating investment success from failure during this time was the mistake of mistaking temporary declines for permanent losses and panicking out of the market. By doing so, investors created the very losses they were trying to avoid. Instead, if they had remained invested, without concern for adding to their investments during market downturns when stocks were effectively on sale (which most individuals should be doing throughout their accumulation phase), the temporary decline would have eventually dissipated. Inevitably, it would have been followed by a period of above-average returns because that's the cycle.

Continued reliance on fixed income, particularly in a prolonged low interest rate environment can jeopardise one's retirement nest egg. While such assets have historically been touted as "safe havens," their real returns, when adjusted for inflation, can often be negligible or even negative. Over-reliance on them can erode purchasing power, which is especially detrimental during retirement when consistent income streams are paramount.

Moreover, in an era characterised by economic uncertainties, monetary policy decisions and unforeseen global events can drastically affect bond yields. A sudden spike in inflation can erode the purchasing power of fixed income returns, leaving retirees vulnerable. On the flip side, a drastic fall in interest rates can further diminish the nominal yields from these instruments, making them even less attractive.

In the context of temporary market downturns, the importance of having a safety net becomes paramount. Fixed income, while providing a steady flow, might not always suffice, especially if the downturn coincides with unforeseen expenses. It's akin to having an umbrella that doesn't quite protect you during a torrential downpour.

Therefore, a more balanced approach that entails holding a liquidity buffer becomes crucial. Just as businesses keep reserves for contingencies, retirees should earmark funds that can be easily liquidated without incurring losses during market downturns. These funds can serve as a bridge, allowing the individual to weather the storm without having to sell off assets at a loss or dip into the principal of their fixed income investments.

In conclusion, while fixed income has its place in a diversified portfolio, an over-reliance, especially in the golden years, can be a perilous strategy. Preparing for the proverbial rainy day, with an adequately funded safety net, ensures that temporary downturns don't result in permanent setbacks. Proper planning, coupled with a comprehensive understanding of market mechanics and individual needs, is essential for a stable and fulfilling retirement.

Human behaviour is a significant problem in this context, as is the reality of life. While it may not matter much during the accumulation phase, it becomes a considerable issue when people reach retirement and need to rely on their portfolio while experiencing a 25% market decline. Withdrawing £20,000 or £30,000 per year from a portfolio that has temporarily lost 25% of its underlying value can be a devastating blow. They will most certainly have to withdraw less or run the risk of depleting their funds much faster. So, how can we address this issue for individuals in the income phase of their lives?

Chapter 34

Equities vs. Bonds: Unleashing the Power of Ownership

"Time is the friend of the wonderful company, the enemy of the mediocre."

Warren Buffett

When it comes to investing, the age-old debate between equities and bonds has captured the attention of financial enthusiasts for decades. While both asset classes have their merits, equities have consistently demonstrated their ability to generate superior returns over the long run. Owning a piece of a great business through equities can be a more lucrative and rewarding investment choice compared to lending to it through bonds.

Over the past century, owning company stocks has yielded a 7% annual real return, while lending to those companies has returned only 3%. This leads us to ask: Why would bondholders voluntarily give up over half the available return? The historical data implies that stockholders capture a significantly higher compound return than bondholders. What motivates the lender to sacrifice so much potential upside?

There may be an assumption that the reduced volatility of bonds offsets the lower returns. Or perhaps other factors like taxes, risk tolerance and time horizons impact this choice.

NOMINAL RETURN VS. REAL RETURN

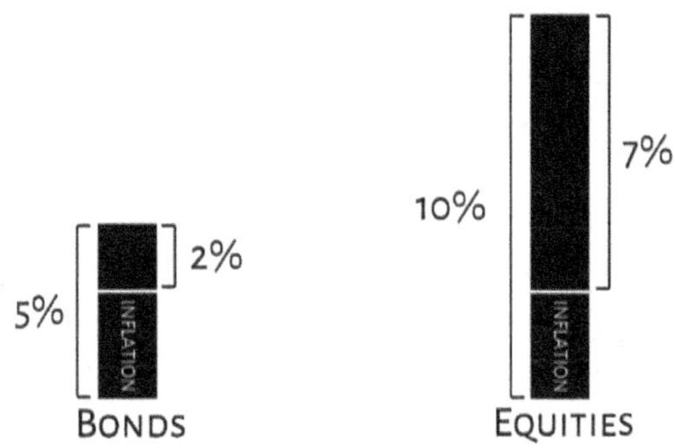

REAL RETURN IS ALL THAT MATTERS.

The numbers reveal an interesting disparity between equities and fixed income - a gap that raises questions about investor behaviour and priorities. You might be wondering why I harbour reservations about holding significant amounts in bonds for investors who intend to stay invested over multiple decades.

Well, here's why:

The Power of Ownership:

Investing in equities means becoming a partial owner of a business, granting shareholders the opportunity to participate in the company's success. By holding equities, investors align their interests with those of the company, sharing in the rewards of growth and profitability. Bonds, on the other hand, offer a fixed income stream but lack the potential for substantial capital appreciation.

Superior Long-Term Returns:

Historically, equities have outperformed bonds over extended periods, delivering higher real returns. While bonds provide fixed interest payments, equities offer the possibility of capital gains and dividend income, which can contribute to compounding wealth over time. As businesses flourish and expand, equities tend to appreciate, delivering substantial returns to shareholders.

Inflation Hedge:

Inflation erodes the purchasing power of fixed income instruments like bonds. In contrast, equities have the potential to act as an effective hedge against inflation. Companies with strong pricing power can adjust their product prices to account for inflationary pressures, leading to increased earnings and, subsequently, higher stock prices. This characteristic allows equities to preserve and even enhance investors' real returns over the long haul.

Diversification and Growth Opportunities:

Equities provide a wide range of investment opportunities across various industries and sectors, allowing investors to build a diversified portfolio. Bonds offer income stability and capital preservation, but typically offer more limited growth prospects. Investing in equities enables investors to participate in the growth of innovative companies, emerging markets, and transformative industries, potentially generating significant wealth in the process.

Psychological Benefits:

Investing in equities can also offer psychological benefits that bonds may lack. As shareholders, investors become active participants in the growth and success of businesses, fostering a sense of pride and engagement. This ownership mindset encourages long-term thinking and helps investors navigate market volatility with resilience, as they have a vested interest in the company's success.

Since 1971 to 2021, bonds have historically achieved an average annual return of approximately 6%, while equities have seen an average return of around 7%. However, when considering the reinvestment of dividends, equities have produced an average return of about 10%. In terms of inflation, the trendline suggests an average rate of 3%.

This means that bonds have typically provided a real return above inflation of around 3%, whereas equities have achieved a real return of 7% above inflation. This indicates that equities have outperformed bonds by more than twice the additional return.

However, it's important to note that achieving this higher return with equities comes at a cost.

Overall, while equities have historically offered higher returns than bonds, investors must consider the associated volatility and risks when deciding on their investment strategy.

Equities, with their potential for capital appreciation, dividend income, and the power of ownership, have consistently delivered higher real returns than bonds and fixed income funds over the long term. Lending to a great business through bonds means forgoing the benefits of ownership and the potential upside of participating in a company's success. By embracing equities, investors not only gain access to higher returns but also the psychological satisfaction of being part of a thriving business. The price one must pay for the additional return is accepting greater volatility or risk. Equities are known to experience more significant price fluctuations compared to bonds.

Therefore, investors should carefully consider their risk and volatility tolerance, investment objectives, and time horizon before making any investment decisions.

Giving up some significant portion of equities' premium long-term return in order to defend yourself against a risk that historically does not exist: long-term permanent loss of capital—is a feared outcome that is unsupported by reason, logic, and the historical record.

INFLATION RISK: MARGIN FOR ERROR

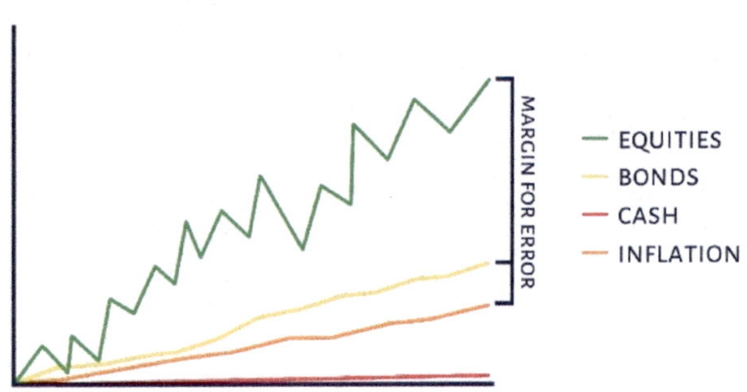

Opting for bonds over stocks, as exemplified in the common 60/40 portfolio split, is primarily a protective measure against what is termed "the risk of equities." However, it's noteworthy that such risk is virtually non-existent over significant time spans, although it can be present in shorter intervals. Consequently, by investing in bonds, one forgoes a substantial portion of the historical consistent returns offered by equities, merely to sidestep their momentary dips. Such a choice does not resonate with the logic of an individual genuinely aiming for wealth accumulation.

Over time, it's clear that an investor's returns hinge heavily on their balance between owning stellar companies and lending to them.

Hold on... isn't owning them riskier?

It's a curious notion that lending to these companies (via bond purchases) is viewed as safer than outright ownership, simply based on the payout sequence if a company dissolves. Think about it: If you genuinely thought a company, you're buying bonds from might go under, would you even invest?

Isn't it wiser, then, to have a stake in these companies, benefiting from their growth, instead of just being a creditor? It's certainly food for thought.

In conclusion, owning mainstream equities has historically been the simplest, most efficient, and least expensive method of building both rising income and rising wealth over time. This is a simple statement of incontrovertible fact. Investing significant amounts in bonds simply cater to investors' irrational fears of short-lived equity market downturns. Anything that restricts an investment's potential to decrease also limits its growth potential. The main risk with alternative investments is that they lure investors into settling for lower long-term returns than what mainstream equities have consistently provided both easily and affordably for over a century.

But What About Generating Income?

The age-old adage tells us:

Bonds = Income

Equities = Growth

But is it time to challenge this deeply entrenched notion?

Consider this provocative thought: What if equities are actually the champions of both growth AND income?

While I could point out that equities have skyrocketed over 70X since 1960 (and that's excluding dividends), today, I want to zone in on the income facet of equities.

Here's the reveal: It's substantial.

Take this in: from 1960, the S&P 500's dividend has catapulted from a mere $1.98 to a staggering estimated $68.34 last year.

This translates to an annual dividend growth of nearly 5.9%, juxtaposed against a 3.75% yearly rise in inflation. Put simply, dividends have trounced inflation by a margin exceeding 2% annually.

Now, isn't a consistently rising income—especially one that outpaces inflation—exactly what retirees seek?

Moreover, the resilience of dividends as an income source is noteworthy, having dwindled only seven times since 1960. And notably, the significant 23% drop in 2009 was an anomaly, induced by government interventions in bank bailouts and ensuing dividend cuts.

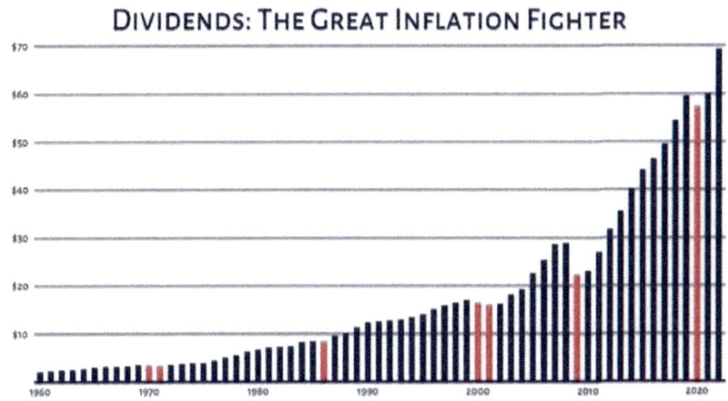

In the financial landscape, dividends have consistently amplified investment returns. Reinvesting these dividends is akin to planting a tree and then sowing its seeds to cultivate an orchard over time. Historically, dividends have accounted for a significant chunk of the stock market's total returns. Reinvestment uses these dividends to help your money grow, especially when you can get more shares for less during times when the stock market is effectively having a sale.

The crux? It's imperative to scrutinise 'established truths.' Delve into the data, and you'll often discover revelations that challenge the norm.

In conclusion, the notion that equities are solely for growth and not income may need re-evaluation. Equities have demonstrated the potential to provide both growth and income, with dividends often outpacing inflation. However, it's important to approach this strategy with a diversified portfolio, an understanding of the associated risks, and a long-term perspective. Tailoring the approach to individual income needs and goals, considering tax implications, and seeking professional advice can help retirees make the most of the income potential offered by equities while managing potential risks.

The story of dividends stands as a testament to the fallacies of accepted wisdom. In retirement, a fixed income equates to a fixed fate: deliberate destitution.

Chapter 35

No Surefire Returns: All Investments Carry Some Degree of Risk

"The biggest risk is not taking any risk. In a world that is changing quickly, the only strategy that is guaranteed to fail is not taking risks."

Mark Zuckerberg

The term "risk-free rate of return" is frequently invoked in the realm of financial planning. However, the idea that any aspect of financial planning—or life in general—can be entirely devoid of risk is utterly ridiculous. After all, no one truly experiences or even seeks out a life that is completely "risk-free." If they did, life would be extremely boring.

That said, embracing uncertainty can also lead to the most significant opportunities. It's often in the unknown spaces, where we push our boundaries, that we experience the most growth – both in life and in investments. While the markets might be unpredictable, it's this very unpredictability that can offer investors opportunities for higher returns.

However, the unpredictability of markets also underscores the importance of having a holistic strategy. Financial success often isn't just about picking the 'right' investment, but about understanding one's personal tolerance for risk and volatility, having clear financial goals, and adjusting strategies as life circumstances change.

Consider this: even the act of driving a car isn't 'risk-free'. Every time we get behind the wheel, there's a chance of an accident. But what do we do? We wear seatbelts, follow the rules, and keep our vehicles well-maintained. Similarly, in the investment world, there's no journey that's completely devoid of bumps or unexpected turns. But with the right 'safety measures' – diversification, research, and expert advice – we can significantly reduce our chances of a financial crash. It's not about avoiding the journey altogether; it's about navigating it wisely.

This isn't to suggest that we should embrace a reckless approach to life or financial planning. On the contrary, with a well-considered plan, one can navigate the tumultuous waters of investment with a level of assurance. Taking proactive steps like continuous education, seeking expert advice, and regularly reviewing one's portfolio can mitigate potential pitfalls.

What remains paramount is the recognition that for many people, the idea of absolute financial security, or being "risk-free", is an alien concept. So, let's be honest about the various investment options available and their inherent risks:

Cash, savings, or bank deposits—usually generate negative returns due to inflation.

Government and corporate bonds—uncertain returns due to fluctuating interest rates.

Property—costly to purchase, maintain, and can be challenging to liquidate, reduced tax breaks and possible tenant issues.

Stocks or equities—values fluctuate frequently, sometimes wildly.

Commodities—do not yield an income and are valued only by what someone else is willing to pay.

Alternative Investments and Emerging Asset Classes:

In recent years, there's been an increasing interest in alternative investments and emerging asset classes. These can include:

Cryptocurrencies and Digital Assets: Digital currencies like Bitcoin, Ethereum, and various altcoins have gained popularity. They offer a new kind of decentralised financial system, but they come with high volatility and regulatory scrutiny.

Environmental, Social, and Governance (ESG) Investing: A growing number of investors are looking beyond financial returns. ESG investing considers the environmental, social, and governance practices of the entities in which one invests. While this approach is geared towards ethical considerations, it also represents a different kind of risk and reward profile.

Private Equity and Crowdfunding: With platforms allowing for smaller investments into startups or projects, this avenue has become more accessible to the average investor. It's essential to understand the illiquidity and the long-term nature of such investments.

Another key consideration is the time horizon. Short-term investments face the brunt of market volatility, while long-term investments can weather these temporary storms, as they potentially offer the luxury of time for recovery. It's akin to embarking on a voyage: those who set out with the understanding that there might be rough seas ahead are better prepared and more likely to reach their destination successfully.

Furthermore, the globalised nature of today's economy means that events in one corner of the world can have repercussions elsewhere. As investors, understanding these interconnected dynamics and being agile in our approach is crucial. Whether it's geopolitical tensions, technological disruptions, or environmental concerns, all these factors can influence investment outcomes.

While none of these options are "risk-free," they each present different types and degrees of risk and reward. Similarly, the potential benefits each offers differ as well. High diversification of different assets will never take away risk altogether, but it does one hell of a job defending against it. Ultimately, an informed and strategic approach, combined with regular reassessment, can steer one's investment journey through the complexities and uncertainties of the financial realm.

In an ever-evolving financial landscape, where disruptive technologies and paradigm shifts in economic policies are common, it's essential to stay informed and flexible.

Knowledge remains an investor's best tool; being aware of market trends, geopolitical shifts, and industry innovations can be crucial in making calculated decisions.

In this dynamic financial landscape, embracing calculated risks and maintaining a balanced, vigilant approach are the keys to harnessing opportunities while safeguarding your financial future.

Chapter 36

The Two Big Investor Mistakes – The Importance of Understanding Risk and Reward

"When you least expect it, nature has cunning ways of finding our weakest spot."

Alan Turing

Investing is filled with twists and turns that can confound even seasoned veterans. The excitement of chasing profits can steer us toward imprudent decisions and overlooked risks. To gain valuable perspective, consider the following two allegories that creatively depict the investing landscape.

The first conveys the volatile ups and downs of certain strategies through a vivid rollercoaster analogy. Strapped in for the ride, one may desperately wish to jump off midway yet have no choice but to stay put. This story underscores critical truths about evaluating risks versus rewards.

The second tale recounts events through the eyes of an unlikely protagonist placed in a lulling environment. When circumstances suddenly shift, grave dangers become apparent too late. This sobering narrative cautions against complacency and assuming the future will resemble the past.

While fictional, these two parables contain universal insights about investing wisely. As you read them, reflect on your own behaviours without the bias of hindsight. Could hidden risks or blind spots be lurking undetected? The simple morals from these creative allegories offer much food for thought. Now, step right up and prepare for a thought-provoking ride!

1. The Rollercoaster Analogy:

Imagine you're lining up with your friends or significant other for a rollercoaster ride, a mix of anticipation and a hint of anxiety stirring within you. You know it's going to be a wild ride. As you settle in, you fasten the safety bar across your chest, it feels a bit snug, and then you begin your ascent up the towering rollercoaster track.

As you climb higher and higher, reaching the pinnacle, your heart drops as you plummet down the other side at a breathtaking speed. As you descend, screams escape your lips, a sense of impending doom filling your thoughts. You experience the first loop-the-loop, then the second, and all that's on your mind is a desperate plea: I need to get off, please let me get off! I think I'm going to die! As you navigate the final loop-the-loop, the rollercoaster gradually slows down to a comfortable stop and you disembark, unharmed.

You're aware that any attempts to extricate yourself during the ride, particularly at the height of those loops, would have had catastrophic outcomes, permanent loss. Yet, you stayed put, weathering the ride to its end. Consider volatility as the rollercoaster-like highs and lows and unpredictability of prices over an upward trend line. Understanding and sticking to an investment strategy during the tumultuous ups, downs, and loops of the market is crucial for successful investing.

The critical point is that exiting the market during downturns can lead to missing out on potential recoveries, which is similar to getting off a rollercoaster at its lowest point, thereby missing the subsequent rise. As previously mentioned in relation to Howard Marks' observation, volatility can be seen as a mere indicator of risk presence, but it does not constitute risk in its entirety. Think of volatility as a rollercoaster journey.

The Hazards of Trend-Chasing in Investments and What's Making Money Now

In the exciting world of investments, it's easy to get drawn into the latest fad, the "what's making money now" strategy, or the tantalising promise of get-rich-quick schemes. The allure of quick and massive returns can be overwhelming, especially when these trends are backed by hyped stories of overnight millionaires. The internet is full of these dangerously alluring and sensationalistic headlines.

However, these investment strategies often carry significant dangers that are not immediately apparent. One critical concern is that such trends are usually powered by speculation rather than grounded in fundamental analysis. When investments are driven by hype rather than intrinsic value, they're subject to sharp price corrections once the hype fades.

Furthermore, chasing the "hot trend" can lead to buying high and selling low – the very opposite of investment wisdom. By the time a particular investment becomes a fad, it's often already reached its peak, leaving late investors exposed to substantial downside risk.

Get-rich-quick schemes are especially perilous. They often hide behind glossy marketing and promise astronomical returns with minimal risk. However, beneath the surface, these schemes frequently lack transparency, have unsustainable business models, and often turn out to be outright scams.

Prudent investing requires patience, thorough analysis, and a long-term perspective. Investing in the latest trends or get-rich-quick schemes often exposes one to considerable risk and potential loss. Remember, if something sounds too good to be true, it probably is. Always conduct due diligence and consult with a trusted financial advisor before making investment decisions.

As a financial advisor, one of the most common questions I get is "Hey Mike, what's the best thing to invest in right now?" If I had a pound for every time someone asked that, I'd be a millionaire! I know the intent is to capitalise on hot trends and what's working at the moment. However, chasing the latest fad or get-rich-quick scheme can be extremely risky, as we discussed earlier. While I understand the appeal of wanting an easy answer, the truth is there's no one-size-fits-all investment for everyone.

Each client has unique goals, time horizons, risk profiles, and portfolios. An investment that seems hot today may be completely wrong for a given individual. That's why a thorough consultation is so important before making recommendations. I need to deeply understand a client's full financial picture and priorities. While it may seem simpler to just name the trendy investment, this carries great danger. Prudent advising requires carefully tailoring a plan to each client's specific needs and circumstances. The right investments are those aligned to one's individual situation and long-term financial objectives, not what happens to be making money now in the market.

2. It Was All Going So Well Until It Wasn't - The Turkey's Story:

Consider this metaphor, inspired by philosopher and mathematician Bertrand Russell, to better understand the risks and the dangers of investment fads and the 'what's making money now' mentality. Imagine you're a turkey living on a farm. It may seem peculiar, but bear with me. Your home is a small coop, and with each passing day, you become more at ease with the farmer and your surroundings. After all, the farmer regularly provides grain and water, demonstrating his care and concern for your wellbeing.

You enjoy a warm shelter, safeguarded from natural predators. The farmer has won your trust. With your fellow turkeys – your family and friends – you live a carefree life. Life is pleasant. With abundant food, you're growing heftier day by day.

Over time, your comfort in this idyllic setting only grows, until something unexpected happens just a few days before Christmas. An odd feeling takes hold that morning; something just doesn't feel right. The farmer, usually punctual, is late. Then suddenly, the shed door swings wide open revealing a large truck outside. One by one, your companions are being loaded into the truck. As Christmas is right around the corner, you're left perplexed, wondering, "What's happening?" What you don't realise is that you're destined to be part of a festive feast. Everything was going along perfectly until today. This sudden turn of events mirrors the feeling of an irreversible loss of capital. Just when you thought things couldn't be any better... WHAM!

Anybody who has ever considered an investment will be familiar with the regulatory warning that the "the past is no guide to the future," and future returns cannot be guaranteed. The turkey would doubtless agree.

However, the predicament lies in the real world where, if the past cannot guide us, we are left floating in an ocean of perpetual uncertainty. Imagine how ineffective a physician would be if their accumulated knowledge and experience became irrelevant each time a patient presented with symptoms. In practice, we all develop rules or short-cuts, heuristics is the technical term, very much based on the idea that tomorrow will, in fact, be like today and indeed, the day before.

Investing in fads can indeed be a lot like the turkey at Christmas. Initially, it might seem like a promising opportunity, with the potential for quick gains and the excitement of being part of something new and trendy. Just like you prepare and cook the turkey with care, investors may put their money into a fad with high hopes.

However, much like the oven breaking down in the middle of cooking, fads can be unpredictable and fleeting. What appears to be a surefire investment can suddenly turn sour as the trend loses momentum or faces unforeseen challenges. Just as you had to scramble to salvage your Christmas meal, investors might find themselves trying to recover their losses when a fad investment takes a nosedive.

Reflect on your investments: do they exhibit the same misplaced trust and false sense of security as the turkey? If so, ponder on whether you could be playing the part of the turkey.

Believe me, I get the appeal of wanting to get rich quickly. We'd all love to strike it big overnight. But aside from winning the lottery, that's just not realistic. We've all seen those cautionary tales of people losing their life savings on the latest investment fad or get-rich-quick scheme gone wrong. I know it's tempting when you hear stories about others hitting the jackpot. But that's the exception, not the rule. The truth is quality investing takes time, discipline, and personalised guidance.

We each have unique situations and objectives. What's hot today could be totally wrong for you and where you are. An advisor's job is to thoroughly understand your full financial picture first—your goals, time horizon, income needs, risk appetite. Only then can they propose investments tailored to your needs, not just chase whatever's skyrocketing this week. Patience and prudence must be your guide. Successful outcomes come to those who follow a customised roadmap, avoiding roads prone to dead ends. Don't be swayed by fantasies of instant wealth. With sound planning and commitment, you can steadily work toward your financial aims. Your financial plan must always come before your portfolio.

Understanding Volatility and Returns Across Asset Classes – The Investing Fairground

Imagine you're at a fairground, and you see a variety of rides, from the gentle merry-go-round to the wild rollercoaster.

The thrill and excitement each ride offers can be likened to the different asset classes in investing. Some promise high thrills (returns) but come with stomach-churning drops (volatility). Others provide a calm experience but don't quite set your heart racing. Before we breakdown these different rides, let’s look at the historic returns of some of the most common asset classes:

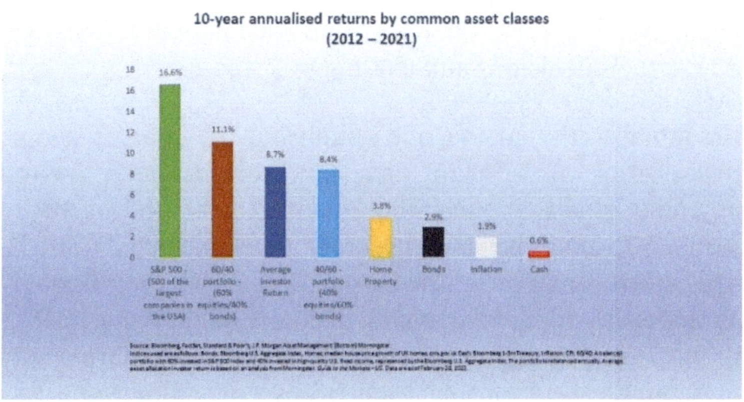

S&P 500: This is like the big rollercoaster in our fairground. Historically, it has given the most thrilling returns over the long term, more than any other asset class mentioned here. But with those returns come big drops and climbs - that's volatility. You're in for an exciting ride, but it can pay off big time.

60/40 Portfolio (60% Stocks, 40% Bonds): Think of this as a slightly tamer rollercoaster. You still get some good thrills (returns), but the presence of bonds makes the ride a bit smoother than just stocks alone.

Average Investor Return: Here's where the fairground analogy gets interesting. If the rollercoaster (S&P 500) is designed to give great returns, why doesn't everyone on it get the same thrill? This is because many riders, out of fear, jump off during the scariest drops or join in when the ride is already at its peak. This decision results in them not experiencing the full thrill the rollercoaster can offer. Carl Richards, the renowned author, and creator of the Sketch Guy, termed this difference as the "Behaviour Gap." It's the gap between the ride's potential and what people actually get due to their decisions and emotions.

Essentially, it's not the ride's fault but the choices people make while on it. Many investors don't achieve the full potential return of their chosen investment; they actually manage to underperform the very investment they are in. This discrepancy or behaviour gap arises from their frequent attempts to time the market, akin to hopping off a rollercoaster during its most daunting twists and turns, only to scramble back on once the ride seems calmer and less intimidating.

40/60 Portfolio (40% Stocks, 60% Bonds): This is like a family-friendly rollercoaster. You'll experience some ups and downs, but it's not as wild as the first two. It offers moderate returns with less volatility.

Residential Property: Imagine this as a spinning ride. It can offer decent thrills and can sometimes go faster or slower depending on the market's "mood" or location of the property.

Bonds: These are like the gentle boat rides. They offer steadier, more predictable returns but typically don't have the high thrills of stocks. They're safer but may not be as exciting in the long run.

Inflation: This isn't a ride but rather the cost of the ticket that goes up every year. If your investments (rides) aren't at least matching or beating inflation, you're losing purchasing power.

Cash: Think of this as the carousel. It's calm, going round and round without any surprising drops. But here's the catch: while you're enjoying this gentle ride, the ticket prices for all the other fairground rides are slowly creeping up due to inflation. So, if you stick to your merry-go-round for too long, you might find that your ticket money doesn't stretch as far, and you can't experience as many other rides as you once could.

While history offers insights, remember no portfolio is perfect. Regular reviews are key to aligning your investments with your goals. Your financial journey may require adjustments. Stay proactive in managing your portfolio for optimal results.

To sum it up, if you want the highest returns, like those historically offered by the S&P 500, you have to be ready for a wilder ride. But remember, it's not just about picking the ride, but also about how you behave on it. Staying on, especially when it gets tough, is the key to making the most of the fairground of investing.

Chapter 37

The Fear of Loss: A Dominant Force in Decision-Making

"There are risks and costs to action. But they are far less than the long-range risks of comfortable inaction."

John F. Kennedy

When it comes to decision-making, whether in investing, personal choices, or everyday situations, the fear of loss often takes the spotlight. This phenomenon, known as loss aversion, deeply influences our choices and the risks we're willing to take.

The legendary psychologist Carl Jung once noted, "What you resist, persists." This observation eerily echoes our relationship with loss. By resisting or fearing potential losses, we often magnify their presence in our psyche, leading to greater apprehension.

Loss aversion doesn't solely revolve around tangible setbacks; it plunges deep into our psychological well-being. Every perceived loss, be it missed opportunities or investment downturns, hits our emotional core, affecting our self-worth and self-perception.

These tendencies towards loss aversion find their roots in our evolutionary past, where, as I mentioned earlier in the book, survival often depended on evading risks and imminent threats. In the modern era, these primal instincts, combined with societal norms that equate financial success to personal value, make any form of loss feel like an assault on one's self-esteem.

Daniel Kahneman, a stalwart in behavioural economics, unveiled this bias through his coin toss experiment. When participants were faced with a loss of $10 if the coin landed on tails, they demanded to gain at least $20 if it landed on heads. This experiment starkly illustrated that the pain of losing was twice as intense as the pleasure of gaining.

The Role of Anticipated Regret

Beyond the inherent fear of loss lies another powerful psychological phenomenon: the anticipation of regret. The potential of looking back and lamenting a decision can be just as paralysing as the immediate fear of loss. This is rooted in our natural desire to avoid emotional discomfort. For instance, an investor might avoid selling a declining investment not just because of loss aversion but also due to the fear that the investment might rebound after selling, leading to regret. The very thought of "What if I had held on a little longer?" can be a driving force in decision paralysis. Thus, our decisions become a balancing act between the fear of immediate loss and the potential regret of missed future gains.

Before we delve further into the implications of this psychological phenomenon, it's crucial to understand its origins. The concept of "loss aversion" was introduced by psychologists Amos Tversky and Daniel Kahneman in the late 1970s. They posited that people feel the pain of losing about twice as strongly as they feel the pleasure of gaining, leading them to make decisions based on the fear of loss rather than the prospect of gains.

Recognising and confronting this anticipatory regret can further empower individuals to make balanced, rational decisions.

Consider a sea captain's experience navigating tumultuous waters. Spotting a distant gleam, an impulsive course change may be executed, fearing a potential threat. However, when dawn breaks, it might reveal that the glimmer was merely a guiding lighthouse, not an impending hazard. Such tales remind us how loss aversion can lead to precipitous, often erroneous decisions.

In the financial sphere, this fear often morphs into conservative tendencies. Investors may cling to dwindling assets, reluctant to confront the reality of a poor choice. Such behaviours, indicative of the "endowment effect," can stifle portfolio growth. Moreover, the trepidation can prevent individuals from embracing promising ventures or calculated risks, even if potential rewards significantly overshadow the prospective losses.

Using aviation as a metaphor, consider pilots navigating dense fog. Adhering to strict protocols, they maintain safe distances to preclude unforeseen collisions. In a similar vein, savvy investors utilise strategies like diversification, ensuring that potential risks are spread out, safeguarding the entirety of their investments.

Yet, loss aversion extends beyond finances. In personal relationships, it may deter individuals from exiting unfulfilling partnerships, plagued by the dread of solitude. Professionally, the fear might stymie one from chasing a passion, daunted by the uncertainties that come with leaving a stable albeit uninspiring job.

Recognising the profound financial and psychological repercussions of loss aversion is pivotal for balanced decision-making. Armed with this understanding, we can embrace proactive measures, be it seeking expert counsel or spreading investments to shield against potential downturns.

Embracing change and growth demands a paradigm shift. Accepting that well-considered risks are the stepping stones to progress is vital. By viewing potential losses as learning curves, we position ourselves to make decisions unshackled by overwhelming fear. It mirrors a pilot's reliance on instruments amidst a storm, guiding them through turbulence.

Aristotle mused, "It is the mark of an educated mind to be able to entertain a thought without accepting it." This insight underscores the essence of understanding loss aversion without succumbing to it.

In summation, the intricate dance of loss aversion, steeped in deep psychological undertones, profoundly moulds our decision-making. By acknowledging its gravity and actively working to neutralise its effects, we chart a course for rational, confident choices, laying the groundwork for enduring accomplishments and successful investing outcomes.

Chapter 38

Beyond the Crystal Ball: Unveiling the Secrets of Long-Term Investment Success

"Patience is bitter, but its fruit is sweet."

Aristotle

Imagine walking into my office in 2013, seeking investment advice for a significant sum of £100,000 that you had available to invest for the long term. Now, suppose I had a remarkable crystal ball that could reveal the tumultuous global events that would unfold over the next 10 years. It would undoubtedly have been a challenging and thought-provoking conversation. Armed with knowledge of the economic hardships, political crises, and unforeseen challenges that lay ahead, the responsibility to guide an investor through such uncertain times would have been substantial.

Between 2013 and 2023, the world experienced a series of significant events that not only tested the resilience of economies and financial markets, but the very fabric of being human. We witnessed political upheavals, trade wars, natural disasters, the Russian invasion of Ukraine, and, of course, the unprecedented global impact of the COVID-19 pandemic. The headlines were often filled with distressing news, uncertainty, and anxiety, which could have easily deterred even the most optimistic and stoic investor.

However, despite the terrible outlook, there was a remarkable development on the financial front. The S&P 500 index, a widely recognised benchmark for the U.S. stock market, stood at 1848 in 2013. Fast forward to 2023, and it had surged to 4500—a substantial increase over those eight years of 143%. If I had managed to share this information with you before you hastily left my office, consumed by a deep sense of dread, and made the decision to invest your £100,000, you would have been thrilled to know that by 2023, it would have grown into an impressive £243,000. This astonishing growth in the S&P 500 despite the turbulent global events underscores the resilience of the stock market and the power of long-term investing. It serves as a testament to the underlying strength of the global economy, which, despite the challenges it faced, managed to recover, and flourish.

Earlier in the book, I highlighted the significance of context in investing. It's essential to re-emphasise its importance here. Many clients, when presented with this information, often inquire about why their portfolio's performance or returns do not fully mirror the reported growth in the stock market. In response, I clarify that most investors maintain split portfolios, such as a 60/40 allocation. In this type of portfolio, only 60% of an investors funds are invested in the stock market. This means that only this portion can capture the full extent of the market's performance. The remaining 40% is allocated to lower risk, lower reward, and lower volatility assets, such as bonds, fixed interest, and other assets that have historically yielded lower returns but experience much lower volatility.

While this allocation strategy aims to balance potential growth with risk management, it also means that their overall returns will not mirror that of an investor who is 100% invested in the stock market. If a client understands and accepts that, for the long-term investor, history has proven the stock market to be the best performing asset class to invest in, the natural question arises: why would an investor not want to allocate most of their funds to an area that has consistently produced the best returns over time? The answer is because this decision comes with a serious trade-off, as the investor must be prepared to accept and endure more volatility in order to pursue these historically higher returns.

Striking the right balance between risk and reward is crucial, and it requires aligning the investment strategy with the client's risk level, tolerance for volatility, and financial objectives. While the stock market has shown impressive growth over time, it also experiences significant fluctuations, which might not be suitable for everyone. A well-informed and measured approach to portfolio allocation considers both historical performance and the individual investor's ability to navigate market volatility effectively.

Clients often hold the belief that having a personal pension, or an investment ISA translates to them being entirely invested in the stock market. However, this is another mistaken notion. In reality, only a portion of their funds is allocated to the stock market, while the remainder is directed towards what is generally lower risk, lower reward, and less volatile areas like bonds and fixed interest. This misplaced belief becomes evident when the media sensationalises headlines like 'stock market has fallen or risen 20%!' – those who are fully invested in the stock will virtually mirror the temporary decline or long-term gains.

This situation is quite common, as such headlines lack context and tend to create unnecessary fear. Clients often assume that if the markets are up 10%, their portfolio is up by the same amount, and vice versa for a 10% downturn. For instance, consider an investor with a portfolio split of 60% stocks and 40% bonds. If the market rises by 10%, only 60% of their invested capital directly enjoys this upswing. This is due to the fact that 40% of their funds aren't directly tied to the performance of the stock market. This explains precisely why many investors often wonder why their investment hasn't realised the full 10% return. The same principle holds true when the markets experience a temporary decline of 10%.

It is crucial to continually educate my clients about these vital matters to help them better comprehend the dynamics of their investments. By understanding the balanced nature of their portfolio and its risk-reward profile, they can make more informed decisions and have realistic expectations and a solid perspective on market fluctuations.

If you're contemplating investing a lump sum, you might find yourself hesitating. After all, it often feels like there's never an ideal moment to invest. Yet, historically speaking, 77% of all market years have been positive, countering our fears.

The real challenge is our preoccupation with perfect timing. However, long-term history indicates that the odds of success for a long-term investor are extremely favourable and improve with the passage of time. It's crucial to emphasise that remaining invested throughout retirement is not just important; it's absolutely essential if you aspire to secure a sustainable and growing income during your golden years. How else can you anticipate the possibility of a sustainable and rising income in retirement?

HISTORICAL PROBABLITY OF A POSITIVE OUTCOME

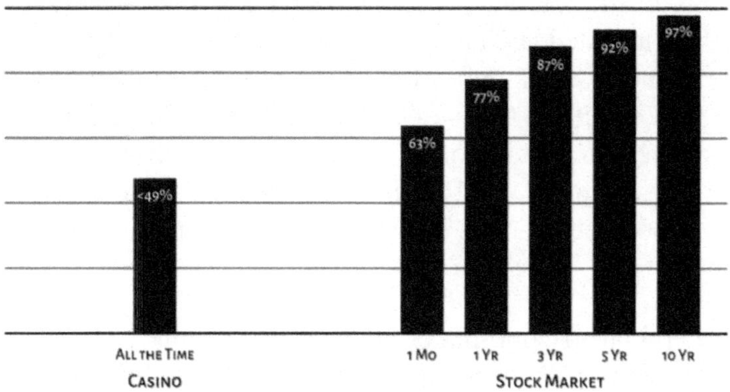

Instead of stressing about the immediate future—be it tomorrow, this month, or this year—shift your perspective to the long term. Consider the probable outcome over the next decade. A decade from now, the precise day you chose to invest will likely seem inconsequential, but the decision to invest at all could make all the difference.

Investing is inherently uncertain, impacted by various factors, and vulnerable to market fluctuations. Regrettably, the real world lacks the crystal ball that would grant us a glimpse into future events. Nevertheless, this hypothetical scenario underscores the importance of staying focused on long-term investment goals and maintaining a disciplined approach. It reminds us that the human spirit is indomitable and that amid adversity, opportunities can still arise, and a diversified portfolio combined with a patient outlook can help weather the storm.

The lesson learned from this imagined situation is that even in the face of significant challenges and disheartening news, the potential for growth and returns in the financial markets can persist. It reinforces the notion that investors should not base their decisions solely on short-term events but should instead adopt a strategic and diversified approach that aligns with their financial goals and risk tolerance. Since its earliest roots dating back to 1698, the stock market has endured numerous tragic events, and yet, with the passage of time, it consistently demonstrates resilience and continues to grow stronger, undeterred by these challenges.

So, take the leap: invest and practice patience. Whenever market uncertainty gives you pause, remember to think long term and the enduring rewards it promises.

Chapter 39

Investing Excellence: How the Best Rise Above

"The illiterate of the 21st century will not be those who cannot read and write, but those who cannot learn, unlearn, and relearn."

Alvin Toffler

In the realm of financial advisors and investment managers, there is often a focus on trying to be brilliant. However, a more effective approach lies in striving to maintain rationality and simplicity. This approach offers significant advantages that should not be overlooked. Some might think that becoming an excellent investor requires off the charts intelligence or some highly proprietary model that leads to an edge that nobody else can replicate. That is not what experience has shown.

Here are some traits and behaviours I have observed that lead to investors excelling over the long-term:

Temperament

The legendary investor, Warren Buffett wisely mused, "The most important quality for an investor is temperament, not intellect."

While I've revisited the concept of temperament multiple times throughout this book, its significance in investment cannot be emphasised enough.

Temperament is the most important quality for an investor to have. My observation of many investors over my 30+ years of advising has led me to believe that temperament cannot be learned, but rather it is an innate characteristic of one's personality. Some people are able to remain rational and continue to follow their process even under great duress or during periods of external upheaval. Others get swept up in the emotion that typically runs amok during such circumstances and abandon their discipline.

Rather than brilliance, the keys to success seem to lie more in cultivating wisdom, discipline, and rationality. As Warren Buffett advised, "Success in investing doesn't correlate with IQ once you're above the level of 125. Once you have ordinary intelligence, what you need is the temperament to control the urges that get other people into trouble in investing."

The feats of brilliant investors like Buffett himself arise more from rational temperament than raw intellect. Maintaining this detached, objective rationality enables investors to stick to their framework despite external noise. As Charles Ellis noted in Winning the Loser's Game, "The greatest enemies of the equity investor are expenses and emotions." Controlling both is critical.

Long-term investing necessitates enduring periods of volatility and resisting reactionary impulses. A temperament of equanimity, patience, and emotional discipline serves investors well through market ups and downs.

Rather than chasing complex models, the most solid investment practices tend to be simple, grounded in common sense principles. As John Bogle emphasised, "The simplicity of investment is critical. Owning the entire stock market through an index fund - owning capitalism - is the ultimate solution." Simplicity enables rationality.

By focusing more on honing wisdom and temperament over intellect and complexity, investors can pursue effective evidence-based principles for long-term growth.

Continuous Learning and Adaptability

In a dynamic world, where markets, technologies, and global events are constantly evolving, the best investors recognise the value of being perpetual students. Peter Lynch, the famed portfolio manager of the Magellan Fund at Fidelity Investments, once said, "The person that turns over the most rocks wins the game." This encapsulates the spirit of relentless inquiry and adaptability.

Continuous learning allows investors to:

Stay Updated: Understanding shifts in the market landscape, emerging technologies, or geopolitical events, ensures decisions are made from a position of knowledge.

Avoid Stagnation: As investment strategies evolve and new tools or metrics become available, a commitment to learning helps to integrate these effectively into one's approach.

Refine Judgement: Regular exposure to varied market scenarios and investment outcomes helps in refining judgement and decision-making abilities over time. This also helps better manage investor's expectations.

Acknowledge Mistakes: The best investors not only learn from their successes but also from their mistakes. Recognising and analysing missteps is essential for growth and future success.

Adaptability complements continuous learning. Markets are not static, and neither should be the strategies. Flexibility in one's approach, while staying grounded in core principles, can help navigate the ever-changing tides of the investment world.

Don't Just Do Something, Sit There – Don't Panic!

In the world of long-term investing, there is an adage that often gets overlooked in the face of market volatility and unexpected events: "Don't just do something, sit there." This seemingly paradoxical statement urges investors to resist the urge to react impulsively and instead embrace patience and a long-term perspective. It emphasises the importance of sticking to a well-thought-out investment plan rather than being swayed by short-term market fluctuations or external events that are beyond an investor's control.

Reacting hastily to events that are outside of an investor's control can introduce significant risks and pitfalls. This contrarian statement underscores the wisdom of resisting reactionary impulses. Hasty reactions to market volatility introduces needless risks such as:

- Selling quality assets at temporarily low prices and locking in losses.

- Chasing fleeting trends and overpaying for investments in the heat of the moment.

- Paying taxes and fees on short-term trades that undermine long-run returns.

- Abandoning one's investment strategy and asset allocation in a panicked overcorrection.

Sitting tight reinforces key investing principles:

- Having conviction in the long-term trajectory of markets and asset values.

- Trusting in one's research, due diligence, and investment selection criteria.

- Maintaining composure and avoiding emotion-based decisions.

- Sticking to a strategic asset allocation built to weather volatility.

While counterintuitive, resisting the urge to react and remaining committed to one's investment philosophy is often the wisest path. As Warren Buffett advises, "The stock market is designed to transfer money from the active to the patient." Cultivating patience over panic is key.

Chapter 40

Live Long and Prosper: Battling Emotions as an Investor

"A man convinced against his will is of the same opinion still."

Benjamin Franklin

In the Star Trek universe, the constantly bickering Mr Spock and Dr McCoy exemplify the dichotomy between pure logic and pure emotion. As investors, we often feel similarly conflicted. Should we let rationality and logic guide our decisions? Or go with our gut instincts?

Spock, with his coldly rational analysis, resembles the ideal disciplined investor. He would use logic, run the numbers, determine an appropriate asset allocation, automate contributions, and stick to the plan without worry over day-to-day fluctuations. Patience and diligence come easily when emotions are ignored.

Meanwhile, McCoy is ruled by his feelings and fears. At the first sign of volatility, he panics and sells his investments in a frenzy. Alternatively, when prices are soaring, he chases returns and buys at the top of the market. Rather than ignoring the 24-hour news cycle, he obsesses over predicting the next crash. Spock would surely raise an eyebrow at such illogical behaviour.

Of course, as humans we cannot fully eliminate emotions like greed and fear from our investing psyche. But we should aim to follow Spock's lead - tune out short-term noise, adhere to an evidence-based investing plan, diversify, and stay the course based on logic rather than feelings. Emotions often serve us poorly in investing.

Reacting to events in real-time can often be driven by emotions, such as fear or panic, which can cloud rational judgment. Emotionally driven decisions may lead to buying or selling assets at inopportune times, potentially causing losses, or missed opportunities.

McCoy would surely argue investing success requires a "gut feeling" and active reactions. But market history proves time and again that patience and unfeeling discipline is better over long time periods. As Spock would say - "live long and prosper" through rational, low-cost investing.

Market Timing

As I have mentioned previously, trying to time the market is notoriously difficult, if not impossible. It requires accurately predicting short-term fluctuations and getting in and out of investments at precisely the right moments. Even professional investors find market timing to be a challenging task and attempting it can result in missed gains or magnified losses.

I would dare to assert that if an investment manager possessed the remarkable ability to consistently time their entry and exit points in the market over a prolonged period, they would likely find themselves among the wealthiest individuals worldwide. It raises an intriguing question: If active fund managers possess such a skill, why do they not utilise it to amass personal fortunes? Furthermore, if they truly had such capabilities, why would they continue to work for a living?

Loss of Focus on Long-Term Goals

Reacting to every market event can cause investors to lose sight of their long-term goals. Markets tend to experience short-term volatility and fluctuations, but over the long run, they have historically shown positive growth. By staying focused on the big picture and maintaining a long-term perspective, investors are more likely to achieve their financial objectives.

Missed Compounding Opportunities

Long-term investing thrives on the power of compounding. By reinvesting dividends and allowing investment gains to accumulate over time, investors can benefit from compounding returns. You should try to avoid interrupting the compounding effect. By not interrupting or halting it, you allow your investments to continue growing and potentially magnify their long-term impact.

While it's important to monitor and review investments periodically, the adage "don't just do something, sit there" serves as a reminder to maintain discipline and avoid knee-jerk reactions to market events that are outside an investor's control. By sticking to a well-constructed investment plan, considering the long-term horizon, and remaining patient, investors can mitigate risks, avoid costly mistakes, and increase the likelihood of achieving their financial objectives.

The focus should be on the process rather than the outcome. Benjamin Graham, a renowned investor once remarked that in the short-term the market is a voting machine, but in the long-term it is a weighing machine. What he meant was that in the short-term security prices fluctuate purely based on the opinions of market participants and can deviate widely from the underlying business values. In the long-term, it is the company's assets and cash flows that determine its true value and exert a force of gravity upon the price of its securities. While stock prices are available on a minute-by-minute basis, ordinary investors often get caught up in analysing random fluctuations, allowing themselves to become emotionally influenced by short-term price movements that may not align with the fundamental soundness of their investment decisions.

On the other hand, successful investors understand the importance of not being swayed by these short-term fluctuations. Instead, they concentrate on improving their investment process and consistently executing it. Their long-term performance is a result of the quality of their process and the discipline with which they follow it.

Another aspect of effective investing is minimising behavioural biases. Although it's challenging to eliminate these biases entirely, the best investors make a conscious effort to be aware of them and take steps to mitigate their impact.

Minimising the Damaging Effects of Behavioural Biases

As discussed earlier, behavioural biases are pervasive and nearly impossible to eliminate. We all have them, but the best investors work hard to be consciously aware of them and to take specific steps to mitigate them.

Prospective clients often enquire about what my ‘edge’ is as an advisor. Sometimes I think the answer they are looking for is some brilliant model, some black box that spits out superior answers or knowledge that nobody else possesses, or an ability to know what the future holds based on some deeply proprietary network of sources. However, the real answer lies in a combination of traits and investor behaviours, as discussed in this book.

One additional trait to consider is maintaining humility while retaining confidence. The best investors possess humility, always seeking to learn and improve while acknowledging their fallibility and potential for mistakes. This mindset helps them guard against complacency and overconfidence. Some may perceive this posture as contradictory to confidence in one's abilities. In an industry where some believe that successful investors must display grandiosity, those I admire the most reject this false dichotomy. They strike a balance between humility, introspection, and confidence, enabling them to continually expand their knowledge and achieve positive financial outcomes.

Part 8

Planning for Retirement

Chapter 41

You Can't Simply 'Save' for Retirement, You Must 'Invest'

"You can be young without money, but you can't be old without it."

Tennessee Williams

I'm dedicated to guiding individuals towards realising their financial aspirations. I constantly encounter individuals who are astounded when they realise that simply saving their cash in a bank account won't get them anywhere near the amount of money, they will need to secure an independent and comfortable retirement. While saving is paramount, the corrosive effect of inflation on funds tucked away cannot be overlooked. The real setback? Missing the potential for growth.

Let's illuminate this with a 30-year historical returns-based illustration. Imagine someone setting aside £300 monthly from the age of 30 until 60.

If deposited in a savings account yielding an average return of 3.5% — a rate prevalent between 1993 and 2023 — they'd amass roughly £190,000.

Conversely, redirecting that same £300 into a globally diversified fund boasting an average 10% annual yield —

echoing the S&P 500 index's performance (with dividends reinvested) from 1993 to 2023 — would burgeon to an impressive sum of about £700,000. However, it's essential to note that past performance cannot determine future returns. They are purely historical.

To put things in perspective, the S&P 500 index magnified a staggering 100-fold since 1957. Dividend payouts to investors soared 32 times during this period, all while inflation surged tenfold.

The narrative alters dramatically with the integration of a tax-advantaged personal pension. Contributions are increased by 20% courtesy of tax relief, transforming £300 into £375 each month. In 30 years, this grows to an approximate £855,000.

Visualise two individuals, Mike, and Mary, who opted for these distinct paths.

At retirement, Mary can access a 25% tax-free cash allowance amounting to £213,750. (£855,000 x 25%) This eclipses Mike's entire savings of £190,000. Should Mary utilise her entire tax-free allowance on some extravagance, she'd still retain a considerable £641,250. Drawing 4% annually, and assuming the pension retained its value, she'd enjoy a yearly income of £25,650.

Mike, on the other hand, drawing his 25% tax-free sum of £47,500, would be left with £142,500. Employing a similar 4% withdrawal strategy yields a mere £5,700 each year. What a difference.

The linchpin here? Maximising the exponential growth power of compounding over time, especially in a tax efficient personal pension. With a thoughtful approach, retirement for individuals like Mike and Mary isn't just a dream — it's an achievable reality.

With this insight into the remarkable power of investment growth and tax advantages, it's also crucial to emphasise another dimension: the pivotal role of time. Time not only dictates the maturity of investments but also the potential gains one could reap. Let's delve deeper into this often-underestimated element in the financial realm.

The Power of Time Invested: Mary versus Mike

The magic of investing isn't just about how much you put in, but when you start. Imagine compound interest as a snowball rolling down a hill—the earlier you set it off, the bigger and faster it gets.

Let's illustrate this with Mary and Mike:

Mary's Smart Start: At 20, Mary began investing £100 monthly. After a decade at a hypothetical 7% return (after fees), she accumulated £17,308. She then stopped contributing but left her savings untouched and remained invested. By the time she's 60, thanks to compound interest, her savings balloon to £140,480.

Mike's Delayed Decision: Mike, however, only began investing at 30, precisely when Mary stopped contributing. Investing the same monthly amount and getting the same 7% return, he continued for three decades. Yet, at 60, his savings totalled £121,997—still falling short of Mary's by £18,483, even though he invested three times longer and three times the amount!

Mary has invested £12,000 over 10 years.

Mike has invested £36,000 over 30 years.

The Future Projection: Assuming the same hypothetical 7% return, if both let their investments grow without adding a penny, by 70, Mary's would be £282,317 while Mike's would be £245,173. Fast-forward to a generous centenarian scenario—keeping their money invested for their grandchildren—they'd have quite a sum. Mary's pot would grow to a whopping £2,291,425, while Mike's would trail at £1,989,946. Mary accumulated £301,479 more simply by beginning her investments 10 years before Mike, even though she contributed just one-third of what he did.

And all this wealth was accumulated from investments of just £12,000 and £36,000, respectively.

The Lesson? The early bird, or in this case, the early investor, gets the worm—or the more significant returns. While both Mary and Mike enjoy the same 7% growth rate, Mary's earlier start gives her a more substantial base, making her returns compound faster and bigger. Mike, despite his best efforts, can never truly catch up because of his late start even though he invested three times more.

So, remember: in the world of investing, it's not just about how much or how long, but *when* you begin. Just let the wonder of compounding do the rest.

The Role of Financial Education and Accessibility

While Mike and Mary's narratives underscore the importance of early investing, diversification, and leveraging tax benefits, another aspect worth noting is the level of financial education and accessibility. Not everyone has the privilege of receiving financial education early on or understanding the nuances of investment.

Recognising these disparities, it becomes essential to address key areas that can empower more individuals to participate effectively in investing. These include enhancing financial literacy, improving accessibility to investment tools, and the crucial role of guidance and mentorship.

Delving deeper into the realms of financial literacy, accessibility, and guidance, let's explore how each plays a vital role in empowering individuals for investment success:

Financial Literacy: Many individuals aren't exposed to the basics of personal finance, let alone the more complex aspects of investment. Offering tools, resources, or workshops can help bridge this gap, making financial education more accessible to a broader audience.

Accessibility of Investment Tools: The past decade has witnessed a surge in user-friendly investment platforms and tools. But not everyone is tech-savvy or trusts online platforms. Ensuring that there are various avenues – both digital and traditional – for people to invest can make a huge difference.

Guidance and Mentorship: The value of a mentor or financial advisor in one's investment journey can't be overstated. Someone to guide, offer advice, and provide reassurance during the turbulent times can significantly impact the choices an individual makes.

It is important to remember that the global economic landscape is influenced by various factors, including geopolitical events, trade wars, global pandemics, etc. While no one can predict these events, being aware of them and understanding their potential impact on investments and retirement planning can prepare investors to navigate uncertain waters.

The lessons here are:

- Start as early as you can.
- Don't just save your money, invest it.
- Remain invested in low cost, globally diversified funds.
- Take full advantage of all the pension and investment tax breaks.
- Persist in your learning journey and seek assistance when necessary.
- Accept that many external factors are beyond your control.

The Power of Financial Framing

The financial journey of Mary and Mike underscores the importance of making informed choices early on, integrating investments with savings, and utilising tax advantages. Yet, while the maths and logic behind these decisions seem straightforward, why do many not tread the same path as Mary? It's often because of the way we perceive, understand, and frame our financial questions and choices.

Building on the narrative of Mary and Mike, let's move to the realm of financial framing, which holds equal weight in the course of our financial decision-making. Every financial decision we make starts with a question we pose to ourselves. How we ask these questions and the context in which we put them can either open doors to opportunities or restrict our vision.

Let’s look at this example:

Question 1: Do you think you could regularly save 20% of your income?

This question, for many, triggers concerns about compromising their current lifestyle. Saving 20% seems like a monumental challenge when framed this way. However, if Mike had been asked this question early on, he might have hesitated, whereas Mary might have seen an opportunity.

Question 2: Do you think you could live comfortably on 80% of your income?

A simple twist in framing and the question suddenly feels more accommodating, echoing the choices Mary made to ensure her financial security. By focusing on maintaining a comfortable lifestyle, the perceived sacrifice of saving is diminished. If you believe you can comfortably live on 80%

of your income, then you're inherently acknowledging that you have the capacity to save the remaining 20%.

Both these questions converge on the same point: allocating 20% of one's income for future benefits. But the response they evoke varies widely due to their framing.

Mary's success isn't just attributed to her informed financial decisions but also to her perception of opportunities over sacrifices. Her mindset resonates with the lessons on the importance of early investment, diversification, and leveraging tax benefits. This example underscores the profound influence of perspective and wording in financial decisions. It reminds us that sometimes, our apprehensions or hesitations about money aren't necessarily rooted in the actual numbers or percentages but in how we perceive them.

In conclusion, when approaching financial decisions or advising others, it's crucial to be mindful of framing. By presenting information or questions in a way that emphasises possibility over sacrifice, or abundance over scarcity, we might find ourselves more open to financial practices that seemed unattainable at first glance.

Post-Payslip: More Than Just Binge-Watching and Bingo

So, why do people work? At the top of the list: cold, hard cash. Once the un-fun adulting bits are sorted (hello taxes, mortgages, and a seemingly endless list of bills and handouts to kids), and after stashing away some for the future, we get to splash out on the fun stuff.

But let's be honest, that monthly boost in the bank balance makes all the workday blues a tad more bearable. If not? Well, maybe you're not quite in the right gig.

Often, it's not until we gleefully dance out of the office for the last time, declaring our freedom from the daily grind and that boss you can't stand, that we realise something is missing. With all that free time, you'd think endless episodes of the latest binge-worthy series or that stack of unread books would suffice. Yet, something is still amiss.

Imagine a bustling street scene in a city. Amid the crowd, there's that one mime artist – peculiar, somewhat irksome, yet oddly captivating. That's how the work environment felt. Unexpectedly, you find yourself reminiscing about the constant chatter from Bob in accounts about his collection of vintage spoons.

A Harvard study (started way back in 1938!) confirms it. As the participants sailed into their golden years, the overwhelming sentiment wasn't about missing the thrill of spreadsheets but the human interaction and camaraderie from their working days.

Retiring 'To' Something: The Importance of Purpose in Your Golden Years

There's a common notion that retirement is a time to step back, to disengage, and to finally relax after decades of hard work. But in this well-deserved rest, many face an unexpected challenge: the vacuum of purpose. It's not just about leaving the daily grind; it's about embracing a new chapter with clarity and intention. Essentially, the question isn’t what you're retiring from but rather what you're retiring to.

Picture this: When we were young, our minds were full of dreams and aspirations. We imagined traveling to distant lands, penning novels, mastering a musical instrument, or diving deep into hobbies that intrigued us. Yet, as life often does, it swept us away with responsibilities, and many of these dreams got shelved, waiting for the proverbial "someday."

Retirement can be that "someday." It offers a golden opportunity to revisit those shelved dreams and give them life. Moreover, rekindling these passions can lend a profound sense of purpose to our later years, ensuring retirement is not just an end but a vibrant new beginning.

Why is this transition so crucial?

Mental Wellbeing: Engaging in activities, especially those we are passionate about, keeps our minds sharp. Learning new skills or honing old ones can be a hedge against cognitive decline.

Physical Health: Many dreams, be it gardening, dancing, or even just traveling, involve physical activity. This movement, fuelled by passion, can contribute to better physical health.

Social Connectivity: Retirement can sometimes lead to social isolation. However, pursuing passions often connects us with like-minded individuals, fostering friendships and strengthening our social networks.

Sense of Achievement: Completing a project, be it a piece of art, a novel, or any long-held dream, gives a sense of accomplishment. This boosts self-esteem and happiness, critical elements in one's golden years.

Legacy Building: More than money or property, the stories we leave behind, the art we create, or the difference we make in communities can be the most valuable legacy.

But how does one transition from retiring from to retiring to?

Revisit the Past: Think back to your younger days. What made your heart race with excitement? Which aspirations got lost in the daily hustle?

Plan Ahead: Before retiring, begin mapping out what you want your retirement days to look like. Setting goals or a bucket list can act as a guiding light.

Stay Open: While it's great to revisit past dreams, staying open to new hobbies and interests is equally vital. Perhaps pottery or digital photography will become your new passion!

Seek Communities: Join clubs or groups aligned with your interests. These communities can offer resources, workshops, and a sense of belonging.

Share and Mentor: Use your years of experience to guide the younger generation. Teaching and mentoring can be incredibly fulfilling.

Today, retirement might span decades. And as a financial planner (or adviser or money guru—take your pick!), I'm here to help clients navigate the financial seas so they can sail smoothly through retirement. But remember, the financials are just one piece of the retirement puzzle. So, the real question isn't just "What are you retiring from?" but rather, "What are you retiring to?"

At the heart of it all, beyond the number-crunching and daydreams of leisurely afternoons, we fundamentally yearn for two things: to sleep soundly at night and to have something—or someone—worth waking up for in the morning.

Whether it's a new hobby, a community project, or just the simple joy of a daily chat over the fence with a neighbour, find your "why" for the golden years. Because retirement is not just an end—it's a brand-new beginning.

In conclusion, retirement is not the closing of a door but the opening of a myriad of others. It's a time rich with potential, waiting to be harnessed. As the famous saying goes, "Age is an issue of mind over matter. If you don't mind, it doesn't matter." So, as you approach retirement, remember it's not about stepping away from the old but rather stepping into the new, armed with dreams and brimming with purpose.

Chapter 42

Unlocking Financial Freedom: Multiply Your Annual Expenses by 25 and Embrace the 4% Rule – A Rough Guide.

"Don't simply retire from something; have something to retire to."

Harry Emerson Fosdick

In this chapter, we'll delve into the powerful concept that can pave the way to financial freedom: the 4% rule. We'll explore its core principle, which involves multiplying your annual expenses by 25, offering a secure path to a prosperous future.

Additionally, we will discuss its limitations, as no financial strategy is without its constraints and considerations.

The "4% rule" is a guideline frequently utilised in retirement planning to determine a safe annual withdrawal rate from retirement savings. This approach, often referred to as the "Bengen 4% rule," originated from the research of financial planner William Bengen in 1994. Bengen's comprehensive study spanned 50 years, from 1926 to 1976, with actual market returns used up to 1992.

His methodology included annual withdrawals, portfolio rebalancing, and projections for years beyond 1993.

How Bengen |Tested the 4% Rule

Through empirical simulations of historical market behaviour, Bengen found that a 4% annual withdrawal rate generally allowed portfolios to sustain over 50 years. Even for portfolios falling short of this duration, they typically lasted for around 35 years, which proves sufficient for most retirees. Published in the Journal of Financial Planning in October 1994, Bengen's research forms the foundation of what is now known as the 4% rule.

Deconstructing the 4% Rule:

The 4% rule is underpinned by several key assumptions, including specific asset allocation strategies. However, factors like fees, inflation, and sequence of returns risk can influence the outcomes of this rule. I discuss these hindrances further on.

Asset Allocation Insights:

Bengen's analysis involved different asset allocations, ultimately favouring a 50/50 split between stocks (S&P 500) and bonds (intermediate term Treasuries). He assessed various initial withdrawal rates:

A 3% rate ensured all portfolios lasted 50 years.

With a 4% rate, most portfolios reached the 50-year mark, though some only lasted about 35 years.

At a 5% withdrawal rate, over half the portfolios depleted before 50 years, the least durable lasting around 20 years.

Only a few portfolios with a 6% rate survived for 50 years, and about 10 lasted less than 20 years.

If a retiree also wanted a secondary goal of wealth creation, Bengen advised increasing the stock allocation to as close to 75% as possible. For some retirees, a 50/50 portfolio is a level of risk and volatility that's hard to stomach, making an allocation to stocks of 75% an even bigger one to contend with. Nevertheless, the 4% rule as Bengen documented it requires a stock allocation of somewhere between 50% to 75%.

The 4% rule is like setting yourself an allowance to ensure your savings last. For example, if long-term investment returns are anything to go by, and you remain in a highly diversified fund while keeping investment costs low, you have a good chance of being able to withdraw £40,000 (4%) every year if you have a £1 million pension pot. This rule is built on the idea that your unspent money continues to be invested, producing returns.

Understanding that this serves as a valuable initial step is crucial, but it's essential to recognise that various factors may come into play and affect its successful implementation.

The goal is that these returns are sufficient to balance the money you're taking out, maintaining your total savings, or potentially even growing them. Now, let's discuss the "25 times your annual expenses" guideline. This is essentially the 4% rule turned on its head. If you can amass 25 times your yearly expenses, you could in theory live off 4% of that sum each year, indefinitely. So, if you spend £40,000 annually, you'd aim to save up £1 million (25 times £40,000) for your retirement.

Both of these strategies rely on your investments increasing enough over time to support your withdrawals. This is where the principle of investing in low-cost, highly diversified funds comes in. A diversified portfolio spreads your money across a variety of investments, reducing risk. Low-cost funds, like index funds, follow wide market indices and generally come with significantly lower fees than actively managed funds. This pairing can facilitate more stable growth of your savings over time, and with fewer costs nibbling away at your returns, you're better placed to attain your financial independence goal.

Don't forget to consider your personal and state pension benefits or any other income-producing assets you might have. These can be included when calculating the 25 times income requirement, reducing the amount you need to save yourself. After all, financial independence isn't just about how much you can save, but also about making the most of all the income streams available to you. For instance, let's consider that you receive state pensions, private pensions, or any consistent income to your household. In such a scenario, you can subtract this additional income from the initial £40k value and then apply the multiplier.

Suppose you have £20k coming in from other sources. In that case, you would require only £500k to generate a 4% net of costs return, which would compensate for the £20k shortfall.

Bear in mind that retirement isn't determined by a specific age, but rather by a certain amount of money. Once your investments have multiplied to 25 times your annual expenditure, you achieve financial independence and can sustain yourself solely from your investments indefinitely.

Conversely, reaching the age of 65 doesn't magically grant you the ability to cease working. If you fail to invest your money wisely and let it work for you, you'll find yourself working indefinitely. Do you believe those Tesco greeters are there because they enjoy spending their days on their feet at the Tesco entrance?

In conclusion, the 4% rule cannot be universally applied as a one-size-fits-all approach. Individual requirements vary significantly, influenced by numerous factors. It is purely a reasonable starting point. Therefore, it is crucial to seek guidance from a knowledgeable advisor who comprehends your unique investment preferences and retirement needs. Working with such an advisor will help tailor the 4% rule to align more accurately with your specific financial situation and objectives.

The Limitations of the 4% Rule

While Bengen's concepts are valuable and a good rule of thumb, you should not rely solely on the 4% rule for your retirement fund withdrawals due to several crucial factors:

Variation in Portfolio:

Your investment portfolio is likely different from the one used in Bengen's research, and this dissimilarity significantly impacts the sustainability of your withdrawal. Not every portfolio construction will be the same.

Longevity Considerations:

Much later in life, your assets could be depleted, but you might find yourself requiring long-term care.

Ignoring Fees and Taxes:

The 4% rule overlooks the impact of investment fees and taxes that are incurred during your retirement journey, which can erode your funds over time.

Fluctuating Expenses:

The money you spend during retirement is not fixed in real terms. It can fluctuate for various reasons, depending on your circumstances and changing needs, but let me ask you a question. How many 80-year-olds do you know who are spending more now than they did at 60? I'd wager that there aren't many. As we get older, we tend to spend less as we slow down. Perhaps more on heating and less on eating. The most common situation that can lead to a huge increase in spending as we get older is the provision of long-term care which can be awfully expensive.

Being aware of additional risks is crucial for investors, and this is precisely where the guidance of a skilled advisor can make a significant difference. A competent advisor can provide valuable insights and support in navigating another significant risk:

Sequence Risk. A Critical Factor in Your Investment Strategy

Failing to fully grasp the implications of sequence risk could hinder your ability to maintain a lifetime income from your investment portfolio. Put simply, sequence risk refers to the possibility of experiencing unfavourable returns due to the timing of your withdrawals from your assets. It's akin to booking a summer holiday and having it rain for the first 3 days. The timing of when you experience the "good" or "bad" events (like sunny days or rain) can impact how much you enjoy or benefit from the whole experience. Just as rain early on can dampen your holiday spirits, poor investment returns early on can have lasting effects on your financial journey.

Understanding Sequence Risk:

The initial years of your retirement are when sequence risk can have the most significant impact. Research indicates that the returns obtained during this period disproportionately affect your overall financial outlook, regardless of the long-term returns over your entire retirement duration. If you achieve favourable returns in those crucial early years, the risk of running out of money decreases. However, poor, or even mediocre returns during this period can present challenges.

Is sequence risk directly related to market volatility?

No, these are different things, though they are often confused, even by some financial professionals. Market volatility refers to the day-to-day fluctuations in your portfolio's value, quantified through standard deviation, which measures the deviation of your portfolio returns from the average over a specific timeframe. Conversely, sequence risk pertains to the specific order in which your portfolio experiences its returns.

Addressing Sequence Risk and Volatility:

A competent financial planner not only assists you in managing market volatility but also safeguards you against the perils associated with sequence risk. By recognising the implications of both factors, a skilled professional can guide you in developing a robust investment strategy that accounts for potential risks and aims to ensure a sustainable income throughout your retirement journey.

It is advisable to maintain a cash reserve equivalent to two years' worth of living expenses. This precautionary measure allows you to navigate through challenging periods when your investments experience a sudden and temporary decline. By temporarily halting withdrawals from your investments and relying on the cash reserve, you can patiently wait for your investment values to recover before resuming income withdrawals. The choice of two years is based on historical data, which indicates that bear markets, characterised by tough economic conditions, seldom extend beyond this timeframe.

Although Bengen's 4% rule does have its limitations, it's important to remember that it doesn't account for the possibility of a retiree choosing to work part-time for additional income. Any extra income during retirement reduces the amount you need to withdraw from your investments. The less you draw, the greater the likelihood of your investments supporting you throughout retirement.

With so many factors in play, what's the best way to plan your retirement income?

This is a question that has perplexed financial experts throughout the modern era. Renowned economist and Nobel Laureate William Sharpe refers to it as the "most challenging, difficult problem in finance".

While many of the commonly available retirement calculators you might come across in your own research are valuable for calculating cashflow projections, they are generally based on the outdated and false assumption that your expected rate of return will remain constant each year. Planning your retirement would be so easy if this was the case. The real world does not operate in such a predictable manner, especially in recent times.

If you are wondering whether it's a good time to invest in a volatile market, the answer is always a resounding YES, IT IS! The market has always experienced declines when we look at it retrospectively. This means that the current prices are lower, allowing you to invest at a discounted rate and ride the upward trend in the future. The market typically moves forward with four steps and occasionally takes one step back. Stay invested for the long term and ensure you are present for the four steps forward.

The aforementioned figures apply if you are starting from scratch. If you already have some savings or investments, you may be closer to reaching your financial independence goal.

Build wealth by adhering to the following three rules:

1.) Live within your means.

2.) Start investing early and consistently.

3.) Remain invested through thick and thin.

As we navigate the intricate web of financial decisions that come with planning for retirement, it is pivotal to understand the broader landscape. This includes considering both external factors, such as state pension contributions, and internal factors like one's risk tolerance.

Typically, there are two primary factors influencing how you should balance your portfolio between stocks and bonds. The first is your capacity for risk and volatility, and the second is your appetite for it. Your capacity for risk is shaped by various elements, such as your current financial standing, impending financial obligations like retirement needs, university fees for offspring, or saving for a deposit on a new home. Generally, if these financial responsibilities are distant, you can afford to shoulder more risk and volatility. Moreover, as your assets grow in comparison to your liabilities, your capacity to bear risk amplifies. Conversely, your appetite for risk is wholly subjective. While some investors remain unfazed by market fluctuations, others lose sleep due to fears over their portfolio's volatility. If you are part of the latter group, you might be overextending yourself risk-wise. Together, your risk capacity and appetite define your overall risk tolerance.

Factoring in State Pensions – Realignment with Desired Portfolio Allocation

As of 2023, the full state pension in the UK stands at £10,600 annually. Guided by the 4% rule, one would require a nest egg of £265k to generate this amount of regular income, and it is essential to remember that the state pension is indexed-linked to help keep pace with the rising cost of living. Should both you and your spouse or partner qualify for the full state pension, your combined income would total £21,200 annually. While the current state retirement age in the UK is 67, it is likely to increase in the coming years. Nonetheless, the assurance of a guaranteed indexed-linked household income of £21,200 for a couple, certainly eases concerns about the financial preparations needed for a comfortable retirement. However, many today aspire to retire well before 67, necessitating plans to bridge the income gap from retirement until the state pension kicks in. Given that we often have higher expenditures in our younger, healthier years, it is crucial to factor this in when calculating the funds required to secure an independent and dignified retirement.

The significance of state pensions within an investment or pension portfolio cannot be understated. Let us delve into this with a practical example. Consider a 62-year-old UK citizen whose average life expectancy is roughly another 25 years. If they retire at 62, they will have to bridge a 5-year gap until they receive their state pension at age 67. This 5-year gap might be funded by a combination of part-time work, savings, and personal and workplace pensions. Based on statistical longevity expectations, they can then anticipate living another 25 years. Taking trendline historic inflationary pension increases of 2.5% per annum into consideration, their state pension at 87 could be approximately £17,239 or £1,447 per month by the time they meet their maker.

Imagine that this individual has accumulated £500,000 in pensions and other investments by the time they retire at the state retirement age of 67. As previously mentioned, I am not a strong proponent of bonds, but for the sake of this example, we'll utilise the 60/40 equity-bond split, which is characteristic of many UK retirees. Without factoring in the state pension and based on this allocation, £300k would be invested in equities (60%) and £200k (40%) in bonds.

However, the equation changes when we account for the state pension guarantee.

Incorporating the £265K imputed value of the state pension, the total investment portfolio value increases to £765k. This adjustment effectively shifts the bond-like portion of the portfolio to £565k, or 74%, leaving only 26% in stocks. To realign to the desired 60/40 investment allocation, the investor would need to channel £459k into equities in this case. In conclusion, it is crucial to factor in the impact of state pension benefits to gain a holistic perspective on a client's retirement income needs and asset distribution.

Additionally, the principle of capitalising guaranteed pensions such as defined benefit/final salary schemes and annuities is crucial. To accurately determine a client's overall equity exposure, this method should always be considered. By valuing these guaranteed income streams, one gains a clearer insight into their tangible worth, their influence on overall equity exposure, and the stability they inherently add to a portfolio.

Recognising the implications of the state pension on one's overall financial strategy is more than just a mathematical exercise; it is about optimising the potential for future financial security. When integrated correctly into an investment plan, the state pension can serve as a sturdy foundation, providing a layer of guaranteed income. However, its true effectiveness is unlocked only when combined with an investment strategy tailored to individual financial goals and risk profiles.

In addition to the aforementioned considerations, it's crucial to recognise the invaluable role of a financial advisor in retirement planning. Tax rules and government pension legislation are not static; they are in a constant state of flux. Attempting to manage your retirement investments independently can inadvertently lead to compliance breaches that come with significant costs and repercussions.

Unwittingly falling foul of current rules and regulations can result in severe tax implications for retirees, potentially undermining years of careful financial planning. It is in this ever-changing landscape that the expertise of a financial advisor shines. By discussing these nuanced and evolving rules with a knowledgeable advisor, individuals can ensure that their retirement plans remain not only robust but also adaptable.

Engaging with a knowledgeable advisor offers a distinct advantage. They can offer insights and strategies that an individual might not readily spot on their own, empowering them to navigate the intricate terrain of retirement planning with clarity and confidence. This collaborative partnership ensures the optimisation of all assets, including state pensions, while ensuring compliance with evolving tax and pension regulations. By discussing these nuances with a financial advisor, individuals can bolster the adaptability and robustness of their retirement plans, safeguarding their financial well-being in the dynamic landscape of retirement planning.

Chapter 43

The Misconception of Retirement: Continuity of Investment

"Retirement is when you stop living at work and start working at living."

Source Unknown

A prevalent belief is that our retirement income must consistently rise each year until our passing. While it is true that inflation will cause many of our expenses, like housing, utilities, and food, to gradually rise over time, our actual spending often decreases in retirement for several reasons.

First, as we age our activity levels tend to decline. We may travel less, eat out less often, and spend less on entertainment and leisure activities. The things we once enjoyed like golfing, skiing or frequent holidays abroad become less feasible. This leads to naturally lower spending on these discretionary items.

Second, by the time we reach our 80s and 90s our physical abilities have often diminished because our knees, hips, and backs are not what they used to be. Getting around is harder so we tend to stay home more. Our appetite decreases so we eat less. Perhaps we spend more on heating but less on eating. We may downsize to a smaller home that requires less upkeep. The result is lower spending on transportation, dining out, housing, and other costs. How many individuals in their 80s do you know who spend more than they did in their 60s? There might be a few exceptions, but I would wager it won't be many.

The one major exception is long-term care in the event of declining health. Nursing home care or in-home caregiving can be extremely expensive and can run into thousands of pounds per month. This is where retirement income needs can spike dramatically. But for healthy retirees, the reality is that more modest inflation adjustments to Social Security, pensions, and retirement savings may be sufficient for daily living expenses. Overall spending tends to moderate as we slow down in later years. How many 80-year-olds do you know who are spending more now than they did at 60?

Investors often struggle with volatility despite knowing that historically, nothing has outperformed the stock market in the long term. They must understand that their investment horizon may span decades, especially when planning for retirement. However, a common misconception arises as many believe that retirement marks the end of investing. In reality, retirees must continue investing, not just up to retirement but throughout it, to provide a sustainable and inflation-proof income during their golden years.

The traditional strategy of de-risking investments as retirement approaches is becoming outdated. While it might have made sense when purchasing annuities (purchasing an income for life from an insurance company), modern retirees prefer to retain control over their funds and have the flexibility to access money according to their lifestyle requirements. They also desire the option to leave remaining funds to their loved ones after their passing, which most annuities do not permit.

Sadly, millions of investors are unaware that they are placed into default "lifestyle funds" within their employer group pension schemes. Left unchecked, these funds automatically de-risk the portfolio as retirement nears, often starting 15 years from retirement leaving investors unknowingly vulnerable to potential pitfalls. Without adequate education or intervention, they unknowingly find themselves blindly navigating a retirement minefield, and the damage has already been done.

Consider this scenario: an investor achieves an average return of 6% per annum throughout their working years by investing predominantly in the stock market. Then, upon retirement, they decide to shift their investments to assets that have historically yielded only 2 to 3% per annum. Such a move could result in an income barely keeping pace with inflation, creating financial challenges during retirement.

While annuities certainly have a place in retirement planning and might work for some individuals seeking a guaranteed income independent of market fluctuations, most retirees prefer more control over their funds and to pass on their wealth to beneficiaries. The inflexibility of annuities and the lack of legacy options lead many retirees to seek more flexible investment strategies.

Investors must be aware of the risks of deliberate and automatic de-risking and the potential drawbacks of annuities. By staying informed, they can make informed decisions, safeguard their financial future, and ensure their retirement years are secure and prosperous.

Retirement is often viewed as the golden phase of one's life, a culmination of years of hard work, dedication, and strategic planning. When we talk about "getting retirement right," we are discussing financial security, maintaining good health, nurturing relationships, and pursuing passions that were perhaps sidelined during one's working years. A well-planned retirement ensures that you live comfortably and can continue to contribute positively to the lives of those around you.

Navigating the Psychological Shift in Retirement

As we approach retirement, we are not only facing a financial transition but a psychological one as well. For decades, individuals work diligently, saving, investing, and watching their nest egg grow. This period, known as the accumulation phase, brings with it the thrill of seeing one's wealth expand. However, upon entering retirement, individuals transition to the distribution phase, the golden years, where they start drawing down on their savings. This shift can be emotionally challenging.

Many retirees grapple with the fear of spending down their assets, especially if market downturns coincide with the early years of their retirement. It is no longer about how much one can save, but how efficiently one can spend without jeopardising future financial security. This requires a mental shift – moving from a mindset of growth and accumulation to one of sustainability and preservation.

The strategies employed during the accumulation phase might not always be apt for the distribution phase. For example, while aggressive investing might be suitable for a young individual with years ahead to recover from potential losses, a retiree might need a more balanced approach to preserve their wealth while still generating necessary returns.

Retirees must learn to navigate this psychological shift effectively, seeking out strategies that match their changed financial landscape and emotional needs. Recognising and addressing this emotional component of retirement planning can lead to more informed, confident decisions during the golden years.

The phrase, "you can forget about leaving a legacy," underscores the importance of adequate retirement planning. A legacy is not just about leaving wealth or assets for the next generation; it's also about the lessons, values, and memories we leave behind. If one struggles during retirement due to financial hardships or health issues exacerbated by neglect, it can become increasingly difficult to focus on building a meaningful legacy. Instead of being remembered for wisdom and generosity, the struggles of one's retirement might overshadow the many accomplishments of their earlier years.

In essence, to make a lasting impact and ensure that our final chapters are just as meaningful as the ones that came before, it's crucial to prioritise retirement planning. A comfortable retirement sets the stage for us to leave behind a legacy of love, lessons, and cherished memories.

Chapter 44

Dream Today, Achieve Tomorrow: Cashflow Modelling for Retirement

"I've got all the money I'll ever need, if I die by four o'clock."

Henny Youngman

When planning for retirement, one of the most important considerations is determining your income needs. There are three main categories to think about:

- Required income - The bare minimum you need to cover basic living expenses.
- Desired income - A comfortable level for your preferred lifestyle.
- Aspirational income - Funds for extra or discretionary spending.

Understanding these income tiers can help you create a realistic retirement budget and savings plan.

Required Retirement Income - What's Your Number?

Planning for retirement means figuring out your personal retirement number - the amount of money you will need annually to fund the retirement lifestyle you envision. This number is different for everyone, based on your unique goals, expenses, and sources of retirement income.

To find your number, first calculate your essential living expenses in retirement like housing, food, utilities, healthcare, and transportation. Account for fixed costs like debt payments and variable spending on hobbies, travel, and entertainment. Consider your desired retirement lifestyle - will you downsize or stay put? Travel extensively or stick close to home? Your number must cover your basic needs and desired discretionary spending.

Next, identify guaranteed income from things like Social Security and pensions. This 'pay cheque' covers some of your expenses. You will need to withdraw the remaining amount from savings and investments. A financial advisor can help analyse gaps between your expenses and guaranteed income to determine the savings you need to generate your total annual retirement number.

The key is saving enough so your withdrawals plus your guaranteed income meets or exceeds your annual number, sustaining you for a retirement lasting 20 or 30 years. Your number will be smaller if you pay off debt pre-retirement. Working part-time in retirement also reduces the needed savings.

Figuring out your personal retirement number takes realistic analysis of your needs and goals. But it gives you a measurable target for building your nest egg. With your number as a guide, you can save and invest appropriately to reach the income your retirement requires.

When creating your retirement plan, consider how major economic factors like inflation and interest rates may impact your finances. The Bank of England provides economic forecasts modelling different potential scenarios. While these predictions are not foolproof, having a personalised wealth forecast based on reasonable assumptions can strengthen your financial planning. For example, factor in various inflation rates to estimate the future purchasing power of your savings. Assume conservative investment return rates when projecting your portfolio growth.

Account for fluctuating utilities and housing costs in your future spending. While no forecast is perfect, thoughtful analysis of economic variables allows you to stress-test your plan and make prudent choices today to better withstand change tomorrow. The goal is not precision, but identifying risks so you can take proactive steps to safeguard your retirement. Whether the economy is booming or struggling, a plan built on realistic forecasts gives your retirement preparations staying power.

Required income covers your most basic living expenses that you absolutely cannot go without in retirement:

- Food - Groceries and basic meals.
- Healthcare - Insurance premiums, prescriptions, out-of-pocket costs.
- Transportation - Car payments, fuel, maintenance, public transport.
- Insurance - Health, life, car, home, pet insurance.

- Debt payments - Credit cards, loans, etc.

Aim to calculate the minimum you would need to get by based on your lifestyle. This provides the foundation for your retirement budget. Identify ways to cover required expenses through guaranteed income sources like Social Security and pensions in payment.

Desired Retirement Income

Once required expenses are covered, you can focus on your desired income. This funds a comfortable lifestyle in line with your preferences:

- Housing - Potentially upgrading to your ideal home/location.

- Food - More flexibility for dining out, day trips, etc.

- Travel - Major trips, visits with family, hobbies.

- Transportation – Newer car.

- Entertainment – Concerts, Cultural events, sports games, shopping.

- Discretionary spending - Spoiling grandchildren, charity.

Desired income allows you to maintain your pre-retirement standard of living. Look at your current budget and identify areas where you may want to spend more, less or the same in retirement.

Aspirational Retirement Income

- Aspirational income covers "nice-to-have" extras above and beyond your typical lifestyle:
- Dream holidays - Round-the-world trips, luxury cruises.
- Second/holiday homes - Beach, lake, or mountain getaways.
- Luxury vehicles, boats, motorhome.
- Lavish gifts to loved ones - University funds for grandkids.
- Significant charitable giving.
- Starting a business or pursuing expensive hobbies.

This tier allows you to splurge on things you have always wanted to do but may not have been able to afford before retirement. Be realistic about which aspirational goals are within reach.

To plan your retirement finances, first calculate your required, desired, and aspirational income tiers; use guaranteed income to cover required expenses first; fill gaps between required and desired with retirement savings; and view aspirational spending as a "wish list" for extra planning.

Determining your income needs across these tiers will provide tremendous clarity for your retirement planning.

Prioritise securing required income, budget wisely for your desired lifestyle and dream big for aspirational fulfilment. With smart planning, all three can be achievable.

Cashflow Modelling

Cashflow modelling, as a financial planning technique, involves projecting and analysing cash inflows and outflows over a specific period, providing individuals with a comprehensive understanding of their financial situation and facilitating informed decisions based on the projected cashflows. This dynamic financial roadmap not only empowers investors to combat the challenges of retirement planning with various scenarios, investment strategies, and income sources, but also visually brings a retiree's plan to life, offering a clear and tangible representation of their financial journey in retirement.

The process of cashflow modelling typically involves the following steps:

Cash Inflows: The first step is to identify and estimate all the sources of cash inflows. For individuals, this may include income from employment, retirement pensions, investments, rental properties, and any other sources of revenue.

Cash Outflows: The next step is to determine and estimate all the cash outflows or expenses. This includes regular expenses such as housing costs, utilities, transportation, food, healthcare, insurance premiums, debt payments, taxes, and discretionary spending. It may also involve considering irregular or one-time expenses like major purchases, home renovations, or holidays.

Projection Period: A timeframe is chosen for the cashflow projection, which could be short-term (months or a few years) or long-term (decades or a lifetime). The projection period depends on the purpose of the cashflow model and the specific needs of the individual or business.

Assumptions: Cashflow modelling requires making certain assumptions about future events that can impact cash inflows and outflows. These assumptions may include factors like inflation rates, investment returns, salary increases, tax rates, and other relevant variables. It is important to base these assumptions on realistic and well-informed estimates.

Cashflow Calculation: Using the identified cash inflows, outflows, and assumptions, the cashflow model calculates the net cashflow for each period. This involves subtracting the total cash outflows from the total cash inflows to determine whether there is a surplus or deficit.

Analysis and Decision Making: Once the cashflow projections are generated, individuals can analyse the results to gain insights into their financial situation. They can evaluate whether their income is sufficient to cover expenses, identify potential shortfalls or excesses, and make informed decisions about savings, investments, budgeting, debt management, or any necessary adjustments to their financial plan.

Cashflow modelling provides a dynamic and forward-looking view of an individual's financial position. It helps in assessing liquidity, managing income and expenses, planning for major life events, making investment decisions, evaluating the feasibility of financial goals, and understanding the potential impact of different scenarios.

Hope for The Best, Plan for the Worst

Calculating your success rate involves harnessing probability, a vital tool used by professionals across various fields. From life-saving surgeons to insurance actuaries and football managers, probability allows you to determine the likelihood of your plans staying on track and enables you to adjust your approach if needed.

In the realm of financial security, the rule of thumb 4% rule is designed to safeguard your portfolio against a range of catastrophic events, including major wars, the Great Depression, a global health pandemic and other global events. However, effective financial planning extends beyond considering worst-case scenarios. It also involves balancing the potential for favourable outcomes.

To evaluate your portfolio's success rate, experts in financial planning leverage extensive empirical data spanning decades of investment history. With this information, they can devise a withdrawal strategy that aims to provide an 80-90% chance of achieving your desired returns, while minimising the risk of poor returns in the early stages.

In practical terms, this means that in approximately 80-90 out of 100 scenarios, your retirement withdrawal strategy is expected to succeed. However, what happens if you fall short of your success rate?

Retirement planning is an ongoing process that requires continuous monitoring and adjustment. Much like when you hit a roadblock and your satnav suggests an alternative route, you may need to make course corrections along the way, such as reducing your withdrawal rate or adjusting your asset allocations. Naturally, the higher your success rate, the lower the likelihood of needing these corrective measures. You possess a unique identity, and your journey towards retirement is just as distinctive.

The path you take will differ from others, even if you are part of a couple. It is crucial to avoid relying on generic solutions when it comes to managing your retirement funds. What you truly need is a personalised and tailored approach that considers various factors, such as:

Financial Preferences:

Consider how you want your money to work for you. What level of income do you desire from your portfolio? Are you planning any one-time lump sum withdrawals? How flexible are you in adjusting your plans if market conditions become less favourable?

Longevity:

While we cannot predict your exact lifespan (if only we could!), it is important to factor in your estimated life expectancy when planning for retirement. This helps ensure that your funds will last throughout your retirement years.

Fees and Taxes:

In addition to the certainty of death and taxes, Benjamin Franklin's famous quote overlooked the impact of fees. It is essential to consider various expenses such as income and capital gains taxes, advisory fees, and other investment costs. These can significantly affect the growth and sustainability of your retirement funds.

Investment Strategy:

Determine your desired asset allocation and whether you want to maintain a cash buffer. Consider the order in which you plan to liquidate your assets and financial products. It is also important to evaluate your comfort level with risk and align your investment strategy accordingly.

Legacy Planning:

Reflect on whether you intend to leave an inheritance for your loved ones or contribute to a cause you care about after you are gone. This aspect of retirement planning ensures that your values and intentions are honoured beyond your lifetime. Remember, your retirement journey is unique to you, and addressing these factors will help create a customised and comprehensive retirement strategy that aligns with your specific needs and goals.

Ultimately, the 4% rule presents a generic starting point, rule of thumb solution to a complex problem that necessitates a personalised approach. To address these concerns, it is beneficial to seek the assistance of a forward-thinking financial planner. By leveraging cutting-edge technology, they can create a highly personalised and adaptable strategy tailored to your specific lifestyle goals and requirements which addresses all the 'what if' questions.

A competent financial advisor will explain concepts and strategies in simple, straightforward terms, enabling you to make fully informed decisions about your future. With complex topics broken down into clear, actionable steps, you can proceed confidently, knowing there will not be any unexpected pitfalls ahead. This clarity empowers you to understand how your choices today will impact your financial wellbeing in retirement and beyond.

By conveying information transparently and confirming your comprehension every step of the way, a trusted advisor provides the insight and perspective you need to craft a retirement plan aligned with your goals and priorities. With a firm grasp of how key decisions can influence your financial life, you are equipped to take purposeful steps towards the retirement you envision.

Spend Less, Invest More

Adopting a strategy of spending less and investing more has a twofold impact. Firstly, you save and invest more to secure a larger sum of money in the future. Secondly, by reducing your expenses, you lower the retirement threshold of 25 times your annual spending. Each pound you transfer from the spending category to the investment category in your budget reclaims a portion of your life!

Chapter 45

Are You Prepared to Weather a Temporary 50% Market Decline?

"Everyone has a plan until they get punched in the mouth."

Mike Tyson

We live in an unpredictable world replete with myriad geopolitical dangers, where situations can change dramatically at a moment's notice. While I may not have the power to avert the proverbial punch in the face, I am very well-equipped to aid in alleviating the ensuing pain. As a behavioural investment coach, my primary objective is to help my clients develop the mental resilience required to navigate through potential temporary stock market declines, which can sometimes reach around 50%.

I believe in preparing clients for such scenarios as they are an inherent part of investing. I guess you could say that you should expect the unexpected. A case in point was the onset of the COVID pandemic. In the short run, anything can occur. Situations that might have been dismissed as inconceivable— or at the very least, extremely improbable—have become the norm.

Consider what has occurred in the few years since COVID rocked our world in 2019:

- A once in a lifetime global health crisis
- A decline of one third in the S&P 500 in a month
- A fiscal response that propelled the S&P 500 back to its previous peak in five more months
- A 19% contraction in U.S. GDP (Gross Distribution Product – the total of all value added created in an economy)—the largest post-war recession by far—that began and ended in three months.
- A 40-year explosion in inflation. The sharpest, fastest interest rate spike ever.
- A 25% temporary stock market decline in 10 months.
- Russia and China—two huge, aggressive autocracies experiencing demographic collapse— essentially opted out of the world community.
- Iran has moved inexorably closer to developing nuclear weapons.

The narrative continues. As long-term owners of conventional global businesses, we are shielded, to the highest degree conceivable, by the sensible decision-making of the management who run these companies.

When a global pandemic emerges, companies will close their doors and place their employees on furlough. When

Russia infiltrates Ukraine, many companies will withdraw from that nation. This reflects the reassuring truth that rational corporations will always act to conserve their owners' capital for the longer term. This is the sole aspect our managers have actual control over, and the only thing investors should be concerned about.

But they aren't, are they? Being simply human—and exposed relentlessly to the damaging discourse of catastrophist financial bile that journalists spout—they closely monitor the utterly erratic "stock market." They perceive "stock market" downturns as "losses" instead of transitory impediments in the enduring rise of shareholder capitalism and relentless growth.

These "losses" induce entirely self-inflicted "pain" that feels doubly harsh as advances feel pleasant. Finally—and most peculiarly— they believe that the more the market plummets, the greater the risk of an even more severe drop. Although this contradicts all historical evidence and logic, it incites them to sell off their investments at fire-sale prices, condemning them to underperforming returns for the rest of their days. They willingly turn a paper loss into a physical loss.

It does make me wonder how people would react if house price values were read out on the news every day. I do not imagine anyone would sell because their house if it fell in value by 25% overnight. Why? Because they were not planning on selling.

I often encounter two recurrent queries: when is the ideal moment to invest and when should one sell and withdraw their money? My responses remain consistent. The prime time to invest is immediately when you have the funds at your disposal, and the optimal moment to sell and retrieve your money is when you require it. It is truly as straightforward as that. Anything beyond this is mere speculation.

Individuals who manage to endure a -20% drop are virtually guaranteed to have bailed out at -30%. And practically everyone has run for the hills at -50%—which, I remind you, has transpired three times in a 50-year-old's lifetime as of 2023. I cannot stress how important it is for an investor to understand and accept this important fact. Even though every fibre of your being is telling you to get out, you must remain resolute and stick to the long-term plan.

Every day you hang in there and resist the temptation of doing something you will regret; your reinvested dividends are buying more shares at fire-sale prices from somebody who is panicking out and making the mistake you refuse to make.

I make it a point to navigate within the realm of uncomfortable truths rather than resort to comforting lies. Upholding transparency in managing my clients' expectations is my utmost priority. My approach is anchored in a "no surprises" policy, ensuring that all conversations with clients are clear, open, and honest.

One of my primary responsibilities is to disrupt this destructive psychological pattern once and for all, for the select few who will let me. That is my main mission. It is my "why." Acknowledging and even welcoming this, I undertake two synergistic challenges:

(1) Preparing my clients BEFOREHAND for the temporary—and always deceptive—vanishing of potentially up to half of their "stock market" values.

It is impossible to start lifeboat drills after the Titanic has struck the iceberg. I cannot genuinely begin to ready clients for significant "stock market" drops once those reductions have commenced.

(2) Providing scheduled, systematic regular doses of reassurance. I refer to this as my "Vitamin C" principle or my 'sanity serum' drawing on the analogy that the body cannot store Vitamin C. I hold the belief that the human mind struggles to uphold the fundamental investing principles of trust, patience, and discipline. Unfortunately, this challenge is further compounded by sensationalist financial journalism, which ultimately erodes the investor's confidence in the rationality of mainstream shares as the ultimate source of genuine (adjusted for inflation) security.

Please note, I am definitely not predicting a 50% market drop. (I am also not predicting that the sun will rise tomorrow, nor that either you or I will be here to witness it even if it does.) Comprehensive financial planners do not predict anything; we prepare for everything. The question is never "Is such a decline imminent?" It is not even "Is such a decline still plausible?" It is "If such a drop were to occur—in response to any 'crisis'—are you absolutely ready to withstand it, with my calm but firm support, as we navigate it together?"

Because we understand that such will be the defining moment in a wealthy family's investing journey. I continue to believe that the best (as it is unquestionably the most realistic) method to communicate this challenge to people is by teaching them about the three occasions in the last half-century during which the S&P 500 temporarily halved in value.

Here are the three instances in the past 50 years where the stock market's value has momentarily halved:

Three US Bear Markets covering the previous 50 years to 2023:

January 1973 to October 1974 S&P 500 -48%

The stock market saw significant turbulence, with the S&P 500 plummeting approximately 48%. Several intertwined events and conditions contributed to this downturn:

Recession: The U.S. economy was gripped by a recession during this period. It wasn't a shallow dip either, with GDP reflecting a notable decline.

Skyrocketing Unemployment: Economic challenges led to a surge in unemployment, which crested at a distressing 9% by May 1975.

Oil Crisis: 1973 marked the year of OPEC's first oil embargo, a decision that sent shockwaves through global economies. Within a short span of just four months, oil prices quadrupled, stoking the fires of inflation, and putting even more pressure on an already struggling U.S. economy.

Watergate Scandal: Adding to the country's economic woes was a political crisis of historic proportions. The Watergate scandal, culminating in President Richard Nixon's resignation in August 1974, created an atmosphere of mistrust and uncertainty. While it's a challenge to delineate its direct impact on stock prices, the scandal undeniably played a role in the overall negative sentiment of the time.

In essence, the period between 1973 and 1974 was marred by a cascade of unfavourable economic, political, and global events. These challenges, in tandem, exerted profound downward pressure on the U.S. stock market.

Markets March 2000–October 2002 S&P 500 -49%

Implosion of the dotcom/technology bubble: This started in 2000 when the overvalued tech sector began to crash, leading to the collapse of many internet-based companies.

Nasdaq/technology index down 80%: Indeed, from its peak in March 2000 to its trough in October 2002, the Nasdaq Composite Index, which had a high concentration of technology stocks, fell by approximately 78%, often rounded to 80% in many discussions.

Recession: The U.S. economy entered a recession in March 2001, which lasted until November 2001.

September 11th, 2001, terrorist attacks: These attacks had a profound and immediate impact on U.S. and global financial markets. Stock markets were closed for several days after the attacks, and when they reopened, there were sharp declines.

Enron and the accounting scandals: Enron filed for bankruptcy in December 2001, and this, along with other corporate and accounting scandals (like WorldCom and Tyco), further eroded investor confidence during this period.

The combination of these events, along with other factors, did lead to a significant drop in the S&P 500. While the exact percentage can vary depending on the specific start and end dates chosen, from its peak in March 2000 to its trough in October 2002, the S&P 500 declined by about 49%, which aligns with your statement.

October 2007–March 2009 S&P 500 -57%

The financial landscape underwent a seismic shift, with the S&P 500 tumbling by a staggering 57%. Several pivotal events catalysed this dramatic decline:

Subprime Mortgage Catastrophe: A wave of mortgage defaults, particularly in the subprime sector, acted as the initial spark, leading to widespread instability in the housing market.

Global Financial Crisis: This housing turmoil snowballed into a full-blown financial crisis. Banks faced insolvency, and financial systems worldwide teetered on the brink.

Unprecedented Recession: The U.S. sank into its most protracted and severe recession since the Great Depression of the 1930s, stalling economic growth and pushing businesses to the edge.

Surge in Unemployment: Reflecting the economic hardships, unemployment rates climbed steeply, cresting at a distressing 10%.

The period between 2007 and 2009 is etched in memory as a time when the very foundations of the global economy were tested. The series of challenges presented not just financial, but also significant societal hurdles.

That concludes the bad news. Here's the good news.

The tapestry of the stock market, through the passage of time, paints a story of contrasts—of highs and lows, triumphs, and tribulations. Yet, even amidst the pronounced volatility, for those willing to view the larger canvas, a narrative of resilience and consistent growth emerges.

Over the course of five decades, from 1972 to 2022, a compelling set of data underscores this very sentiment:

S&P 500 Value: The index value at the close of 1972 stood at 118. This value, despite facing myriad challenges, catapulted to 3,840 by the end of 2022, marking an impressive ascent to 4,500 by September 2023. This trajectory, more than mere growth, exemplifies the market's tenacity.

Earnings of Companies: Mirroring the overarching health of corporations, earnings expanded from $6.17 per share in 1972 to a robust $219 by 2022, bearing testimony to businesses' adaptability and the spirit of innovation that fuels them.

Dividends Paid by Companies: From 3.19 in 1972 to 66.92 in 2022, dividends have grown exponentially. These dividends, beyond being mere numbers, encapsulate the consistent rewards reaped by long-term investors, emphasising the power of patience and commitment.

Inflation: While inflation grew from 43 in 1972 to 297 in 2022, the growth witnessed in the stock market and earnings significantly outstripped it, ensuring that wealth creation wasn't just nominal but real.

Pivoting to a broader time horizon, the stock market's journey over the past half-century is illustrative. Industries, in the face of global challenges, have showcased an impressive ability to evolve and flourish. The very foundation of financial systems might have trembled during turbulent times, but the stories of growth and evolution penned by various sectors and corporations stand in stark contrast.

S&P 500's Journey: Capturing global economic strength, the S&P 500 saw a monumental 35-fold rise, illustrating the market's dynamism.

Dividend Payouts Surge: The dividends, a direct reflection of corporate confidence, witnessed a 21-fold surge, comfortably outpacing inflation that grew seven times in the same duration.

Consistency Amidst Chaos: The S&P 500's average yearly compound rate of total return remained at a firm 10.2%, aligning with the century-long average, even as the index faced significant reductions three times!

Timing vs. Time: One of the most profound lessons from this journey is the futility of trying to time the market. The real key lies in enduring the short-lived declines with an unwavering focus on the long-term horizon.

A Look Back from 1957: Since the S&P 500's inception in 1957, the metrics are awe-inspiring. By 20/06/2023, the index value multiplied 100-fold. Dividends amplified 48 times, and in the same period, the cost of living, as represented by inflation, grew 18-fold. This disparity speaks volumes, highlighting that investments in top-tier global corporations delivered returns that magnified over five times relative to the cost of living.

Concluding this chapter of financial history, the narrative is clear. Investing in a broad spectrum of the world's foremost companies has proven to be not just a defence against inflation but a significant avenue for wealth augmentation. Challenges, while daunting in isolation, form just transient episodes in a much larger, compelling story of growth, resilience, and innovation.

Part of my role as a Lifestyle Financial Planner is not to talk you down from the ledge when times get tough. It is to make sure you never feel the urge to climb up onto it in the first place. The present situation in the economy and the markets is never the main concern. It's how you, as an investor, react—or, with proper guidance, choose not to react—to what's transpiring. I maintain that there's no trustworthy route to superior wealth management other than this: continuously conditioning my clients not to react to significant market shifts, whether they're frightening or euphoric.

The tendency to make decisions that align with the prevailing market trend, especially during its peak, is very strong and often feels like the right move. Resisting such impulses is a significant challenge. However, having the foresight to stay the course and avoid rash decisions can bring immense satisfaction and potential benefits in the long run. You'll likely look back with gratitude for your patience and prudence.

My message:

- The long-term growth trajectory of earnings, dividends, and values of the prominent businesses, collectively, is robustly positive.

- The stock market is considerably more unpredictable than the enduring values of the companies themselves. Meaning, the market for the companies' shares is far more volatile in both directions than the actual companies.

- However, the most erratic element in investing—from the heights of euphoria to the depths of despair—is human nature itself.

- We can't (and don't need to) do anything about the companies. Population growth, economic progress, innovation/productivity, and the law of creative destruction are driving that, while logical managers are doing the rest.

- We can't do anything about "the stock market." It will forever excessively discount both positive and negative economic cycles and the companies' fortunes. "The stock market" thus elevates much more, and then plummets much more, than it "ought to," based on the fundamentals of the companies. These alternating cycles can't be timed, they just have to be weathered. Given time, market prices will always gravitate back toward fundamental values.

- The only aspect an investor can potentially control—and the crucial determinant of their lifetime return—are their own emotions. The challenge here is human nature itself, which—left unchecked —is an unsuccessful investor.

- Rescuing the investor from themselves. Training clients to endure the alternating extremes of the stock market is how I can most dependably accomplish my mission.

It's also important to be aware that negative sentiment in investing can become a self-fulfilling prophecy as it leads to panic selling, market declines, and further reinforcement of pessimistic beliefs. Positive sentiment can have a similar effect, driving prices up. Long-term factors and strategies should always be considered over short-term sentiment.

The profound reality is that the premium return of investing in a vast collection of the world's great companies is earned purely by a willingness to withstand their temporary downturns. Yet, it is these temporary downturns that human nature obsesses over. So, the next time you begin to feel a bit nervous, don't just do something, SIT THERE, and wait it out!

Part 9

Avoiding Financial Scams and Mastering Investor Psychology

Chapter 46

Guarding Your Nest Egg: Navigating the Minefield of Financial Scams

After years of diligent saving and investing, many people anticipate a peaceful retirement, enjoying the fruits of their labour. However, for some, this dream can shatter in the blink of an eye and become a living nightmare, all because of falling prey to a financial scam. The promise of extraordinary returns and guarantees can be alluring, but if an opportunity sounds too good to be true, it almost certainly is.

In our ever-evolving technological landscape, the advent of artificial intelligence (AI) has ushered in unparalleled advancements. But with these advancements comes a new frontier for scams. With AI, fraudulent schemes have not only increased in frequency but also have become infinitely more devious and sophisticated. Techniques such as deepfakes, where AI generates eerily realistic but entirely fake content, can be employed to produce deceptive videos or voice recordings of trusted figures.

Scammers are not always faceless strangers behind a screen; sometimes, they're well-dressed professionals armed with cutting-edge technology. The elderly, raised in an era of handshake deals and person-to-person interactions, are particularly vulnerable to these modern, AI-enhanced scams.

Common Financial Scams:

The Ponzi Scheme: A scam where returns are paid to earlier investors using the capital of newer ones. This continues as long as new investors keep coming.

Fake Lottery or Prize Wins: Scammers notify victims that they've won money or a prize, but they need to pay a fee to claim it.

Phishing: With AI, phishing emails can now be tailored to match a recipient's habits, making them far more convincing.

Deepfake Voice Scams: Using AI, scammers replicate a trusted person's voice and make fraudulent calls.

Tech Support Scams: Scammers pretend to be from renowned tech companies, claiming there's a virus or other issue and charging for unnecessary services.

Inland Revenue Scam: Individuals are contacted, often by a convincing automated call, suggesting they owe a significant tax bill or are due a tax refund. They are then asked to provide bank or personal details, sometimes under the guise of 'clearing the dues' or 'receiving the owed amount.'

Bank Transaction Scams: Scammers pose as bank representatives and mention suspicious activities like parking in an unfamiliar location or dining in a distant town. They capitalise on your fear, urging you to close your account and open a new one, directing your funds to their accounts instead. Always hang up and call your bank on a different handset. If using the same phone, they might stay connected, intercepting your call to the bank. For safety, visit your bank or ensure you're dialling a verified bank number.

Safety Sense Checklist:

Scepticism is Your Ally: Always be wary of unsolicited offers, especially those promising high returns with no risk.

Verify Visual Content: With deepfakes on the rise, be cautious with videos or audio clips urging financial transactions or revealing sensitive data. Cross-check using trusted channels.

Personal Information is Gold: Never provide personal or financial information unless you're sure of who's asking and why.

Check Credentials: In an era of deepfakes and AI-powered scams, verifying through independent sources becomes even more crucial.

Second-Opinion Safeguard: Unsure about a financial opportunity? Discuss it with a trusted family member, friend, or financial advisor.

Change is Good: With AI's predictive capabilities in play, regularly update passwords and ensure they are complex and unique.

Trust but Verify: If contacted by someone claiming to be from a trusted institution, call back on the official number, preferably using a different handset.

Educate Yourself: Stay updated about the latest AI-driven scams. Knowledge remains a powerful defence.

Regular Account Check: Monitor bank and credit card statements meticulously for unauthorised transactions.

Reporting Matters: In this digital age, your experience can shield countless others. Report any suspicious activity.

The modern era, with all its technological marvels, brings with it modern challenges. Yet, with vigilance and a commitment to education, you can ensure that your hard-earned savings remain securely in your grasp.

Chapter 47

It's About Behaviour, Not Brains – Master Yourself, Not the Market

"Investing isn't a test of financial acumen but a continuous journey of mastering oneself. Amidst the numbers and charts, lies the true challenge: taming our own impulses."

Mike LeGassick

Throughout this book, we've delved deep into the intricacies of investing. As we draw to a close, it's vital to recentre our focus on the heart of the matter. As the esteemed investment guru, John Bogle, famously remarked, "The market is a huge distraction from the business of investing."

Reflect upon the essence of successful investing: It's less about one's intellectual prowess and more about mastering one's own behaviour. The patience to think long-term, the discipline to consistently save, and the embrace of uncertainty are paramount, often outweighing even the brightest IQ or the most prestigious credentials.

While chasing monumental returns may seem tempting, it's your consistent saving habit that creates a fertile ground for compound interest. Wealth isn't achieved in a singular moment but cultivated over time. Patience and resilience are the cornerstones of this process. It's essential to focus on goals that span a decade or more, steering clear of knee-jerk reactions to fleeting market moods.

Market unpredictability is inevitable. Yet, embracing this uncertainty, rather than resisting it, can pave the way to long-term rewards. Worry less about the market's whims and more about honing your saving habits. And while it's natural to rue past mistakes, channel that energy into making informed decisions today, rather than dwelling on bygones.

The real challenge in mastering money is psychological. It's not so much about sheer intelligence but controlling one's emotions. Embody humility, adaptability, and a purpose that transcends mere profits. After all, the riches you amass are best measured by the company you keep and the memories you make.

History resounds with tales of great investors. Their secret wasn't extraordinary intellect but consistently exemplary behaviour. Warren Buffett once noted that after reaching a certain level of intelligence, what truly sets you apart is the temperament to avoid pitfalls that ensnare many. Similarly, Benjamin Graham, the pioneer of value investing, prized a methodical approach. For Graham, the key lay in steadfastly adhering to foundational principles. Sir John Templeton, another stalwart in the investment world, believed that an overconfident attitude often led investors astray. To him, humility and adaptability overshadowed raw intelligence.

Just as these giants of investing have shown us, it isn’t the knowledge of arcane financial details that creates lasting success, but the application of timeless principles with consistency. The journey of investing is as much an exploration of one's character as it is of financial markets. Embrace the lessons and let them guide your path forward.

In conclusion, let me underscore ten fundamental principles every investor should grasp:

1. Prioritise establishing a transparent dialogue regarding your risk tolerance and appetite for market volatility with your advisor. Being open about this will help tailor a strategy that best aligns with your comfort level and will remain consistent with your expectations.

2. Ensure that your life's goals and aspirations drive your investment strategy, not the other way around. Your portfolio should serve as a tool to realise your life plan, and not dictate it.

3. Prior to investing, secure an emergency fund. This cushion ensures you don't have to prematurely withdraw from investments during market downturns, letting you benefit from potential long-term gains. Ideally, this should cover at least 6 to 12 months of living expenses.

4. Understand that as an investor, your influence primarily lies in managing costs and your behaviour. Extraneous factors often fall beyond personal control, so resist becoming overly absorbed by market fluctuations. Remember to stay grounded in facts, not myths.

5. Maintain ongoing communication with your advisor and promptly share any changes in your personal

situation or financial goals. Effective advising is a collaborative process.

6. Always be cautious of the allure of 'hot tips' or the next 'big thing'. The most reliable investment strategies are often grounded in thorough research, not passing fads.

7. Regularly reassess your plan with your advisor but avoid the temptation of daily evaluations. Overemphasis on daily investment fluctuations can lead to undue stress and distract from your overarching life plan.

8. Empower yourself through financial literacy. The more knowledgeable you are about your finances, the better positioned you'll be to make informed decisions and stay composed during volatile periods. Use my investor education website: www.saverbehaviour.co.uk to improve your knowledge.

9. Take the time to identify and understand your investing biases. Acknowledging these innate biases can help you make more rational decisions and prevent costly mistakes.

10. Stay committed to your long-term investment plan. It's easy to become seduced by the allure of new, 'revolutionary' strategies or to react impulsively to temporary market upheavals. But true financial stability is built on patience and perseverance.

Be sure to savour the present moment while planning for the future. Life is happening now. It’s prudent to keep one eye on the future but not both. This isn’t a rehearsal and it's essential to enjoy and appreciate the here and now. As Ferris Bueller wisely noted, "Life moves pretty fast. If you don't stop and look around once in a while, you could miss it."

Investing is not just a pathway to financial prosperity. It's a testament to our belief in the future, a commitment to our goals, and, above all, an ongoing journey of self-discovery. As you move forward, armed with the knowledge and insights from this book, always remember to balance ambition with gratitude, planning with living.

I hope the principles and strategies discussed here serve as valuable companions on your journey. Should you find value in these pages, I'd be honoured if you'd share it with others who might benefit. And for those keen to delve deeper or seek further guidance, I'm here to help. Feel free to contact me directly at mikelegassick@gmail.com. Together, we can navigate the intricacies and opportunities of the financial world.

USEFUL RESOURCES

Saver Behaviour. My client financial education website:

www.saverbehaviour.co.uk

Office for National Statistics. Calculate your life expectancy:

www.ons.gov.uk

State Pension forecast. Discover how much State Pension you will receive:

www.gov.uk/check-state-pension

Action Fraud. 24-hour reporting website for fraud and cybercrime:

www.actionfraud.police.uk

Money Saving Expert. Money saving website for consumers:

www.moneysavingexpert.com

Bank of England. Multi-faceted financial information website:

www.bankofengland.co.uk

Retirement Living Standards. Find out what retirement looks like at three different levels:

www.retirementlivingstandards.org.uk

Restless. Digital community for the over 50's:

www.restless.co.uk

MyBNK. Empowering young people to take charge of their future by bringing money to life:

www.mybnk.org

Index

1 to 10 risk scale, 226
4% Rule, 315, 316, 317, 319, 320, 322, 324, 340, 342
Accumulation phase, 255, 257, 331
Active funds, 85, 99
Active investing, 22, 97, 98, 99, 103, 109
  Defined, 22
  Risks, 99
  Strategies, 97
Active management, 99, 100, 113
Adair, Red, 186
Adaptability, 8, 74, 80, 236, 294, 327, 352, 363
Advice
  Behavioural, 4
Analysis paralysis, 6
Anchoring, 199
Annual rebalancing, 192
Annuity, 29, 30
Anticipated regret, 283
Aristotle, 76, 285, 286
Arnot, Robert, 226
Asset allocation, 105, 129, 235, 239, 252, 255, 297, 316, 341, 342
  Overcorrection, 296
  Risky, 235
  Strategic, 296
Asset classes, 26, 86, 182, 226, 234, 235, 242, 243, 258, 269, 279
  Common, 23
  Definition, 23
  Diversification, 27
Automation, 80
Bank transaction scams, 359
Bear markets, 22, 41, 42, 44, 48, 65, 210, 349
  Defined, 22, 41
  Enduring potential, 8
  Investor confidence, 41
Benchmarking, 105, 204
Bezos, Jeff, 161
Biases, x, 104, 116, 170, 197, 200, 203, 218, 238, 300, 365
  Behavioural, 10, 116, 160, 189, 196, 197, 233, 238, 300
  Emotional intelligence, 9
  Evolutionary, 15
  Familiarity, 199
  Natural, 4
  Overcoming, 11
  Recency, 200
Bogle, John, 109, 114, 294, 362
Bonds, 44, 45, 46, 47, 86, 92, 182, 216, 239, 240, 241, 242, 243, 258, 259, 260, 262, 263
  40/60 Portfolio, 280
  60/40 Portfolio, 279
  Active investing, 22
  Asset allocation, 252, 316

Asset classes, 23
Corporate, 268
Defined, 24, 141, 241, 280
Diversification, 260
Fears, 263
Government, 179, 234, 239, 240
Income, 264
Inflation hedge, 260
Investment ISA, 29
Investment risk, 239
Long term returns, 260
Long-term success, 287, 288
Market volatility, 26
Ownership, 260
Portfolio, 26
Portfolio allocation, 325
Psychological benefits, 261
Volatility, 259, 261, 324
Brandeis, Louis D., 217
Buffett, Warren, 10, 65, 90, 94, 97, 101, 160, 161, 168, 178, 207, 232, 258, 292, 293, 296, 363
Bull markets, 40, 41, 43, 44, 46, 64, 246
Buyer's paralysis, 6
Buyer's paralysis, 6, 7, 68
Cameron, James, 134
Capital preservation, 260
Cash fund, 25
Cash ISA, 29
Cash reserves, 192
Cashflow modelling, 338, 339
Caveman investor theory, 181
Coaching
Behavioural, 4
Cognitive biases, 3, 104, 116, 200, 205
Cognitive load, 5
Collective memory, 67
Competition, 96
Composure, 233, 296
Compound growth, 145, 146, 147, 149
Compound interest, 5, 149, 156, 305, 362
Compounding, 27, 48, 57, 62, 107, 108, 122, 127, 128, 147, 148, 149, 176
Defined, 27
Effect, 299
Exponential growth, 305
Growth, 145
Inflation, 139
Long-term returns, 231, 260
Market returns, 173
Patience and discipline, 249
Power of, 125, 299
Process, 192
Starting early, 145
Time invested, 306
Compounding charges, 148
Compounding effect, 127, 137, 139, 146
Confirmation bias, 10, 104, 198
Consistency, 94, 363
Consumer society, 136
Continuous learning, 238, 295

Contributions, 304
Corporate profits, 40, 41
Cost of living, 25, 26, 247, 324, 354
COVID, 41, 59, 286, 344, 345
Critical thinking, 15, 173, 244
Cryptocurrency Bubble, 64
Cultural factors, 6
Cultural influences, 79
Da Vinci, Leonardo, 84, 88
Daltrey. Roger, 95
Davies, Robertson, 203
Debt instruments, 24
Decision-making, 7, 9, 11, 14, 20, 22, 53, 93, 159, 174, 205, 208, 282, 285, 345
  Abilities, 33, 295
  Financial, 9, 197, 309
  Judgement, 295
  Patterns, 238
  Processes, 72, 159
  Rational, 18, 32, 48, 104
Deepfake voice scams, 359
Discipline and patience, 10
Distribution phase, 331
Diversification
  Defined, 27
  Geographic, 92
  Global, 92
  Market, 97
  Myths, xi
Diversified portfolios, 46, 167, 173
Dividend growth, 264
Dividend income, 127, 260, 262
Dividends
  Defined, 24
  Ethics, 72
  Income, 264, 265
  Risks, 208, 241
DIY investing, 187, 189
Downturn
  Economic, 33, 53
  Temporary, 45, 48, 257, 356
Early investing, 145, 307
Economic cycles, 355
Economic forecasting, 168
Economic forecasts, 335
Economic growth, 250
Economic hardships, 286, 351
Economic uncertainty, 227
Economics, 134, 152, 191, 283
Efficiency, xi, 108, 159, 176, 250
Efficient Market Hypothesis, 116
Efficient Market Theory, 174, 175
Efficient markets, 105, 175
Einstein, Albert, 144
EMH. See Efficient Market Hypothesis
Emotional Bias, 199
Emotional decisions, 91
Emotional factors, 104
Emotional intelligence, 8, 9, 10, 11, 67
Emotional spending, 79

Emotional triggers, 9
Enron, 123, 350
Environmental, Social, and Governance. *See ESG*
Equity-based portfolio, 192
ESG, 68, 269
Investing, 269
Ethical considerations, 73, 74, 269
Ethical investing, 73, 74
Evolutionary roots, 5
Exponential growth, 126, 144, 145, 152, 154, 155, 156, 305
Exposure, 103, 125, 210, 226, 234, 243, 249, 294, 326
Fads, 210, 239, 240, 242, 276, 277, 365
Fake lottery scams, 359
Fight-or-flight response, 3
Finance Education, 17
Financial advice, 4, 9, 170, 179
Financial advisors, 19, 68, 85, 91, 104, 234, 292
Financial data platforms, 97
Financial education, 17, 18, 68, 79, 307, 367
Financial experts, 51, 118, 165, 170, 173, 194, 322
Financial freedom, x, 315
Financial future, 17, 57, 63, 101, 146, 168, 187, 188, 194, 238, 271, 330
Financial habits, 4, 79
Financial illiteracy, 17
Financial literacy, 67
Financial losses, 39, 159, 170
Financial missteps, 4, 194
Financial planning, 3, 36, 186, 191, 193, 267, 268, 327, 335, 338, 340
Effective, 340
Intricacies, 195
Rational, 51
Risks, 51, 267, 268, 327, 335
Financial Pundits, 165
Financial returns, 68, 72, 269
Financial scams, 357, 358, 359
Financial security, 57, 81, 137, 190, 268, 309, 326, 331, 340
Financial stability, 128, 163, 365
Financial strategies, 80
Fixed income, 234, 252, 255, 256, 257, 259, 260, 262, 266
Flexible access drawdown, 30
Fluidity of money, 80
Forecasts, 119, 163, 166, 171, 210, 335
Fosdick, Harry Emerson, 315
Franklin, Benjamin, 16, 95, 125, 237, 297, 341
Galbraith, John Kenneth, 168
Gambler's Fallacy, 199
GDP, 25, 345, 349
Geopolitical events, 115, 294, 308
Global economy, 33, 126, 177, 222, 287, 351

Global events, 33, 116, 256, 286, 287, 294, 340, 350
Global financial crisis, 59, 351
Global giants, 126, 127, 128
Global stock market, 22, 106, 110, 177, 238, 239, 242, 243
Globalisation, 68
Gold, 91, 92, 141, 142, 143
Gold Rush, 64
Gold standard, 91, 142
Gold vs. Stocks, 141
Goleman, Daniel, 9
Graham, Benjamin, 32, 252, 300, 363
Greed, 9, 58, 64, 65, 71, 104, 199, 298
Gross Domestic Product. *See* GDP
Growth potential, 8, 40, 126, 127, 264
Hawking, Stephen, 49
Herd mentality, 10, 14, 39, 48, 242
Herding, 198
Historic returns, 73, 74, 279
Holistic, 9, 49, 68, 191, 200, 267, 326
Housel, Morgan, 165
Humility, 160, 167, 168, 301, 363
Hurdles, 189, 352
Hype, 108, 121, 166, 274
Illusion of Safety, 137
Impact investing, 72
Income tiers, 333, 337
Indecision, 7
Index funds, 21, 97, 101, 102, 111, 176, 179, 318
Index tracking funds, 99, 100, 179
Individual Savings Account. See Cash ISA
Information overload, 6, 12, 98, 172
Inland revenue scams, 359
Interest rates, 29, 151, 173, 256, 268, 335
Investing strategy, 83, 175, 239
Investment charges, 100
Investment choices, 4, 68, 70, 87, 115, 159, 179, 184, 226
Investment coach, 44, 344
Investment fees, 110, 175, 320
Investment funds, 23, 102, 123
Investment ISA, 29
Investment managers, 97, 113, 114, 158, 176, 292
Investment philosophy, 102, 296
Investment principles, 90, 94
Investment returns, 90, 95, 105, 143, 145, 150, 172, 173, 265, 321, 339
Investment risk, 212, 226, 238, 239, 240, 244
Investment risks, 133, 244
Investment strategies, 9, 48, 62, 74, 77, 159, 207, 217, 274, 294, 330, 338, 365
Investment tools, 11, 307

Investment volatility, 23
Investor Mindset, 54
ISA. See Investment ISA or Cash ISA
Journal of Financial Planning, 316
Jung, Carl, 282
Kahneman, Daniel, 283
Kennedy, John F., 282
Knee-jerk reactions, 86, 183, 299, 363
Legacy planning, 68, 205
LeGassick, Mike, xi, 362
Liquidity, 127, 256, 339
Long-term gains, 66, 288, 364
Long-term investment, 141, 143
  Goals, 290
  Plan, 200, 365
  Returns, 317
  Strategy, 117, 162, 210
  Success, 97, 286
Long-term signal, 201
Long-term vision, 42, 125
Loss aversion, 116, 282, 283, 284, 285
Low costs, 84, 86, 102, 108, 122
Low-cost funds, 95, 107, 114, 125, 126, 127, 128
Market analysis, 22
Market bubbles, 10, 201
Market cap. *See* Market capitalization
Market capitalisation, 24
Market crashes, 10, 18, 50, 52, 53, 69, 201, 248
Market cycles, 247
Market decline, 46, 57, 182, 254, 257, 344, 345
Market downturn, 34, 39, 44, 181, 182, 199, 201, 202, 228, 253, 255, 256, 263, 331, 364
Market dynamics, 67
Market fluctuations, 5, 9, 14, 33, 61, 109, 182, 192, 195, 222, 232, 240, 289, 290, 324, 330, 364
  Emotional responses, 9
  Short-term, 9, 235, 295
Market news, 232
Market timing, 28, 203
Market trends, 9, 239, 271
Market volatility, 3, 26, 56, 198, 208, 209, 226, 228, 232, 253, 261, 270, 288, 295, 321, 364
Marks, Howard, 2, 45, 93, 274
Marx, Groucho, ix
Media, xi, 11, 12, 13, 14, 52, 113, 165, 166, 168, 169, 171, 172, 173, 180, 181, 182, 184, 185, 208, 209, 216, 237, 250, 288
  Hype, 121
  Hysteria, 173
  Landscape, 11, 12, 180
  Modern, 13
  Role, 18
  Strategy, 12
media pundits, 168
Mentorship, 80, 307

Misconceptions, 19, 48, 49, 53, 77, 206, 226
Money fund, 25
Monthly savings, 92
Munger, Charlie, 101, 173
Myths, xi, 19, 52, 92, 95, 211, 212, 364
Newton, Isaac, 197
Oil Crisis, 349
Outperformance, 99, 103, 104, 105, 130, 131, 170, 174, 175, 176
Overconfidence, 104
Paradox of Choice, 68
Passive funds, 103
Passive investing, 21, 96, 97, 99, 103
  Defined, 21
Past performance, 116, 121, 170, 199, 304
Peer pressure, 79
Pension savings, 30
Perception of value, 110
Performance illusion, 203, 204, 205, 206
Persistence, 104, 254
Philanthropy, 80
Phishing, 359
Pitfalls in investing, 10
Placebo effect, 110, 111, 112
Ponzi Scheme, 359
Portfolio allocation, 132, 239, 288
Portfolio rebalancing, 132, 315
Portfolio returns, 233, 321
Property, 25, 269, 280
Prudence, 63, 67, 158, 163, 209, 249, 278, 355
Psychological comfort, 111
Psychological factors, 115
Psychological pressure, 116
Psychology, 9, 152, 160, 172, 198
Purchasing power, 25, 26, 60, 135, 138, 140, 141, 163, 215, 235, 242, 256, 260, 281, 335
Purposeful spending, 80
Randomness, 6
Ravikant, Naval, 65
Reagan, Ronald, 134
Real rate of return, 26
Rebalancing, 117, 121, 129, 130, 131, 132, 167
  Periodic, 132
Recession, 61, 345, 349, 350, 351
Retirement income, 30, 253, 322, 326, 328, 329, 333, 334, 336, 337
Retirement lifestyle planning, 334
Retirement planning, 188, 308, 315, 327, 330, 332, 337, 338, 342
Retirement savings, 29, 187, 188, 315, 329, 337
Retirement withdrawal, 340
Return on investment, 28
Risk ladder, 226, 230, 233, 234, 238, 239
Risk management, xi, 287

Risk tolerance, 9, 27, 105, 209, 213, 228, 233, 249, 259, 291, 324, 364
Robo-advisors, 67, 91
ROI. *See* Return on investment
Rollercoaster analogy, 272
Rule of 72, 150, 151, 152, 157
Russell, Bertrand, 212, 276
S&P 500 index, 179
S&P 500 index fund, 22, 41, 84, 142, 179, 183, 214, 215, 241, 247, 264, 279, 280, 281, 287, 304, 316, 345, 349, 350, 351, 352, 353, 354
Safety, 360
Samuelson, Paul, 89
Savings account, 23, 28, 137, 138, 151, 204, 303
Savings habits, 81
Savings rates, 138
Scepticism, 18, 40, 173, 246, 252
Seneca, 33, 34, 36, 71
Sensationalist financial headlines, 184
Sensationalist headlines, 18
September 11th, 350
Sequence risk, 320, 321, 322
Short-term noise, 201, 249
Short-term pain, 65
Simplicity, 84, 86, 294
Snakes and Ladders, 237, 238
Social media, 14, 53, 98, 99, 218
Societal factors, 6
Societal values, 68, 70
Speculation, 38, 85, 98, 115, 167, 170, 274, 347
Speculative investments, 239, 242
Standard & Poor, 46, 182, 213
State pension contributions, 324
State pensions, 318, 324, 325, 326, 327
Stock picking, 21, 84, 105
Subprime mortgages, 351
Sunk Cost Fallacy, 199
Sustainability, 72, 73, 319, 331, 341
Sustainable growth, 237
Tax strategies, 195
Tech support scams, 359
Technology, 67, 68, 70, 102, 164, 217, 218, 342, 350, 358
Temperament, 10, 292, 293, 294, 363
Templeton, Sir John, 246, 363
Temporal discounting, 5
Temporary volatility, 149, 252
Time horizon, 28, 37, 105, 176, 230, 249, 262, 270, 278, 353
Trend-chasing, 274
Truman, Harry S., 254
Turing, Alan, 272
Tversky, Amos, 283
Twain, Mark, 12, 39, 169, 180

Tyson, Mike, 344
Tzu, Lao, 165
Unpredictability, 43, 91, 135, 162, 267, 273, 363
Volatility composure, 228, 232, 233
Watergate Scandal, 349
Wealth accumulation, 161, 162, 188, 263
Zuckerberg, Mark, 180, 267

Printed in Great Britain
by Amazon

34201050R00215